THE MAKING OF MISSION COMMUNITIES IN EAST AFRICA

The Making of Mission Communities in East Africa

Anglicans and Africans in Colonial Kenya, 1875–1935

ROBERT W. STRAYER

Associate Professor
State University of New York
College at Brockport

HEINEMANN
LONDON · IBADAN · NAIROBI · LUSAKA
STATE UNIVERSITY OF NEW YORK PRESS
ALBANY

Heinemann Educational Books Ltd
48 Charles Street, London W1X 8AH
P.M.B. 5205 Ibadan · P.O. Box 45314 Nairobi · P.O. Box 3966 Lusaka
EDINBURGH MELBOURNE TORONTO AUCKLAND SINGAPORE JOHANNESBURG
HONG KONG KUALA LUMPUR NEW DELHI KINGSTON

ISBN 0 435 94801 6 (cased)
ISBN 0 435 94802 4 (paper)
© Robert W. Strayer 1978
First published 1978

Published with assistance from
the University Awards Committee
of State University of New York

Published in the United States of America by
State University of New York Press
Albany, New York 12246

Library of Congress Cataloging in Publication Data

Strayer, Robert W.

The making of mission communities.

Includes bibliographical references.
1. Missions—Kenya.
2. Church of England—Missions.
I. Title.
BV3625.K4S77   266'.3'6762   77-12979
ISBN 0-87395-245-6

Set in Ehrhardt 10 on 11 point
Filmset in Great Britain by
Northumberland Press Ltd,
Gateshead, Tyne and Wear
Printed by
Richard Clay (The Chaucer Press) Ltd,
Bungay, Suffolk

Contents

Acknowledgements

In the process of research and writing, one becomes acutely aware of the collective nature of the scholarly enterprise. Here then I should like to acknowledge, albeit inadequately, the contribution of others to this work. None of them, however, is in the least responsible for any errors of fact or judgement which may appear in the book.

Among the major professional obligations I have incurred are those to the following people and institutions:

- Professor Robert Koehl for his assistance and encouragement not only during the dissertation stage of my research but over the course of our association since 1964.
- Miss Rosemary Keen and the staff of the Church Missionary Society Archives for gracious and able assistance.
- Mr Nathan Fedah, Crampton Tamba and the staff of the Kenya National Archives who helped to make my research in Nairobi enjoyable and profitable.
- Professor B. A. Ogot and the History Department of the University of Nairobi for facilitating my research in Kenya.
- The History Department of the State University College, Brockport, New York for a stimulating and friendly atmosphere in which to pursue historical inquiry, and Brenda Kingman, the department's secretary, for her cheerful, able and repeated typing of the manuscript.
- The University Awards Committee of the State University of New York for helpful financial assistance.
- Dr Jocelyn Murray of the Department of Religious Studies, University of Aberdeen, Scotland, my collaborator in Chapter VIII, for her kindness in supplying me with important documents and the benefit of her own long experience in mission affairs.
- Those who read this work in whole or in part and generously gave of their professional advice and criticism, including Professors Felix Okoye, Matthias Ogutu, Frank Salamone, John Kutolowski, T. O. Ranger, J. M. Lonsdale, David Sandgren and Donald Schilling.
- Mr James Currey of Heinemann Educational Books who ably guided the transformation of this work from manuscript to book.

I have also received much assistance from people outside the world of professional scholarship who patiently put their time and knowledge at my disposal. Among these I should like to make special mention of the following:

- All of those listed in the bibliography who kindly shared with me their accumulated experience in interviews.
- Mr Humphries Mbuchi, who acted as translator, guide and companion.

- Reverend and Mrs Alan Page for their generous hospitality at Weithaga.
- Mrs M. C. Hooper who most graciously opened to me her home, her personal papers and her memories.

My grateful thanks are also due to *African Historical Studies* for permission to use their maps.

My greatest debt, however, is to my wife Dana, who over the past decade shared in every phase of the process which produced this book. It is with gratitude and affection, therefore, that I dedicate it to her.

Robert W. Strayer
Brockport, New York

Abbreviations

ACC	African Church Council
AIM	African Inland Mission
AMS	Alliance of Missionary Societies
CMS	Church Missionary Society
CSM	Church of Scotland Mission
EAA	East African Association
EAI	East African Industries
IBEAC	Imperial British East Africa Company
IMAS	Industrial Missions Aid Society
IMC	International Missionary Council
KA	Kikuyu Association
KCA	Kikuyu Central Association
KISA	Kikuyu Independent Schools Association
KNA	Kenya National Archives
LNC	Local Native Council
PCEA	Presbyterian Church of East Africa Archives
UMCA	Universities' Mission to Central Africa

1. Rev. H. K. Binns and Mission Agents at Rabai c.1881
(*Back row*) Edward Cantella, Jonah Mitchell, Carus Farrar, unknown
(*Centre*) Polly Nyondo, H. K. Binns
(*Seated, front row*) Jeremiah Mangi, Mary (?), Ann (?) with Tom (Price's dog, inherited by Jones)

2. J. R. Streeter, in front of an early house at Freretown c.1878–9

3. Freretown Police

4. Sewing Class in Rabai – Mrs A. D. Shaw

5. Mr & Mrs A. D. Shaw and Mission Agents at Rabai; among them Jonah Mitchell, seated far left and Jeremiah Mangi, standing centre

6. Drill classes at Kahuhia School for Girls

7. Kahuhia School for Girls, 1927

8. Church Council, Kahuhia

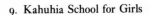

9. Kahuhia School for Girls

10. Government Road,
Nairobi, 1917

12. A Christian wedding,
1920s – Kahuhia

11. Rev. Handley Hooper
(CMS) and Dr Arthur
(CSM) on duty with
Carrier Corps during
World War I

13. Building CMS Church,
    Mutira

14. Going to church at
    Weithaga, 1906

15. Rev. and Mrs Handley
    Hooper

16. Teacher training class,
    Kahuhia

CHAPTER I

✂✂✂✂✂✂✂✂✂✂✂✂✂✂✂✂✂✂✂✂✂✂✂✂✂✂✂✂✂✂✂✂✂✂✂✂

Introductions

MISSION HISTORIOGRAPHY

The historical study of the encounter between Christian missions and African societies has from its beginning paralleled closely the wider tendencies of African history generally. It was of course missionaries and their supporters who initiated formal examination of the subject and thus gave rise to a metropolitan-ecclesiastical school of mission history.[1] Focused on European strategies for the planting of Christianity in Africa, and on heroic missionary efforts to implement these plans, this literature seldom examined the theme of encounter at all. In this respect it resembled the early colonial history which regarded Africa as a stage on which Europeans of all kinds played out both their interests and their fantasies.

Taking vigorous exception to this view was what might be loosely called the 'nationalist' perspective in African historiography. In accord with a new emphasis on African initiatives, historians of mission activity began to probe the ways in which African perceptions and reactions conditioned the pattern of mission expansion, the extent to which evangelization was an accomplishment of African catechists rather than Europeans and the kinds of protests that were generated against mission policies and attitudes. Concerned to puncture the pious pretensions of the earlier approach, nationalist historians delighted in showing that missionaries were no less racist than other Europeans and that they were intimately linked to imperial pressures and colonial governments. Finally the nationalist perspective has emphasized the extent to which mission activity has transformed traditional patterns of African life by undermining the cultural self-confidence of their converts and by generating an educated and modernizing elite which eventually brought down the colonial system that had spawned them.[2] The nationalist posture towards the missionary presence has thus been ambivalent, for while its practitioners have been bitterly critical of missionary arrogance and have deeply regretted aspects of the world they have lost, partly through mission activity, they regarded mission-inspired efforts at modernization as fundamentally progressive and believed that missions had contributed, albeit unwittingly, to political independence, the great denouement of nationalist historiography.

The importance of African efforts in the making of mission communities and churches, the relation of missions to protest and nationalist movements, the connexions both ideological and institutional among elements of the colonial establishment – these were and remain important themes in mission history. But more recent research has added new items to the historiographical agenda as well. Among these the most exciting has been that of African religious history and here again developments in the wider field have stimulated new modes of inquiry in mission history.[3] Nationalist historians had largely ignored the mission-African inter-action at the level of religious encounter, in part at least in an effort to reaffirm the validity of traditional religious systems against European presumptions of the superiority of Christianity. Acknowledging African interest in Christianity *qua* religion meant accepting missionary definitions of traditional belief systems as inadequate or worse. Yet we now know that the expansion of Christianity in Africa had important popular religious dimensions as both individuals and societies found on occasion in the immigrant religion symbols, techniques and ideas which seemed appropriate to meeting old needs and which could facilitate their adjustment to the new and wider world increasingly impinging upon them. Likewise the many conflicts that punctuated the relationship between African Christians and their missionary mentors derived as much from the incompatibility of mission Christianity and traditional religious sensibilities as from a sense of political and social grievance. Thus, the two great facts about the twentieth-century history of Christianity in Africa – its remarkable success compared, for example, with India and China and its dramatic divergence from 'orthodox' European models in a massive proliferation of independent churches – both require explanations that in some measure touch on fundamentally religious concerns.

In other ways, too, the nationalist analysis of mission history is being refined. A more subtle and highly differentiated picture of mission inter-action with colonial authorities and with the process of social change is emerging on the basis of continuing case-study research, thus laying the foundation for genuinely comparative mission history. The degree of integration between mission and colonial institutions varied widely depending on the particular mission and issues involved as well as on the nature of the colonial situation. The subservient relationship of Catholic missions to Belgian authorities in the Congo, for example, was a very different matter from the frequently antagonistic stand of German Protestant missions towards their own governments in Tanganyika or the Cameroons. Nor were missionaries everywhere and always in the vanguard of progressive social change despite their association with such agencies of modernization as schools and hospitals. The energetic efforts of Scottish Presbyterians, with their abiding faith in the value of education, to create a middle class elite contrast sharply with the concern of many Catholic and Dutch Reformed Church missionaries to produce rather a contented Christian peasantry.[4]

This study represents a contribution to the literature of mission history by examining the evolution of those communities associated with the Anglican Church Missionary Society on the coast and in the highlands of Kenya between 1875 and the mid-1930s.[5] Such communities were among the most significant of those institutional innovations that served as networks of inter-action between Europeans and Africans in colonial Kenya. It is in fact difficult to think of any important aspect of the modern history of Kenya which did not in some way involve these mission communities. In terms of institutional development they gave rise to schools and churches of both an independent and an orthodox variety. They participated in most of the political crises of the colony and reflected within themselves many of the tensions and conflicts of a colonial society. They were in a position to channel and direct, if not control, those multiple processes of social and cultural transformation that everywhere accompanied a measure of economic change. And they served both to bind colonial society together and to erode its structures and values. The profound loyalties and vehement antipathies which mission communities generated are ample testimony to their central position in the history of twentieth-century Kenya.

AFRICAN SETTINGS

In one way or another the CMS encountered most of the major peoples living in the area encompassed by contemporary Kenya. When Johann Ludwig Krapf landed in Mombasa in 1844, he initiated CMS contact with the Arab–Swahili coast. To the mission, Swahili society represented a frustration since it was almost impervious to the Christian gospel, an affront because of its slave-holding and slave-trading economy and a threat as it seemed to them a likely base for the expansion of Islam in the interior. Yet it was also a social order that contained a recognizably 'civilized' pattern of life – an urban social structure, a commercial economy linked to the trading patterns of the Indian Ocean, a hierarchical political system, a certain cosmopolitan outlook and a religion of the book. Beyond the coast, however, missionaries felt themselves among wholly different kinds of people and societies. In the immediate hinterland lay the country of the Mijikenda, nine culturally related peoples who had migrated from Singwaya in the seventeenth century and settled in a series of nine *kayas* or fortified villages on a ridge next to the coastal strip.[6] Krapf and Rebmann had worked among one of these groups, the Rabai, while later CMS missionaries encountered the Giriama and the Digo. The Taita people lived on a series of steep hills about eighty miles (one hundred and thirty kilometres) south-east of Kilimanjaro, while the Taveta inhabited a heavily forested strip along the Lumi River. Before the end of the nineteenth century, the CMS had entered into an intense relationship with both of these peoples. The highlands of central Kenya, where the CMS developed in the twentieth century its most successful work, had been occupied by the Kikuyu and related Embu, Ndia, Gicugu and Mbere peoples who, migrating generally southward, arrived in the Kiambu region only around 1800. The Kamba and Masai occupied the region between the coast and highlands and while the CMS had only brief and abortive contacts with them, they very largely created the economic and military conditions within which nineteenth-century missionaries had to work.

Outside the Swahili coastal settlements, the peoples of the interior shared certain basic structural similarities which contained implications for their encounter with the CMS. Their high degree of political decentralization – the absence in fact of a separate or autonomous political sector – meant for the intruding missionaries that, unlike Buganda, there was no centre to conquer, no necessary focus to their efforts, but on the other hand no single political authority whose hostility might forbid their penetration. It was not the state but the cross-cutting links of age and kinship, institutionalized in corporate descent and age groups, which provided cohesion for these rural communities. But stateless though they were, these societies did not lack certain patterns of differentiation and potential conflict which served on occasion to funnel discontented persons into the alternative community of the mission. While young Kikuyu women may have ideally been free to choose their marriage partners, this was frequently not the case in practice and as a result many of the women who found their way to a mission station were attempting to flee an unwelcome marriage.[7] The closure of the Kikuyu frontier by extensive European settlement had a far greater initial impact on *ahoi* or tenants than on those who held *mbari* or kinship-group rights to a piece of land. Consequently many of the earliest mission adherents came from the less affluent sectors of Kikuyu society and represented people seeking an alternative to the traditional means of achieving status.

The institutionalization of religious expression paralleled that of politics, for as Ranger has written about the peoples of Masasi in southern Tanzania, they 'combined a profound religious sense with a minimum of formal religious apparatus'.[8] Thus there were no territorial cults and no separate and competing hierarchy of religious specialists, such as those officials of the M'Bona cult among the Manganja of Malawi who chased UMCA missionaries off their sacred hill in the early 1860s.[9] The possibilities of religious inter-action were no less available, but they were less focused. In the fundamental assumption that unseen forces and purposes informed the events of the material world lay a point of contact with mission Christianity. Periodic famines during the last quarter of the nineteenth century, for example, activated a search for an appropriate religious technology which did not exclude the resources of resident missionaries. That Africans could believe in a variety of causal agencies – God, lesser spirits, ancestors, witches – and an even wider variety of ritual means to invoke or control their powers meant that they could appropriate aspects of Christian technique and symbol with little sense of betraying a received tradition. A pattern of ritual experiment and exchange was in fact part of that tradition and constituted one source of wider links among the disparate communities of East Africa. The use of coastal Moslems and their charms in religious ceremonies was common among the Mijikenda, while Krapf recorded how a Mijikenda invitation to an Usambara rainmaker led to the opening of commercial relations between the two areas.[10]

Awareness of such religious inter-action represents only one reason why it is no longer possible to view East African society as a series of discrete and self-sufficient 'tribes' occupying clearly defined territories. Colliding patterns of migration had for centuries made of the East African interior a place of fluidity and movement. The Kikuyu and Masai, for example, since at least the middle of the eighteenth century had inter-acted in terms of war, trade and cultural borrowing, and careful historical study of most East African peoples reveals a pattern of heterogeneous and diverse origins very far from notions of ethnic purity.[11] In such an environment of movement, mission stations could on occasion become at least temporarily another focus for new loyalties and identities, particularly if they could provide a measure of physical and material security.

But the major motor of historical change and regional integration during the nineteenth century lay in the elaboration of an extensive Kamba commercial system, a pattern of trade that closely linked for the first time the economies of the interior with those of the Swahili coast and the world beyond East Africa. When Arab and Swahili caravans penetrated the interior later in the century, it was for the most part along routes that had been pioneered by the Kamba.[12] Much of the positive reception accorded nineteenth-century CMS missionaries by the Kamba, Taita, Taveta and Mijikenda peoples derived from the belief that these outsiders could somehow facilitate their burgeoning commercial contacts. Moreover, the development of market-oriented trading systems encouraged the growth of new and more individualistic bases of political power and led to the emergence of such 'new men' as Kivoi among the Kamba, Ngonyo and Mwakikongo among the Mijikenda, Karuri in Kikuyuland and Gutu and Kathathura among the Embu.

4

With their power based in large part on the control of the new trade routes and their consequent ability to attract diverse people into new social units, such people were readily seized upon by the invading British, became in some cases the earliest collaborators with the new regime and were thus in a position either to facilitate or frustrate mission penetration.

MISSIONARY BACKGROUNDS

The missionaries of the CMS experienced no easy accommodation to African ways of life. Neither their social origins, religious outlook nor their preconceptions about Africa and Africans facilitated the making of harmonious mission communities. On the contrary, these elements in their background rendered inevitable some clash of cultures.

'The missionary movement', wrote Max Warren, 'was an expression of a far wider development – the social emancipation of the underprivileged classes.' During the first half of the nineteenth century, he concluded, the great bulk of missionary recruits came from the 'aristocracy of labour' and the *petite bourgeoisie*, those emerging classes for whom a missionary career certified a change in status towards 'that great middle class'.[13] During the last quarter of the century, when CMS efforts in East Africa began in earnest, the social background of its missionaries there was somewhat but not substantially more diverse.[14] Between 1870 and 1910, sixty-nine male missionaries were appointed to the East Africa Mission, of whom forty-nine had previous occupations listed in the CMS Register of Candidates. Among these, twenty-eight or fifty-seven per cent indicated occupations that might reasonably be regarded as 'aristocracy of labour' or lower middle-class, including clerks, carpenter, shipwright, mechanic, grocer, printer, leather-cloth worker, tailor, bootmaker's manager and several curates without university training. Among the attractions of a missionary career for such people was the possibility of ordination with a much less rigorous examination than prevailed at home. East African bishops in the early years were bombarded with insistent requests for ordination by anxious but not very well prepared candidates, most of whom in fact received the title they so ardently desired. Nor were other Europeans in East Africa unaware of the status increment to be obtained by missionary service and ordination. Most missionaries, wrote the big game hunter Sir John Willoughby, have been

> manufactured out of traders, clerks and mechanics. The process is not a difficult one: a man, thinking he can improve his position by missionary work, has only to go to a school for a year or two and learn a certain amount of medicine and carpentry, flavoured with a little theology, and he is turned out a full-blown missionary and orthodox deacon by the local bishop.[15]

Yet there was an important minority of missionaries who were already more solidly entrenched in the middle class. Four doctors, a solicitor, several school-masters, a well-to-do Bulgarian merchant and a captain in the Royal Navy served the CMS in its East Africa Mission during this period of forty years. Furthermore, seventeen per cent of the total male missionary population had university degrees, most from Oxford and Cambridge. There was, however, a tendency to send better educated recruits to India and China where an allegedly more sophisticated paganism apparently called for more highly trained missionaries.

Those with an A1 life at Lloyd's went to Africa, wrote T. A. Beetham, while those with a first at Oxford and Cambridge were sent to the East. This policy was resented in East Africa where the missionary leaders wanted the sort of man 'who will be respected by the East African white population, having some standing of his own, varsity fellow, and what the Indian officers say a "Sahib"'.[16] Following the First World War, the growth of the CMS educational system and the pressures of cooperation with the government resulted in a much higher percentage of university-trained male missionaries amounting to fifty-one per cent of those recruited during the 1920s and 1930s. Even then, however, fully a third of those whose earlier occupation was listed came from artisan backgrounds.

It is more difficult to say anything definite about the social backgrounds of the approximately one hundred women who served the CMS in Kenya before the 1930s. Only twenty-four had earlier occupations listed and of these there were nine nurses, three governesses, three weaver-seamstresses, three with 'clerical' experience, two teachers, two deaconesses, one musician and one YWCA superintendent. Yet without information on fathers' occupations it is difficult to assign the others to a particular social category. If most of the seventy-six women for whom no occupation is listed were 'at home' before marriage or missionary service, one might infer that they were of at least middle-class origin. Whatever their social backgrounds, if these women looked to a missionary occupation as a means of emancipation from the limits of sexually defined roles, they were to be sorely disappointed, for women were clearly treated as second-class missionaries. Though by 1913 they outnumbered the men by twenty-four to nineteen, their authority over Africans was sharply circumscribed, and they were completely unrepresented on the decision-making bodies of the local mission and could affect policy only through the recommendations of a Women's Conference which met once or twice a year. But the men regularly disregarded these recommendations even when they concerned the work among African women and girls. If Christian women workers with an average amount of common sense cannot see such issues clearly, wrote an infuriated Florence Deed, then we are not worthy of the name missionary. 'Our position is intolerable', declared Miss Mason in 1920, but despite local protests and appeals to the Parent Committee women remained in a distinctly subordinate position within the mission, a fact that had no small effect on the mission's efforts among the African female population.[17]

In other ways as well the patterns of recruitment to the CMS engendered tensions and conflict within the small and very status-conscious community of Anglican missionaries in Kenya. Ordained missionaries engaged in 'spiritual work', for example, were much more highly regarded than their lay counterparts whose efforts in teaching or bookkeeping were seen as secular. This local stratification system only enhanced the desire of laymen for ordination. Resentment against 'domineering and unreasonable clergymen' persuaded J. A. Wray, a layman who had entered the CMS as a twenty-three-year-old mechanic in 1880, to join the ranks of those who had provoked his indignation. On occasion these ecclesiastical conflicts coincided with resentments based on education and social class. The lay schoolmaster at Mombasa, W. E. Parker, whose education had terminated with a course at the CMS training college at Islington, complained bitterly about the interference of one whom he regarded as an unsuccessful Oxford man.[18] The creation and protection of personal spheres of influence, whether geographical or institutional, consumed an inordinate amount of missionary energies, rendered rational and long-range planning difficult and was in part responsible for the haphazard nature of mission expansion.

For the bulk of Anglican missionaries in pre-war Kenya, neither their education nor their class backgrounds provided them with much in the way of broad vision, imagination or sympathy with alien cultures. At the CMS training college at Islington, attended by almost a third of the men who were appointed to the East Africa Mission before 1910, it was not until 1905 that any systematic study of comparative religions was initiated and even then African religions, regarded as 'mere superstitions', were excluded. Christian theology, technical training and a smattering of medical knowledge were the major elements in the curriculum.[19] Many missionaries were particularly sensitive and insecure when confronted with Africans of equal or better education. If, as Max Warren suggests, Africans replaced the lower classes as a group against which aspiring missionaries defined themselves, then the prospects for Henry Venn's self-governing African church were not very bright. For the most part local missionaries were technicians not strategists, operating on the basis of an uncritically accepted set of goals and assumptions.

The constraints of their social and educational background were not substantially modified by their theology or religious experience. Before the Great War they were almost without exception conservative evangelicals, what the Americans called fundamentalists, though with a shade less rigidity and belligerence than that term often implies. As such they were concerned chiefly with personal conversion. Asked why he wanted to offer himself to the CMS, W. A. Pitt-Pitts said, 'Because I understand that CMS goes in for spiritual conversion of the natives working on 'lines stated in the Word of God'.[20] An acute sense of guilt and sin and a corresponding yearning for spiritual wholeness and 'real communion with the Lord' was an integral part of both their theology and experience. Missionaries regularly lamented their own 'wretchedness' and decried the dryness of their religious life. 'We have got lots of organization and plenty of work going on', wrote Miss E. Mayor in 1927, 'but we don't seem to have very much life.' Thus periodic conferences for 'spiritual renewal' – mini-Keswick conventions, in fact – punctuated the routine of missionary life in East Africa.[21] None of this was particularly helpful in dealing with cultures where shame was a far more potent emotion than guilt.

While evangelical Christianity was very largely a religion of communion, its missionary adherents were not reluctant to proclaim that God's power might directly affect the material affairs of men and nations. On a tour of East Africa in 1930, Julian Huxley was appalled. 'What! We attempt to wean the negro from his addiction to magic and yet allow him to be preached at and converted by people who solemnly believe in prayer for rain, the literal inspiration of the Bible, the historical truth of the Genesis account of Creation and all the rest of it.'[22] Yet particularly in the early years it was more the missionaries' willingness to pray for rain than their teachings on sin and damnation that afforded them a hearing among people for whom religion was at least in part both science and technology.

Adventism was another important element in evangelical theology and expectation. 'We know the end of the struggle', wrote Krapf from East Africa in 1853. 'The Lamb shall overcome them who fight with him and the word of the Most High shall stand against all the gates of hell.' Seventy years later Canon George Burns of Nairobi was opining that the 'amalgamating of businesses' was a sure sign of the quick return of Christ to earth.[23] Adventism thus encouraged a sense of urgency, a certain reluctance to be distracted from the main task, and a perception of the need for constant struggle. 'Living Christianity is an aggressive force and living Christians are essentially military', wrote a CMS missionary from Taveta in 1896. And yet there was hope and encouragement too, for as Owen Chadwick has written, the minds of evangelicals were both 'dark with shadows and brilliant with sparks from the Second Coming'.[24] Such a highly eschatological Christianity was difficult in the extreme to translate into the cultural categories of people whose concept of time was anything but linear and progressive.[25]

If evangelicals were aggressive, it was in part because they felt themselves on the defensive, under attack from modern science, Anglo-Catholics, and higher criticism of the Scriptures. 'We evangelicals always seem to be giving up something', complained the veteran missionary H. K. Binns in 1922.[26] There was thus a tendency in evangelical missionary circles to an increased rigidity in matters of culture and doctrine, especially on the question of the inspiration of the Scriptures. As a denominational mission linked to a state church, the CMS was saved from the extremes of such a reaction. In fact some of the more fundamentalist of the missions' supporters broke away from the parent body to form the Bible Churchmen's Missionary Society in 1922 when the CMS refused to commit itself to recruiting only people with a conservative view of biblical authority.[27] Thus in Kenya the CMS was never quite as legalistic or rigid on matters of theology and culture as the other major Protestant missions, a distinction that would have important consequences for intra-mission relations as well as for the cohesion of Anglican mission communities.

Furthermore, among the new generation of post-war missionaries, according to the official historian of the CMS, 'there were not a few who were beginning to discover new elements in their working theology in which wholeness in this world was tending to replace the adventist hope'.[28] In Kenya this new dimension was best exemplified in the person of Handley Hooper, a young, energetic, perceptive and diplomatic recruit who in 1916 was appointed to Kenya where his father had worked for almost a quarter of a century. We are too fond of defining Christianity in terms of certain dogmas, he wrote in 1928. 'All that is asked is that a man shall be convinced of the unique pre-eminence of Christ in any estimate of the values of human conduct and shall undertake to make him known with entire dependence in faith upon him.'[29] His father, a product of the Moody–Sankey revivals at Cambridge in 1882, had of course asked far more in terms of theological commitment. The newer views allowed missionaries to embrace education, agriculture, community development, even politics as genuine missionary concerns significant in their own right, for the older dichotomies between church and world, evangelism and education, secular and religious work seemed far less sharp than they had for the conservative evangelicals of the pre-war era.

In their perceptions of Africa itself, CMS missionaries in Kenya reflected the larger movement of European ideas about the possibilities of African development. The East Africa Mission of the CMS caught just the tail end of the 'conversionist' thrust of mid-nineteenth-century missionary thinking. It was a pattern of thought that was positive in its assessment of African capacities for absorbing western civilization and looked forward with optimism to the creation, in Henry Venn's famous phrase, of a self-supporting, self-governing and self-propagating African church.[30] By the 1880s, however, missionary thinking was much more pessimistic about African capabilities, for it was conditioned now by the pseudo-scientific racism of the day, the narrowness and exclusivity of the Keswick movement, and the growing thrust of European imperialism in Africa. 'Paternalism was the rule', wrote Max Warren in describing the new missionary mentality, 'barely masking a complete scepticism as to the capacity of the African to take any form of responsibility. . . . In particular the vision and practice of Henry Venn was allowed to lapse. . . . A recrudescence of puritanism, especially in evangelical circles, reinforced the doubt as to the moral capacity of Africans and Asians for leadership.'[31] These attitudes had precipitated the crisis in the CMS Niger Mission which drove Bishop Crowther to his grave and they had a similar though less well known impact in East Africa. Experience did count for something, however, and sensitive and secure individuals on occasion came to a more realistic appraisal of African life. The Giriama, wrote Miss Florence Deed in 1906 after thirteen years' experience in East Africa, 'are a people worth reaching, rapid learners, intelligent and most interesting to talk to, with a dignified code of manners of their own which one learns by living among them'.[32] But few indeed were able to transcend on any sustained basis the influence of a racially defined and pessimistic paternalism.

In Kenya much of this thinking persisted well into the inter-war period, for many of the pioneer missionaries of the turn of the century were still active in the 1920s and 30s. But there were as well new pressures on missionary beliefs about African capabilities. The war itself had dealt a blow to western presumptions of moral superiority: Africans were becoming more assertive both ecclesiastically and politically. A new generation of younger missionaries arrived lacking the immense prestige of the pioneers but possessing a better education, sometimes a more secure sense of self and certainly a more flexible and this-worldly theology. All of this led to a certain softening of the harshness and rigidity of earlier missionary attitudes. Not that their assumptions were fundamentally different, for when Handley Hooper, clearly among the best of the new breed in Kenya, was asked what he had done to prepare himself for missionary service, he replied, 'I have tried to gain as much experience as possible in children's and boys' work . . . because it seemed quite probable that a native African's processes of thought would run on childlike lines.'[33] Africans then were still children but, as Hooper put it, growing rapidly in bulk and mental perception. The emphasis now was on the problems associated with the coming of age rather than on the static fact of a limiting childhood. In a book significantly entitled *Leading Strings* Hooper argued that 'the negro must be allowed the infinite hope of a fully equipped and unfettered manhood for his race'.[34] Thus a new kind of paternalism was called for – sympathetic rather than critical, conciliatory rather than threatening, subtle rather than overt – though it was, if anything, even more concerned to maintain missionary guidance and leadership in the affairs of the mission community during this critical stage of 'vigorous adolescence'. But such nuances in attitude produced major consequences and where they prevailed among CMS missionaries in Kenya, the mission-African relationship was profoundly affected.

Finally, the organizational patterns of the mission conditioned their activities in East Africa. The ultimate authority in the CMS was the Parent Committee in London, which exercised its power primarily through detailed control of the finances of the mission. The local governing body was normally an annual or biennial Missionary Conference, composed of all males who had passed the required

9

language examinations and had completed a prescribed probationary period. Between meetings of the conference business was handled by a body known variously as the Finance, Executive or Standing Committee. These local authorities were engaged in a constant tug of war with CMS headquarters primarily over resources of money and manpower and less frequently over policy. While initiatives, except for retrenchment, almost always came from the field, the Parent Committee insisted on approving the financial and personnel arrangements for each project or institution separately since they refused to give bloc grants to their field representatives. Within the local governing organs there was the persistent problem of securing adequate representation for the various elements within the mission. Conflict between men and women, up-country and coastal, clerical and lay, educational and evangelical, junior and senior interests were reflected in the governing bodies of the mission. Though many East African bishops had been CMS missionaries, usually in India, they were appointed as ecclesiastical representatives by the Archbishop of Canterbury and had no official connexion with the CMS. But each of them negotiated with the Parent Committee in an effort to secure as much power as possible in the affairs of the local mission and was generally appointed chairman of all committees and regarded as the senior missionary in the field. Coupled with the traditional deference paid to bishops, this authority gave them a strong position, though circumstances required that they use this strength as mediators of conflicting interests as much as initiators of policy. On the other hand, the bishops' independent position gave them a certain leverage with the Parent Committee and on one occasion Bishop W. S. Peel threatened to collect funds for educational work on his own if CMS headquarters cut its grants for teachers.[35] All of this, however, lay well in the future, for the earliest CMS inter-action with East Africa was almost wholly the work of two individuals living in conditions largely untouched by European influences.

THE LEGACY OF THE PIONEERS

In 1875 the CMS moved to establish its presence more forcefully on the eastern coast of Africa by establishing a colony for freed slaves near Mombasa. This action, however, represented not simply a new beginning but rather the reinforcement of an existing work. For thirty years the CMS had been represented in East Africa by a handful of German missionaries, most notably Johann Ludwig Krapf and Johann Rebmann. When Krapf first arrived in Mombasa in 1844, it was in an effort to reach the Galla from the south, for he had failed to do so from his earlier base in Ethiopia. Soon however he abandoned this notion and together with Rebmann and a few others turned his attentions to the peoples of the immediate coastal hinterland and beyond. From their base at Rabai, for three decades (Krapf until 1855 and Rebmann until 1875) they travelled, translated and preached in a remote part of the world that held a very low priority in the minds of their superiors. Their reputation such as it was, grew out of their journeys of exploration along the coast, towards Kilimanjaro and in the Ukambani country of upland Kenya, though the temptation to become 'great travellers' caused the missionaries severe pangs of guilt and led Rebmann to pray that he might 'condemn such thoughts as carnal'.[36]

The impact of these few strangers on the peoples among whom they worked was minimal. In fact, to their immediate Mijikenda neighbours, the motives for their coming were something of a mystery. Some identified them with the earlier Portuguese intruders and thought they wanted to retake Fort Jesus. Most credited them with a desire for gold and silver, while others regarded Krapf as an exiled king and Rebmann as his only follower.[37] Despite this uncertainty, attempts were made to utilize whatever religious resources the strangers might possess and the missionaries thus found themselves implored to produce rain, heal the sick and foretell the future.[38] But few became what the missionaries would recognize as 'converts'. There was Mringe, a badly crippled but attentive young man who was baptized on his deathbed in 1851. More promising was Abbe Gunja, a Giriama outcast who had attached himself to Rebmann as early as 1850 and, incurring the intense displeasure of his fellows, remained the missionaries' most faithful disciple. Living alone in the forests of southern Giriamaland, he taught what he had learned and by 1874 had collected around him a small band of people who had given up their fetishes and 'joined the Book'.[39] It was in part the desire of this group for missionary attention that drew the CMS further into Giriamaland in the 1870s and 80s.

The most important legacy of these early efforts, however, was neither geographical knowledge nor a handful of converts but an idea. Krapf was a man of continent-wide vision and soon after his arrival in Mombasa he argued that 'the coast mission must have a broad basis toward the West and be the first link of a mission chain between East and West Africa'.[40] This idea was assimilated into official CMS thinking and functioned both as a stimulus for and a justification of later efforts at expansion in the interior. As early as 1848, Krapf urged the CMS to make this 'first link' in the chain a 'large establishment for redeemed slaves' somewhere along the east coast. Aware of the growing influx of slaves from the south into the coastal region, Krapf himself purchased five boys whom he hoped would form the nucleus for such a settlement, though his plan was soon squashed by Atkins Hamerton, the British consul at Zanzibar, who told the missionary that his actions were contrary to English law.[41] Not for another twenty-seven years would Krapf's first link be forged and a CMS freed-slave settlement be planted on the eastern shore of Africa.

FOOTNOTES

1. In this genre, for example, see such standard mission histories as Eugene Stock, *The History of the Church Missionary Society* (London, 1899–1916), A. E. M. Anderson-Morshead, *The History of the Universities Mission to Central Africa, 1859–1909* (London, 1909) and to a lesser extent C. P. Groves, *The Planting of Christianity in Africa* (London, 1948–58).

2. The best examples of this approach include J. F. A. Ajayi, *Christian Missions in Nigeria 1841–1891* (London, 1966) and E. A. Ayandele, *The Missionary Impact on Modern Nigeria* (London, 1966). See also F. K. Ekechi, *Missionary Enterprise and Rivalry in Igboland, 1857–1914* (London, 1972) and Arnold Temu, *British Protestant Missions* (London, 1972). Roland Oliver's pioneering *Missionary Factor in East Africa* (London, 1952) while not falling wholly in this category does touch on many of its concerns.

3. The religious dimension in mission-African inter-action is examined in J. F. A. Ajayi and E. A. Ayandele, 'Emerging Themes in Nigerian and West African Religious History', *Journal of African Studies*, I:1 (Spring 1974), pp. 1–39; Robin Horton, 'African Conversion', *Africa*, XLI:2 (April 1971), pp. 85–108; T. O. Ranger and John Weller, *Themes in the Christian History of Central Africa* (Berkeley, 1975); M. L. Daneel, *Old and New in South Shona Independent Churches* (The Hague, 1971).

4. Representative examples in this area include Marcia Wright, *German Missions in Tanganyika, 1891–1941* (Oxford, 1971); Ian Linden, *Catholics, Peasants and Chewa Resistance in Nyasaland, 1889–1939* (Berkeley, 1974); Marvin Markowitz, *Cross and Sword* (Stanford, 1973); T. O. Beidelman, 'Social Thought and the Study of Christian Missions', *Africa*, XLIV:3 (July 1974), pp. 235–49; Erik Hallden, *The Culture Policy of the Basel Mission in the Cameroons, 1886–1905*, (Uppsala, 1968).

5. CMS stations in western Kenya originated as an offshoot of the mission's work in Uganda and were administered from Uganda until 1921 when they were transferred to the Kenya Mission and ecclesiastically to the Diocese of Mombasa. But even then a policy of decentralization allowed the Nyanza region of Kenya to retain much of its previous autonomy in matters of mission policy.

6. Thomas T. Spear, 'The Mijikenda, ca. 1550–1900', in *Pre-Colonial Kenya*, forthcoming.

7. Jocelyn Murray, 'The Kikuyu Female Circumcision Controversy', Ph.D. dissertation, UCLA, 1974, pp. 53–4.

8. T. O. Ranger, 'Missionary Adaptation of African Religious Institutions: The Masasi Case', *The Historical Study of African Religion*, eds T. O. Ranger and Isaria Kimambo (Berkeley, 1972), p. 223.

9. Matthew Schoffeleers, 'The Interaction of the M'Bona Cult and Christianity, 1859–1963', *Themes in the Christian History of Central Africa*, eds T. O. Ranger and John Weller (Berkeley, 1975), pp. 18–19.

10. CMS/M, Rebmann Journal, 31 December 1847; Krapf to Venn, 11 September 1852; 1887/11, Parker to Lang, 21 December 1886. See also David Parkin, 'The Politics of Syncretism', *Africa*, XL (1970), pp. 217–33.

11. Godfrey Muriuki, *A History of the Kikuyu 1500–1900* (Nairobi, 1974). William Lawren, 'Masai and Kikuyu', *Journal of African History*, IX:4 (1968), pp. 571–83.

12. John Lamphear, 'The Kamba and the Northern Mrima Coast', *Pre-Colonial African Trade*, eds Richard Gray and David Birmingham (London, 1970), pp. 75–102.

13. Max Warren, *Social History and Christian Mission* (London, 1967), pp. 37–55.

14. These and subsequent calculations have been based on information contained in CMS, *Register of Candidates of the CMS, 1859–1941* and *Women's Register, 1905–1956*.

15. Captain Sir John C. Willoughby, *East Africa and Its Big Game* (London, 1889), p. 26.

16. T. A. Beetham, *Christianity and the New Africa* (New York, 1967), p. 12; CMS/1883/46, Binns to Lang, 26 February 1883; 1916/49, Verbi to Manley, 5 May 1916.

17. CMS/1904/186, Deed to Baylis, 29 August 1904; 1920/43, Mason to Manley, 7 August 1920; 1905/14, Minutes of Mission Conferences, 13–16 December 1904.

18. CMS/1877/2, Handford to Wright, 5 November 1876; 1896/124, Wray to Baylis, 24 March 1896; 1903/38, Parker to Baylis, 23 January 1903.

19. Alison Hodge, 'The Training of Missionaries for Africa: The Church Missionary Society's Training College at Islington, 1900–1915', *Journal of Religion in Africa*, IV (1971), pp. 81–96.

20. CMS, Candidates' Papers, W. A. Pitt-Pitts, September 1915. See also Gavin White, 'Kikuyu, 1913: An Ecumenical Controversy', Ph.D. thesis, University of London, 1970, p. 36.

21. CMS/1886/165, Shaw to Lang, 14 April 1886; M, Krapf to Venn, 16 November 1848; Annual Letters, Miss E. Mayor, 9 October 1927; PCEA: Specials, Pitt-Pitts to Arthur, 18 June 1928.

22. Julian Huxley, *Africa View* (London, 1931), p. 336.

23. CMS/M, Krapf to Venn, 14 March 1853; Bowden Papers, LBD to Mother, 2 March 1924.
24. CMS/1897/55, *Taveta Chronicle*, Christmas 1896; Owen Chadwick, *The Victorian Church* (New York, 1966), p. 451.
25. For a study of this difficulty, see J. S. Mbiti, *New Testament Eschatology in an African Background* (London, 1971).
26. CMS/1922/35, Binns to Manley, 10 April 1922; 1913/31, Peel to Manley, 21 March 1913.
27. Gordon Hewitt, *The Problems of Success: A History of the Church Missionary Society, 1910–1942* (London, 1971), pp. 409, 460–71.
28. Hewitt, ibid., p. xviii.
29. CMS, Acc. 85, Hooper to Pitman, 6 November 1928.
30. For a delineation of nineteenth-century European attitudes towards Africa, see Philip Curtin, *The Image of Africa* (Madison, 1964), and H. A. C. Cairns, *Clash of Cultures* (New York, 1965).
31. Warren, *Social History*, op. cit., p. 144. See also J. B. Webster, *The African Churches Among the Yoruba* (Oxford, 1964).
32. CMS, *Extracts*, Miss F. Deed, 31 December 1906; 1906/57, *Mombasa Diocesan Magazine*, April 1906.
33. CMS, Candidates' Papers, H. D. Hooper, 25 May 1915.
34. H. D. Hooper, *Africa in the Making* (London, 1922), p. 22; *Leading Strings* (London, 1921), p. 8; CMS, Annual Letters, H. D. Hooper, 1923.
35. CMS/1908/108, Peel to Baylis, 21 October 1908.
36. CMS/M, Rebmann to Venn, 17 December 1851; Krapf to Venn, 8 August 1849.
37. CMS/M, Rebmann to Secretary, 22 March 1851.
38. J. L. Krapf, *Travels, Researches and Missionary Labours* (Boston, 1860), pp. 148–9; CMS/M, Rebmann Journal, 12 December 1847.
39. CMS/M, Rebmann to Secretary, 22 March 1851; Rebmann to Venn, 28 April 1856; Krapf to Venn, 11 September 1852; Eugene Stock, *History of the Church Missionary Society* (London, 1899–1916), III, p. 58.
40. CMS/M, Krapf to Venn, 28 February 1849.
41. CMS/M, Krapf to Venn, 16 November 1848.

CHAPTER II

ᵡᵡᵡᵡᵡᵡᵡᵡᵡᵡᵡᵡᵡᵡᵡᵡᵡᵡᵡᵡᵡᵡᵡᵡᵡᵡᵡᵡᵡᵡᵡ

Bombay Africans and Freed Slaves: A Missionary Prelude to Colonial Rule, 1875–1900

The year 1873 was one of new departures in British inter-action with the eastern side of Africa. The death of David Livingstone stimulated a great outpouring of support for the missionary enterprise in terms both of money and recruits. The Church Missionary Society, for example, established a Special East Africa Fund and in half a decade over £10,000 was subscribed for a renewed effort in that hitherto remote corner of the world. In the same year, the British concluded a treaty with the Sultan of Zanzibar legally abolishing the seaborne traffic in slaves, an agreement that represented the culmination of gradually increasing British pressure over the course of more than half a century. It is as a result of these developments that the origins of renewed CMS activity in East Africa can be found. The treaty clearly necessitated some provision for slaves rescued from Arab dhows attempting to escape the new prohibitions on the slave trade and the CMS saw in this situation an opportunity to establish a base in East Africa from which to pursue Krapf's vision of a chain of mission stations extending inland from the coast. In close cooperation with the British government the mission decided to reinforce its East African Mission with the aim of founding a settlement for freed slaves on the model of Sierra Leone. To both Edward Hutchinson, the CMS Lay Secretary who had long been active in the abolitionist movement for East Africa, and Sir John Kirk, the British Consul in Zanzibar, the settlement's location on the mainland opposite Mombasa island was appropriate 'both in respect of protection and control and strategical position with regard to the coast-wise land traffic [in slaves]'.[1] Kirk hoped to use the settlement as an instrument of controlled pressure on the Arab slave trade, but events soon showed that it was not so amenable to manipulation and was in fact the occasion for frequent embarrassment for the British consul.[2]

A PROTO-COLONIAL SOCIETY

Founded in 1875, the settlement was named after Sir Bartle Frere, who had negotiated the Treaty of Abolition with Zanzibar. To oversee the establishment of Freretown, the CMS called on W. S. Price, superintendent of its Sharanpur Christian Village on the west coast of India near Bombay, which itself had been a settlement for slaves rescued from Arab dhows since 1855. Price took with him some residents of this institution, as well as a number of freed slaves in the area who took this opportunity to return to Africa. Most prominent among these 150

14

'Bombay Africans', as they were called, were William Jones, George David and Ishmael Semler, who had been sent in 1864 to assist Rebmann at Rabai. Many of them were well educated, speaking several Indian languages in addition to English, while others had practical training in such trades as agriculture, carpentry and mechanics. They were expected to form the solid Christian core of the settlement and to assist Price in getting Freretown off to a good start. In that dual role – were they merely settlers or rather the special associates of the missionaries? – lay the seeds of much future difficulty.

In September 1875, the first freed slaves were handed over to the mission and within a few years, Freretown was a community of over 450 residents. Covering about a thousand acres just north of Mombasa island, it was a well planned settlement complete with church, schools, cricket field, prison, cemetery and mission *shambas* (farm plots) as well as individual gardens for married couples. To Bishop Hannington who first saw it a decade ·fter its founding, Freretown was 'one of the most lovely spots I have seen', though he did 'shudder slightly to see such palatial residences'. Between 1875 and 1890, 921 freed slaves were received by the mission, most of whom were settled at Freretown. A number of freed slaves and Bombay Africans were also sent to Rabai, Rebmann's old station fifteen miles (about twenty-five kilometres) into the interior where their numbers were considerably supplemented over the years by the arrival of a great many runaway slaves from nearby Arab and Giriama plantations. By the early 1890s Freretown had a population of over nine hundred while Rabai numbered some twelve hundred.[3]

This was the setting for a quarter of a century's sustained inter-action between Africans and English missionaries. The significance of the encounter, however, lies less in the realm of consequence than of precedent. Unlike their more numerous counterparts in Sierra Leone, the freed slaves of Freretown and Rabai left little traceable impact on twentieth-century Kenya. Even within the mission there was little continuity between this early coastal experience and later expansion in the interior, for by 1910 there were no freed slaves or their descendants in the employ of the CMS. But examined as proto-colonial societies, as an indication of things to come in Kenya, the history of these early settlements is rich and instructive. In their patterns of conflict, expressions of protest, attitudes towards cultural change and processes of institutional development, the freed-slave communities of Freretown and Rabai bear marked similarities to the colonial society of twentieth-century Kenya into which they were eventually absorbed. Underlying these parallels was a common 'colonial' social structure in which racial and stratification categories very largely coincided. The consequent lack of social mobility gave these societies a caste-like character, for within the framework of a single political system there existed two groups – the colonizers and the colonized – whose political rights, social roles, economic functions and cultural possibilities were defined essentially on the basis of race.

At the apex of this hierarchy in Freretown and Rabai the missionaries, never numbering more than twenty, occupied the position of a European ruling elite, their status reflected in their superior material conditions. Bishop Hannington, for example, referred to their living 'in every comfort'.[4] Culturally, however, missionaries were both isolated and lonely, alienated not only from local African society but also from other Europeans. Even for their fellow Anglicans of the UMCA at Zanzibar, they could muster 'no sympathy'. Rather pathetically,

H. K. Binns valued a large bell rung hourly at Rabai as it helped to 'keep away feelings of loneliness in this foreign land'. The tight boundaries of this small and beleaguered community of missionaries were disclosed most dramatically on those several occasions in which individuals reached out to Africans for sexual companionship, only to find themselves ostracized by their own colleagues.[5]

Within the social structure of the settlements, the function of the missionaries was to rule, a prerogative which they arrogated exclusively to themselves. African deacons or pastors were never accorded the powers or privileges of their European counterparts while missionaries, whether lay or clerical, consistently refused to serve under African pastors regardless of their qualifications. Such attitudes, which can hardly be considered other than racist, were not initially apparent at Freretown. While the settlement was directed by William Price (1874–6) and his successor William Lamb (1876–8) such racial consciousness was not evident. Perhaps Price's earlier connexion with the Bombay Africans in India and the absence of any substantial challenge to mission authority in part accounted for this situation. But both Price and Lamb were older men, veteran missionaries from India and Yorubaland respectively, who had formed their ideas and values in an earlier and more liberal missionary tradition. It was when they were replaced by younger and more inexperienced missionaries such as John Streeter and John Handford that conflict between mission authorities and the better educated Africans emerged. With the appointment of Streeter in 1877 to the post of Lay Superintendent, a position designed to oversee the secular side of mission affairs, Price's benevolent authoritarianism yielded to outright brutality. The rules of the settlement were defined under Streeter in 1881 giving discretionary power to himself. Punishments ranged from fines for first offenders to ten lashes and fourteen days in stocks for wife-beating, the most severely punished crime. The stocks, wrote Price, were the 'most prominent object' in the settlement, and the lash was in frequent use.[6] Streeter and his supporters defended their methods in terms of the new European understanding of Africans as essentially and racially different from themselves. 'The polished rules and laws of ten centuries of civilized life are hard to apply', he wrote. African adults, added W. E. Taylor, 'are morally speaking children and must be treated as such as they fail to understand any other method'. Given these sentiments, it is not surprising that investigations in the early 1880s by both CMS authorities and British officials from Zanzibar disclosed an administration which had become heavy-handed at best and was frequently cruel and brutal. 'Anything approaching this in the way of severity I had never before witnessed', reported one of the investigators, while another referred to the treatment of Africans at Freretown as 'simply brutal' and 'a disgrace to the honour of Englishmen'.[7]

It was this administration that gave rise to a serious conflict between the missionaries and the second distinguishable group in the settlements, the Bombay Africans. As catechists, teachers, interpreters, preachers and artisans, they had been in large measure responsible for the successful establishment of Freretown and Rabai. By 1882 they numbered some 145, equally divided between the two settlements. Several of them, particularly George David and Ishmael Semler, purchased large pieces of land just outside the mission estate and others engaged in some petty trading. They represented an aspiring mission-trained middle class, confident of their abilities, devoted to the mission but anxious to make the most of their new opportunities. Under the leadership of Price and Lamb, their interests were not seriously compromised. Initial steps were taken towards the development of an African church organization and it was anticipated that George David would become the first bishop, 'the Crowther of the East Coast'.[8] But with Streeter's ascent to power, tensions began to develop and by 1881 an incipient rebellion of at least the better educated and more highly placed section of the Bombay Africans was well under way.

On one level, the revolt grew out of Streeter's harsh disciplinary measures which were applied to Bombay Africans as well as to freed slaves. Yet there was another and more fundamental aspect of the Freretown situation which provoked their indignation – their ambiguous position within the settlements. Missionaries considered them primarily as model citizens, living affirmations of the beneficial results of missionary effort and the model for the newly freed slaves. Thus they were both disappointed and threatened when the Bombay Africans proved 'insubordinate' or when they demonstrated a desire for economic improvement that missionaries translated as evidence of a 'love of money' and a lack of spirituality. In any event they were apparently unwilling wholly to accept their assigned role in the settlements. For their part, the Bombay Africans regarded themselves as co-labourers with the European missionaries in the work of establishing Freretown and as such felt they had a claim on European recognition and gratitude. But such expectations ran counter to racial condescension and stereotyping which was becoming increasingly characteristic of European thought about Africans in general and educated Africans in particular. It was the appearance in a CMS publication of certain generalized derogatory remarks about the Bombay Africans which, together with Streeter's brutality, triggered off their protest.[9]

As an initial move the Bombay Africans contacted the British vice-consul in Zanzibar accusing Streeter of exceeding his legal authority and were successful in obtaining an investigation which resulted in a recommendation for his removal from Freretown. But more significantly, they appealed in a long memorandum over the heads of local missionaries to the Parent Committee in London.[10] Their complaints were primarily twofold. First, they deeply resented the lack of recognition accorded to their efforts by local missionaries. After detailing their many contributions to the settlements, they summarized:

> In short the work which has already been done here and what is being done now by the Europeans are done through the Bombay Africans. For all this why should the missionaries be ever murmuring against the Bombay Africans?

Second, they were offended at the generalized, negative and stereotyped picture which their missionary mentors painted of them. 'It is the omission of this one good word *some* which has been given all the B[ombay] Africans a very bad name and a bad certificate throughout the world.' The authors of the memorandum proposed either that they be stationed in a different location under a God-fearing, unordained missionary or that they be removed completely from the mission. Finally they stated their refusal to receive communion until their letter was answered.

Claiming neither power nor equality, what the Bombay Africans sought fundamentally was an affirmation of their status as valued subordinates. They were not so much rejecting missionary paternalism as claiming its privileges, for they felt they had more than fulfilled its responsibilities. They were the fore-runners not of anti-colonial nationalists but of the most moderate collaborators. Yet such was the antipathy of missionaries to anything that narrowed the gap between themselves and Africans that they could perceive in this protest a 'serious social conflagration ... really far worse than the Swahili invasions'. And while the Bombay Africans were eager to work within the existing structure, they felt driven almost to the point of rupture with the mission. In fact in 1882 George David, who only a few years earlier had been destined for the office of Bishop, submitted his resignation to the mission after Binns indelicately informed him of 'his besetting sin – the love of money'. At least twenty others who had been turned out of Freretown or fled its restrictions found their way to Zanzibar where they obtained work with the UMCA.[11]

The protest of the Bombay Africans provoked an unusually quick response from mission headquarters. William Price was sent out to investigate and his report resulted in the removal of Streeter and the reconciliation of the Bombay Africans, for it represented a thorough defence of their character and accomplishments.[12] Yet the problem of the relationship between the mission and its African employees persisted, since missionary attitudes did not substantially change and there were still no institutional structures through which Africans could contribute to the making of mission policy.

At the bottom of the social pyramid of Freretown and Rabai and at the heart of mission plans for the settlements were the freed slaves. The general model that missionaries had in mind for the settlements seems to have been that of an idealized, rural, pre-industrial England in which the church had played an important social as well as religious role. Overtones of such sentiments were evident, for example, in an 1880 grammar examination given at Freretown in which students were asked to supply the gender of such words as King, Count and Jew and to parse such sentences as 'When the miller brought the flour, I gave him a nice flower from my garden'. These images of an 'earlier and happier England' were common in Anglican circles during the second half of the nineteenth century when efforts were also being made to apply them in urban situations.[13] In Freretown and Rabai they found expression in the attempt to create a class of self-supporting peasant proprietors. 'Every man his own landlord' became the unofficial motto. Each married couple had their own cottage and a small plot of land and were assisted by the mission until the first crop came in, after which they were theoretically on their own. Apart from orphan children who were housed in dormitories and attended school, the independent monogamous family was to be the basic social unit.

The central aspect of this scheme, its self-support feature, soon proved a failure. The soil, weather and available technology yielded only a marginal subsistence to most freed slaves and even this was rendered precarious by frequent crop failures. By the mid-1880s it was the consensus of missionary opinion that the land in and around Freretown could not support the number of people living on it. But what was an observation to the missionaries was desperate experience for the Africans. Like the Bombay Africans, their reaction was to claim the rights of the subordinate in a paternalist relationship and to depend ever more heavily on their missionary patrons. Seeking alternative forms of economic security, the freed slaves took advantage of a visit to Freretown by Bishop Royston in 1884 to insist that 'unless the mission gave them work, they must starve'. To a certain extent, local missionaries did not resist this pressure, for it provided them with a ready source of cheap labour to work on the considerable amount of mission land at Freretown. Under constant pressure from the Parent Committee to reduce expenditure, and provided with only very limited funds, the CMS paid wages described by one missionary as such 'that no man out here who is *really free* would think of receiving'. But the supply of needy workers often exceeded the mission's demand for their services, and when the CMS in 1886 limited the amount of mission employment available, the intense hostility of the freed slaves was provoked. They protested to the bishop, boycotted church, and in a 'drunken brawl' almost attacked the missionary in charge of Freretown.[14]

Nor were the better educated freed slaves, who worked for the mission usually as teachers or catechists, satisfied with their economic position in the settlement. When James Deimler, a young, bright and aspiring teacher, was denied a raise in salary in 1887, he was incensed at what he regarded as a breach of promise, observed that 'Europeans are thieves and stole the black peoples' money', and indicated that he was not willing to 'lick the Europeans' feet' even if the Bombay Africans did. Mission policy on the question of wages for its spiritual agents was clear enough – 'the CMS does not undertake to pay them for the value of their work'. Thus it is not surprising that the arrival of the Imperial British East Africa Company in 1888 and its willingness to pay far higher salaries for clerical help than the mission created a serious situation at Freretown, and by 1890 all but one of the African teachers had left.[15] The Company also provided an alternative source of employment for the mission's surplus unskilled labour force. Concerned about the impact on Christian character of this exposure to a wider world, and feeling the difficulty of obtaining labour for their own purposes, the mission attempted to regulate the flow of workers from the settlement to the Company, and, making a virtue of necessity, re-emphasized the importance of 'industrial work' within Freretown. In such ways, the CMS acknowledged the failure of settlements based on a concept of agricultural self-sufficiency.

Disappointed in the economic aspirations of the freed slaves, missionaries were no less frustrated with the cultural ambitions of their charges. In this area, however, positive mission goals were not so well defined. What was clear, however, was their strenuous opposition to the emergence of 'black Englishmen', people whose dress, education and standard of living compromised the social and psychological distance between Africans and Europeans and thus threatened the distinctions on which missionary paternalism was based. A variety of efforts informed the missions' attempt to forestall this development. In the first place, missionaries tried, at least initially, to reinforce certain aspects of traditional ethnic identities, largely in the hope that the freed slaves would thereby be rendered less susceptible to the influence of Islam, which was in the missionary view a serious disadvantage to Freretown's location. Each of the several 'tribal' groups at Freretown lived in its own quarter of the village and along streets bearing its own name. Traditional dances were occasionally encouraged and were certainly not viewed with the same moral opprobrium as they later came to possess in missionary eyes.[16] Though it was neither possible nor, from the mission viewpoint, desirable to maintain traditional cultures intact, much mission energy was expended on efforts to restrict African access to western culture.

What particularly agitated the missionaries was the propensity of Africans to adopt European modes of dress. Almost from the beginning dress had been a significant symbol of relative status within the settlements. Price distinguished among the well dressed Bombay Africans, the 'better class' of freed slaves who were beginning to 'affect clean clothes', and the others who were 'just emerging from barbarism with little save their black satin skins'.[17] It was one thing for the Bombay Africans to wear European clothes, but when a number of the freed slaves began in the early 1890s to use trousers, hats, boots and walking sticks, the missionaries determined to draw the line. Binns urged that all mission employees be required to wear loin cloths on the grounds that 'many think our religion consists of wearing a pair of trousers'. Though it might 'shake the mission to its foundation', Binns insisted on making the matter of dress a test of nothing less than 'who are truly on the Lord's side'. Bishop Tucker was no less disturbed, for he feared that the adoption of European dress by mission adherents would compromise the African character of the church he hoped to build. In 1895 he issued a circular urging all missionaries to discourage 'indulgence in European luxuries of either food or dress' among mission adherents. Tucker apparently forbade all Africans in the settlement from wearing shoes, while all teachers at Freretown were required to wear a *kanzu*, a long white garment which they detested for its association with Arab and Swahili slave dealers. Restrictions on clothing were slack, however, in comparison with the rules at Jilore in northern Giriamaland where the CMS missionary Douglas Hooper forbade girls to wear corsets, use beads, or plait their hair and complained that authorities at Freretown were insufficiently strict in the matter.[18]

As a potent symbol of both modernity and social mobility, the wearing of European clothing was as attractive to many Africans as it was threatening to missionaries. Those most directly affected by such CMS restrictions on their aspirations were the mission's own employees – the *bourgeoisie* of Freretown – whether Bombay Africans, recently freed slaves or local converts. In 1895, for example, four such employees were licensed as lay readers in the mission and as a condition of their appointment had to agree to a series of rules which forbade their wearing European clothing, cultivating land and building their own houses. The mission also asked them to take a twenty-five per cent cut in salary owing to its financial difficulties. This slash reduced their wages to Rs. (Rupees) 12 per month, a figure below that of common labourers who were then receiving Rs. 15–25 per month.[19] It was in connexion with the imposition of these restrictions that the employees of the CMS drew together under the leadership of James Deimler in an organization they called the African Workers Council, the purpose of which was to unite all the African agents of the mission. 'No one is to take a matter of difficulty and answer by himself', read one of the Council's rules which went on to forbid members from resigning their positions without the Council's permission. Thus the Council sought to defend its members against the authoritarian and individualistic mode of mission administration. But they also wanted 'to consider and report to the bishop or the E.C. [Executive Committee] what we think is the best method to carry on this work'.[20] In the absence of sanctioned channels for African participation in decision-making, the mission's own employees had created for themselves an institutional means of helping to shape the development of the church.

EDUCATING FREED SLAVES

Nowhere were the colonial dimensions of Freretown's social structure more apparent than in the development of its educational system. By the late 1880s Freretown and Rabai boasted a total of more than 350 students in separate boys' and girls' schools and education had become a central, if subordinate, function of the settlements. At the heart of the curriculum, at least initially, was literacy in Swahili and English. Dictation and translation represented the major modes of instruction, and grammar was taught in the upper classes. Arithmetic completed the 'three Rs' to the point of fractions, abstract and concrete numbers, and money exchange. Religious instruction in the form of scripture lessons and catechism was of course the *raison d'être* of the entire curriculum and so assumed a prominent place within it. These freed slave children soon learned to 'write a short life of Joab', to 'relate the Parable of the Tares together with its meaning', and to define such terms as Almighty, Catholic, chastity, Articles of the Christian Faith and grace. In the two upper classes of the Freretown Boys' School geography was an additional subject, while bell ringing, the effects of which were described as 'truly sublime', rounded out the curriculum. This last item was believed to counter the alleged chaos and disorder of Africa, for it was thought to inculcate ideas of harmony, concentration, exactness and uniformity of action.[21] Two aspects of this curriculum were subjected to criticism in the early years of the mission – its overall academic thrust and the question of language. Together, these issues offer an indication of the type of education missionaries believed to be most suitable for their students.

When J. W. Handford, Freretown's first European schoolmaster, began his work in early 1876, students attended classes in both the morning and afternoon. Within a year, missionaries had concluded that this programme entailed 'too much school and too little work', and a number of the older boys were set to cultivating in the afternoons. Within a few years, school boys were making mats, bags and baskets and a certain number were removed from academic training each year to be taught trades. From the beginning, girls had spent their afternoons sewing, but in 1887 their outside work was increased even more at the expense of their general education.[22] If the CMS blunted its academic programme, it also moved sharply away from the teaching of English. Handford reported in 1879 that he intended to make Swahili 'the chief element' in the secular side of mission education, while the following year, the mission announced that 'the use of English will be relinquished' in religious services as well.[23]

Reinforcing these moves away from an academic curriculum was the presence in the settlements of a sizeable number of young men who either had little aptitude for school or had completed their education. In any case, they had no work and represented to the mission an early form of the unemployed school leaver problem. In the creation of industries and the encouragement of industrial training lay the most persistently advocated solution to the problem, though it did not go without opposition from those who felt that an industrial programme deflected the mission from its real work and distorted its image in the eyes of Africans. What finally solidified missionary support for a renewed emphasis on vocationally-oriented technical training was the impact of the Imperial British East Africa Company on the settlements. The CMS experienced the Company's presence in two contradictory ways. On the one hand, the heavy demands for artisans provided a practical opportunity for the mission to engage in this kind of training. On the other hand, many missionaries shared Binns's fear that young people working for the Company in Mombasa 'will be taken captive by the Devil at his will'. Everyone agreed however that industrial training represented the salvation of the settlements, both socially and morally and in 1893 the missionaries resolved that in all schools from the very start a strong point should be made of the dignity of work and the boys trained in habits of industry, self-reliance, punctuality, and general helpfulness so that they grow up to look on idleness and helplessness as a disgrace.[24]

But there was considerable debate as to whether subsequent employment opportunities should be located in the settlements themselves or whether mission-trained artisans might be safely allowed to work in the shops of the Company. A plethora of proposals for industries and industrial training explored these various positions in the years immediately following the arrival of the Company in Mombasa in 1888.

Thus in about fifteen years the mission's educational emphasis had been transformed from one stressing an academic education largely in English to one which focused much more heavily on technical and vocational training with Swahili as the dominant language of both schools and settlements. Here then were early manifestations of what became enduring doubts about the suitability of an academic education for Africans. The change in policy represented the abandonment of an earlier missionary tradition, which, based on a more open-ended and optimistic assessment of African capabilities, sought to 'westernize' its converts. Increasingly the model for African education adopted by missionaries was one 'designed to meet the needs of the British working class' with an emphasis on basic literacy, denominational religion and industry.[25] Applied to the world beyond Europe, it was an educational philosophy which questioned the racial ability of Africans to profit from an academic education in English and doubted the wisdom of letting them try. The freed slaves of Freretown qualified doubly for such an education, for they were 'lower class' both by racial definition and with respect to their position in the settlements. Initiatives in the area of non-academic education for Africans acquired an ideology in the 1920s which drew heavily on the American southern experience and was best summarized in the Phelp–Stokes Commission Reports of 1922 and 1925. But schemes of technical and industrial training, including those of the CMS at Freretown, preceded by many years the 'adaptation' movement which subsequently informed so much of British educational thinking in the colonies. This suggests that many of these practices, as well as much of the later ideological justification for them, represented less an adaptation to African conditions than the racial attitudes and class structure of colonial or proto-colonial society.

Yet the nature of missionary goals imposed limits on the extent to which a basically academic education could be abandoned. As a religion of the book, of course, Christianity demanded a heavy emphasis on literacy. Furthermore, the CMS as an Anglican body had a commitment to building an institutional church which would become, in Henry Venn's classic formulation, self-supporting, self-governing and self-propagating. The necessity for an educated leadership in an indigenous church, and one that would remain loyal to the parent body in matters of doctrine, ritual and government, led to a heavy emphasis on the training of a 'native agency' in 'sound theological doctrines and ecclesiastical principles'.[26] Thus the educational system at Freretown was expected to perform two functions. First the mission was committed to providing a modicum of education consisting of literacy, religion and industry for all of the freed slave children. Early moves away from an academic orientation indicated the direction which missionaries felt this aspect of their programme should take. But the immediate need for teachers, evangelists and catechists in an expanding mission system and the long-term commitment to creating an African church required the education of a mission elite at a higher level and in a manner that would of necessity be largely literary and academic. Until 1894, both approaches were pursued, often in an *ad hoc*, improvised way. By then, however, a serious conflict had emerged between these two lines of development and their respective supporters.

Despite repeated expressions of concern and even urgency regarding the training of a 'native agency', the CMS had by 1890 almost completely failed in this area. No sustained training programme had been developed and at the beginning of 1890 only one trained African teacher remained in the employ of the mission. One explanation for this dismal record lies in the absence of any sustained missionary leadership. Those who most vigorously advocated training programmes – William Price and Bishops Hannington and Parker – were unable to exert a continuing influence on events at Freretown. Price left East Africa in 1876 only to return for short periods in 1882 and 1888. Bishop Hannington was killed in 1885 on his way to Buganda, while his successor Bishop Parker died on the shores of Lake Victoria only three years later. By virtue of their leadership roles and ecclesiastical responsibilities, these were men genuinely interested in creating a corps of well trained Africans. Commitment to this ideal was rather more questionable at the level of ordinary missionaries whose positions could possibly have been threatened by too much activity in this direction. Hannington hinted at this in 1885 when he wrote privately to the Parent Committee that one European was sufficient to supervise both Freretown and Rabai and that not enough was being done to 'develop the natives'. Bishop Parker agreed and urged that promising Africans be put in positions where they could develop their powers and not be overshadowed by Europeans. And Price, back in East Africa for his third time in 1888, deplored the conversion of educated Africans into cooks and donkey boys and suggested that 'many of our good friends have not yet fully realized that the evangelization of Africa is to be done by Africans'.[27]

Related to the failure of mission leadership was the frequent unwillingness of educated Africans to take up careers in the mission. The racial, social and economic discrimination they encountered or saw others undergoing must have dissuaded many from joining training programmes designed as preparation for such careers. In 1889, for example, a group of untrained mission teachers, prospective students for a divinity training course, refused to commit themselves to the programme until the matter of salary, then under dispute, was resolved.[28] Subsequently a number of them left the mission altogether.

The arrival in East Africa of Bishop Alfred Tucker in 1890 brought into the open the bankruptcy of the mission's efforts to create an indigenous African leadership. In a devastating review of the Freretown settlement, Tucker focused largely on what he regarded as the complete failure to train teachers, catechists and pastors. In his view the dormitories were at the root of this failure and freed slave orphans were the worst possible material for 'native agents'. The orphans, he recommended, should be boarded out with Christian families and the dormitories turned into a full-time training institution which would recruit its students entirely from outside the settlements. He was also appalled at the moral and spiritual condition of Freretown – low attendance at church, no missionary spirit and a large number of settlers who 'turned out very bad'. The girls' dormitories, he felt, were little more than a 'feeder for the ranks of prostitution'.[29]

In thus criticizing the work of fifteen years and proposing a radical alteration in the original purpose of Freretown, Tucker incurred displeasure from several quarters. Binns, for example, accused him of condemning everything wholesale while really knowing nothing of the place or people. And the Parent Committee of the CMS in a studiously moderate response to Tucker's report was not disposed to view the situation as nearly so serious and in fact suggested that things could have been far worse. The bishop was furious! Not only had his report been 'practically ignored', but he soon discovered that he was being bypassed on matters concerning the industrial programme of the settlement. Tucker accused CMS headquarters of breaking their promise to consult him before going ahead with an industrial training scheme. 'I would say as with a considerable amount of emphasis', he wrote, 'that I disapprove under present circumstances of the whole thing – root and branch – and can have nothing whatever to do with it.' Spiritual work should come first, he insisted, then the industrial. Finally he strongly hinted that Binns was usurping the leadership role in mission affairs more properly reserved for the bishop and reminded the Parent Committee that 'there is a bishop out here whom they have made the director of the mission'.[30] As an ecclesiastical figure whose basic concern was the future African church rather than the mission, Tucker regarded the development of an indigenous leadership as a matter of the first priority and the educational efforts of the mission as a means to that end. Missionaries such as Binns, however, associated with Freretown almost from its inception, were concerned to see the settlement flourish as a colony for freed slaves and regarded industries and industrial training as a more appropriate agency for that purpose. While the two positions were not necessarily incompatible, the scarcity of financial resources and a certain subtle competition for leadership between Tucker and Binns turned the debate over educational priorities and the future of Freretown into a local impasse which could only be resolved at a higher level. Anxious to mollify an angry bishop, the Parent Committee capitulated entirely to Tucker's position by calling a halt to further industrial developments and by establishing a new, and this time permanent, Divinity School in Freretown. The whole affair pointed out the difficulty for missionaries in achieving a balance between the literary and academic education which the nature of their enterprise demanded and the industrial or vocational training which the nature of their society seemed to require. It would not be the last time that CMS missionaries in Kenya found their calling in some measure of conflict with the constraints of a colonial social order.

PROTEST OF THE 'AGENTS'

Just as the proto-colonial societies of Freretown and Rabai were being incorporated into the larger framework of the British East Africa Protectorate, tension in the settlements again erupted and in the years immediately surrounding the turn of the century, the CMS found itself forced to confront the discontents and protests of its most promising adherents. At the heart of these events was William Jones, the senior African employee of the CMS. A Bombay African originally trained as a blacksmith in India, Jones had been sent to Rabai in 1864 to assist Rebmann, was ordained as a deacon in 1885 and a decade later became the first African priest in British East Africa. For most of his career in the mission, Jones was stationed at Rabai, where in the absence of sustained European leadership he exercised a large measure of secular as well as religious authority. Though his administration at Rabai was no less authoritarian than that of Europeans elsewhere, it was tempered by a sustained rapport with the people of the settlement. 'His influence over the people was remarkable', testified a missionary on the occasion of his death in 1904.

> They called him their 'big father' and looked to him as their great friend and adviser in all their troubles and difficulties. No other man can ever occupy the same place in their hearts and lives. In fact some of the more ignorant people seem to have largely depended on him for their religion, for when he was called to higher service numbers of them went wrong and no longer took any interest in the services of the church.[31]

Much of this esteem derived from his consistent defence of the many runaway slaves who sought refuge at Rabai. Against the orders of his European superiors, he persistently refused to give up runaways to their masters but rather assisted their assimilation into the mission community by baptizing and confirming them with what Europeans regarded as excessive haste and zeal. Nor did Jones neglect the improvement of his own position during his years in East Africa. He purchased a considerable amount of land around Rabai, some of which he rented to Indian shopkeepers, and built himself a large stone house. He sent several of his children to India for education, one of whom returned to become an interpreter in the High Court of colonial Kenya.

While Jones had encountered the insensitivity and even racism of CMS missionaries earlier in his career, in the years after 1895 his sense of grievance mounted. In large part this derived from his relationship with the missionary then in charge of Rabai, the Rev. A. G. Smith, for Jones felt that Smith was deliberately attempting to usurp his position of authority. Smith, he charged, 'worked very hard to put me down in Rabai as he thoroughly knew what influence I had among the people. He blocked me on every side.' When people came to him for counsel, he said that Smith reprimanded them for having gone to a black man and ordered them to obey only the government officer. With the establishment of British administration, Jones must indeed have lost much of his former authority, for the Commissioner of the Protectorate admitted that Smith was 'voluntarily' doing the work of an assistant district commissioner at Rabai. Moreover, Jones resented Smith's suspicious inquisitiveness as to how he built his house and acquired his money.[32] And there was the matter of a dispute between Jones and the mission over the ownership of a piece of land at Rabai. At Smith's suggestion the case was submitted for arbitration to the sub-commissioner of Mombasa who, after considering a great deal of conflicting testimony, decided in favour of the CMS on presumption rather than evidence and charged Jones with costs. Jones's comment on the case revealed his growing awareness of the racial dimensions of conflict in the settlement: 'The sub-commissioner, Mr Hollis, and Smith – three Europeans against one black man – ought to prevail anyhow ... for to say the least, Europeans will side with Europeans.'[33] Finally Jones resented the unwillingness of the mission to meet his needs on the question of salary. When he had been ordained a priest in 1895, he had not been granted the stipulated increment and by 1897 felt that his stipend of Rs. 46 per month, equivalent to what a cook in European service might receive, was insufficient to support his family of seven children. Moreover the CMS stopped an allowance he had been receiving to support the education of his children in

India and refused to pay his passage there to remove them from school, forcing him to make the journey as a deck passenger.

'I fought for Rabai', he wrote to the Parent Committee, 'I fought for the slaves with their masters; I did all I could for mother CMS; and now after many years to be told that I have proved myself an unfaithful servant was unbearable, hence I resigned.' Jones spurned a quick mission offer to raise his salary, and in late 1898 took up a new position with the government at Rs. 150 per month, more than three times his mission wage. As in the case of Bishop Crowther's encounter with missionary racism in West Africa, Jones had been harassed out of the CMS by missionaries whose unwillingness to incorporate him into their structure of values had been exacerbated by the advent of colonial rule.

Jones's resignation touched off a series of demands for increased salaries among the hierarchy of mission employees and provoked mass resignations when those demands were not met. James Deimler's comment was not untypical: 'If one is quiet and works patiently on, is it the cause of his being forgotten till he shouts and threatens to leave?'[34] By 1900, the entire corps of CMS agents on the coast had submitted their resignations 'as the salaries they considered too small'. Yet it seemed unlikely that money was the only or even the major complaint of these mission employees, for within a year they had all returned to the CMS at salaries far below what they could have received elsewhere. While they were solidly committed to many of the goals and values of the mission, they actively resented the mission's persistent attempts to frustrate their efforts at self-improvement in terms of clothing, housing, cultivation, and salary. These people, furthermore, had frequently experienced the unwillingness of missionaries to accord them on a personal level the courtesy and dignity readily granted to other whites. Finally they were not usually regarded as co-workers but as agents or instruments of mission policy without any means of contributing to the formation of that policy. After a quarter of a century of effort a new bishop, W. G. Peel, who arrived in 1900, found that 'there is no real Native Church Council Organization in the whole of the Mission'.[35]

That this pattern of conflict was rooted less in the structure of the mission than in the attitudes of the missionaries was reflected in the ease with which Bishop Peel was able to woo the disaffected men back into the CMS. As a person of more moderate views and conciliatory disposition than many of the local missionaries, Peel had a certain respect for the 'spirit of independence' he observed in leading African Christians and felt that it could be a positive force 'if rightly and *lovingly* guided'. Such attitudes gave him a rapport with the mission's African employees that had been lacking before. Furthermore Peel agreed to an increase in salary of approximately twenty per cent for the African staff.[36] While this move by no means made mission salaries competitive with those in government offices, all of those who resigned returned to the mission's employ by October of 1900.

In the resolution of this particular crisis lay the roots of yet another, for Bishop Peel had assured the returning staff, some of whom were chosen for further training, that the teaching of English and its use as a medium of instruction would figure prominently in the curriculum of the Divinity School. By this time, the knowledge of English had both a cash and prestige value and, like the wearing of European clothing, was a potent symbol of modernity and a perceived means of mobility in the new order of colonial East Africa. For precisely these reasons, many missionaries proved exceedingly reluctant to engage in the widespread dissemination of their own language. It was Peel's misfortune that among those most adamantly opposed to the teaching of English was the Rev. J. E. Hamshere, the twenty-nine-year-old principal of the Divinity School. Only forty-five minutes of English instruction per week, and this in the form of dictation, was included in the timetable of the school. Even in personal discourse, Hamshere refused to speak English to his students but answered them in Swahili when they addressed him in his own tongue. In other ways as well, the regimen of the Divinity School was stern and rigid. Hamshere planned his students' activities in detail, from seashore bathing at 5.30 every morning to a prayer meeting at 8.30 in the evening. That many of his students were married men with families made not the slightest difference to Hamshere who felt that 'we are a sort of nursery father and mother to these people who lean on one as children do'.[37]

Led by Levi Mwangoma and Josiah Rimba, the Divinity School students sharply protested at both the lack of English instruction and the strict regulations of the institution, and there soon developed what Hamshere called a 'tense spirit of insubordination', followed by a series of resignations from the training faculty. Furthermore the African Workers Council was activated. Hamshere himself testified to the effectiveness of their organization when he indicated that 'none would act without the other'. At this juncture, the missionaries perceived a serious dilemma. On the one hand there was little sympathy for Hamshere among his colleagues, who recommended that he be removed from the Divinity School. Likewise, Peel had concluded that the quarrel had been 'more, much more the result of his action than of theirs'.[38] Yet they felt their own authority was at stake. Anxious inquiries regarding the activities of the African Workers Council were initiated in the fear that its members 'might turn it to some of the disadvantages that trade unions have been thought to bring'.[39] Thus it was decided to retain Hamshere and to suspend Levi and Josiah from CMS employment. As the issue of authority loomed larger in missionary eyes, the original question of English was increasingly forgotten, a development which facilitated the resolution of the crisis, for the protesting students had never intended to challenge the authority of the mission. Under the careful handling of Peel, who wanted to 'pass the matter over lightly', Hamshere was rebuked but retained, Levi and Josiah were reinstated as CMS employees but not required to re-enter the Divinity School, and through a policy of calculated but very limited conciliation mission authorities arrested yet another crisis.

The persistence of social conflict in Freretown and Rabai was only indirectly related to their 'colonial' social structure, for the aspiring members of these communites never really sought to challenge the unequal distribution of power in the settlements. What activated their protest was rather, in E. E. Hagen's perceptive phrase, 'the withdrawal of status respect',[40] for in both word and action the missionaries had demonstrated a lack of regard for the sensibilities and aspirations of their African subordinates which was keenly and bitterly felt. It was the colonial character of the settlements that rendered them vulnerable in this way, for it made them dependent on the missionaries for an affirmation of their value. And so the CMS's African employees reacted in anger, protest and sometimes withdrawal as they sought to challenge the paternalism of condescension which informed the attitude of so many Europeans towards their African associates. Such was missionary insensitivity, insecurity and cultural arrogance, an outlook conditioned in various degrees by their class background, narrow evangelical training and the impact of a rigid racial anthropology, that they not only repeatedly provoked their

African employees but also perceived in their remonstrations an assault on the very social order of the settlements. Yet when local CMS leadership was in the hands of men such as Price and Peel, whose paternalism was one of conciliation and who affirmed their respect for the roles of their subordinates, African grievances were easily accommodated with no loss of missionary authority.

By the turn of the century, Freretown and Rabai had lost much of their individuality as they were absorbed into what became colonial Kenya. Nor were they any longer of such central significance to the CMS itself as the mission turned to the possibilities of expansion in the interior.

FOOTNOTES

1. CMS/LI, Hutchinson to Price, 12 February 1875.
2. For an examination of the 'foreign policy' problems of the mission's settlement with both Arab–Swahili society around Mombasa and British authorities at Zanzibar, see Norman R. Bennett, 'The Church Missionary Society at Mombasa, 1874–1894', *Boston University Papers on African History* (Boston, 1964).
3. CMS/1885/25, Hannington to Lang, 9 February 1885; 1881/89, Map of Freretown; 1890/91, Binns to Lang, 9 April 1890.
4. CMS/1885/25, Hannington to Lang, 9 February 1885.
5. CMS/1881/38, Binns to Hutchinson, 21 February 1881; 1886/339, Jones to CMS, October 1886; Binns Journals, 9 November 1878.
6. CMS/1881/96, Rules of Feretown; 1882/26; Price Journal, 6 June 1882.
7. CMS/1881/71, Streeter to Stock, 12 July 1881; Taylor to Stock, 12 July 1881; Foreign Office 541/49, Holmwood to Kirk, 7 July 1881; Byles to Brownrigg, 12 July 1881.
8. CMS/017, Lamb to Wright, 4 November 1876.
9. 'The East Africa Mission', *Church Missionary Intelligencer* (January 1881); CMS/1883/47, Binns to Lang, 17 March 1883.
10. Foreign Office 541/49, Holmwood to Streeter, 6 July 1881; CMS/1881/30, Memorandum of Bombay Africans to the CMS, 28 February 1881. Five of them signed the letter: George David, Thomas Smith, J. Ainsworth, Ishmael Semler and R. Keating.
11. CMS/1881/59, Menzies to Hutchinson, 21 June 1881; 1882/3, Price to Wigram, 14 December 1881; Binns Journal, 10 September 1882.
12. CMS/1882/65, Report on East Africa Mission, 6 October 1882.
13. CMS/011, Examination Papers, 1880; K. S. Inglis, *Churches and the Working Class in Victorian England* (London, 1963), pp. 21–4.
14. CMS/1884/115, Shaw to Lang, 22 November 1884; 1885/120, Shaw to Lang, 1 August 1885; 1887/14, Shaw to Lang, 9 December 1886.
15. CMS/1887/107, Shaw to Bishop (enclosure), 2, 3 February 1887; 1890/7, Binns to Lang, 1 January 1890; 1889/195, Pruen to Lang, 6 June 1889.
16. *Proceedings of the Church Missionary Society* (hereafter *Proceedings*), 1876–77, p. 41; Binns Journals, 8 November 1878.
17. CMS/1882/58, Price Journal, 9 May 1882.
18. CMS/1891/89, Binns to Lang, 28 February 1891; 1896/394, Hooper to CMS, 29 October 1896; KNA: CMS 1/634, Rabai Logbook, 7 February 1895; Alfred R. Tucker, *Eighteen Years in Uganda and East Africa* (London, 1908), I, p. 357.

19. CMS/1895/102, Tucker to Baylis, 4 March 1895.
20. CMS/1901/153, African Workers Council.
21. CMS/1888/98, Account of Schools; 1877/37, Handford to Wright, 3 February 1877; CMS/011, Grade Book, 1878; Examination Papers, 1880.
22. CMS/M5/1877/31, Russell to Lay Secretary, 1 February 1877; 1881/1, Binns to Lang, 19 December 1887.
23. *Proceedings*, 1878–79, p. 36; 1879–80, p. 23.
24. CMS/1893/272, Scheme for the Management of CMS Boys.
25. Philip Curtin, *The Image of Africa* (Madison, 1964), p. 264; Mary Sturt, *The Education of the People* (London, 1967), pp. 27–9; G. A. N. Lowndes, *The Silent Social Revolution* (London, 1937), p. 5.
26. E. Stock, 'Future Independent Churches in the Mission Field', *Church Missionary Intelligencer* (April 1901), pp. 246, 257.
27. E. C. Dawson, *The Last Journals of Bishop Hannington* (London, 1888), pp. 324–5; CMS/1886/300, Parker to CMS; 1887/357, Price to Lang, 6 September 1888.
28. CMS/1889/217, Fitch to Lang, 3 July 1889.
29. CMS/1892/197, Tucker to Lang, 16 May 1892; 1892/238, Tucker to Wigram, 5 June 1892.
30. CMS/1892/435, Binns to Lang, 7 November 1892; 1893/242, Tucker to Baylis, 31 August 1893; P4, Resolution regarding Freretown, 18 July 1893.
31. *Proceedings*, 1905, p. 78.
32. CMS/1899/112, Jones to Baylis, 9 May 1899; Great Britain, *Parliamentary Papers*, 1897, LX, cd. 8683, *Report on the British East Africa Protectorate to July 20, 1897*.
33. CMS/1899/112, Jones to Baylis, 9 May 1899.
34. CMS/1898/96, Deimler to Finance Committee, 9 April 1898.
35. CMS/1900/31, Peel to Baylis, 1 March 1900.
36. CMS/1901/72, Report by the Bishop of Mombasa, 26 March 1901.
37. CMS/1897/104, 105, Hamshere to Baylis, 24 March 1897.
38. CMS/1902/40, Divinity School Diary, 1 April 1901; 1903/151, Hamshere to Baylis, 5 October 1903.
39. CMS/L9, Baylis to Burt, 1 November 1901.
40. Everett E. Hagen, *On the Theory of Social Change* (Homewood, Ill., 1962), p. 185.

CHAPTER III

꓀꓀꓀꓀꓀꓀꓀꓀꓀꓀꓀꓀꓀꓀꓀꓀꓀꓀꓀꓀꓀꓀꓀꓀꓀꓀꓀꓀꓀꓀

The Dynamics of Mission Expansion, 1875–1914

The 'scramble for Africa' was a religious as well as a political phenomenon for, paralleling the imperial partition of the continent, a variety of European and American missionary groups competed intensely to divide and occupy Africa for their respective churches. The initial result of this religious scramble was the establishment of hundreds of mission stations which, manned usually by Europeans, were everywhere the local agency of the missionary purpose. Only after this had been accomplished could the work of attracting converts and founding a church begin. The process of creating these outposts has naturally not received the attention accorded to the partition and conquest of Africa. Yet it was not a simple, automatic or an insignificant movement and deserves study in its own right for a variety of reasons.

In the first place, it offers an opportunity to examine a neglected and misunderstood dimension of European–African contact in the years immediately surrounding the era of conquest. Mission expansion, after all, was not simply a product of the evangelical imperative of the Christian gospel but was conditioned by an interplay of local forces prominent among which were the attempts of African societies to manipulate the missionary presence to their own advantage. In West Africa, for example, Ajayi and Ayandele have related the progress of mission advance among the Yoruba to the military balance of their civil wars, while Ekechi has pointed to the connexion between mission penetration of Igboland and the political and economic rivalry of various Igbo towns. Similarly, Marcia Wright has sought to explain the pace and direction of early German mission expansion in southern Tanzania by reference to the complexities of local ethnic politics.[1] By examining such local as well as metropolitan roots of mission expansion, new discoveries in this early period of contact can be made.

Second, a study of mission expansion touches on the question of the relationship among the various agencies of imperialism, for in the early years of the colonial era the courses of both mission and political and economic expansion intersected at various points as each attempted to exploit the other for its own ends. The West African studies already mentioned point to the frequent alliances of English missionaries with British consuls on the coast and the Royal Niger Company in the interior as a factor which alternately facilitated and frustrated mission expansion in Nigeria. On the other hand, certain English mission groups in Leopold's Belgian Congo and several German societies in Tanganyika came into serious and intense conflict with both local and metropolitan colonial officials.[2] Thus the converging and conflicting interests of consul, company, colonial government and mission society, as well as African reaction to these relationships, played an important role in determining the timing and direction of mission expansion.

Finally, the study of mission expansion is important because it has had long-term political, social and religious consequences. Operating through a 'sphere of influence' policy, the pattern of mission competition largely determined the geographical distribution of the various denominational expressions of Christianity and influenced the access to educational opportunities within a given territory.[3] Where nationalist political organizations at least partially followed denominational lines, as in Uganda, the impact of earlier patterns of mission expansion is clear.[4] On a more local level in Kenya, the incidence of independent schools growing out of the female circumcision crisis largely followed denominational lines. Those parts of Kikuyu country which had earlier fallen within the Anglican sphere produced far fewer independent schools than those under Presbyterian or American fundamentalist control, owing to the more tolerant Anglican attitude towards female circumcision.

THE EXPANSION OF THE MISSIONARY FRONTIER

Between 1875 and 1914 the Church Missionary Society's operations in what became the Diocese of Mombasa[5] grew from its two initial stations in the environs of Mombasa to sixteen resident mission centres widely dispersed throughout eastern and central Kenya. The earliest such attempts were naturally focused on the neighbouring Mijikenda peoples, particularly the Rabai, Giriama and Digo, as well as among the immigrant Kamba communities in the area. These efforts did not issue in real success until 1890 when the Jilore station was established at the northern end of Giriama country. In the meantime the CMS had pressed inland with an isolated outpost at Sagalla in the Taita hills in 1883 and, after an abortive attempt to locate one among the Chagga, planted a station at Taveta in 1892. The first decade of the new century saw the most dramatic outburst of mission energies as the Uganda Railroad and the new colonial administration opened up the previously inaccessible Kikuyu highlands to mission penetration. When baldly summarized in this fashion, the process of mission expansion may appear to be a straightforward matter of implementing a clearly articulated mission policy. On the contrary, however, it was a highly tentative process characterized by a variety of short-term considerations rather than by rational long-range planning and its results were determined far more by the inter-action of local groups than by direction from either mission headquarters or colonial metropoles. While the conditions under which expansion took place varied considerably from place to place, an analysis of the process suggests that three factors need to be considered: the nature of mission initiatives and policies, the presence of European economic and political interests, and the attempts of African societies and their leaders to turn the coming of these various Europeans to their own advantage.

At the centre of the complex of motives impelling mission expansion lay a dynamic ideology, which was particularly compatible with the energetic, self-confident, even arrogant dimensions of nineteenth-century European consciousness. The biblical injunction to 'make disciples of all nations' found widespread reception perhaps best reflected in the slogan of the late nineteenth-century Student Volunteer Movement for Foreign Missions which proclaimed as its goal nothing less than 'the evangelization of the world in this generation'.[6] In CMS circles concerned with East Africa this ideology found its clearest expression in Krapf's vision of a 'mission chain between East and West Africa'. Originally conceived in the mid-nineteenth century, the idea was an important element in the CMS justification for establishing Freretown a quarter of a century later, and early missionaries there were clearly instructed that the settlement was a means 'for carrying out their long contemplated plan of a chain of missions from Mombasa towards the Victoria Nyanza'.[7] The degree to which this ideology had been absorbed by individual missionaries was reflected in the guilt which many experienced when they were either required or tempted to remain long in any one place.[8]

Such an ideology, however, was frequently used to justify mission expansion growing out of very different concerns. Expansion could be, for example, a means of social promotion for individuals within the very small and status-conscious community of European missionaries. Mobility from lay to clerical status could be more easily achieved if a layman opened up a new station in the interior where the neeed to serve communion, conduct baptism, and perform marriages strengthend his case for ordination. After establishing two new stations among the Kikuyu, a lay missionary called McGregor supported his request for ordination with the claim that it would add greatly to his influence with government officials.[9] Of seven lay missionaries who opened up-country centres, six were subsequently ordained.

Another indication of status within the CMS involved having sole control over a particular mission station, and individuals' desires to create or defend their own outposts further contributed to the process of mission expansion. The CMS pattern of creating many lightly staffed stations rather than a few well-manned centres permitted and reinforced this petty empire building. The CMS station at Wusi in Taita country, only three hours' walk from another Anglican establishment, was created in 1904 solely because of an inability to resolve the problem of authority among three male missionaries.[10] For whatever reasons, the desire to move up-country was so intense that the veteran missionary H. K. Binns complained in 1906 that no one wanted to remain at the coast.[11] The observation that imperial expansion afforded opportunities for individuals to escape the constraints of authority and the limits of their social position at home finds confirmation in the missionary movement and helps to account for the haphazard nature of mission expansion.[12]

If the frontier beckoned ambitious or frustrated individuals, it also stimulated competition among various mission societies. As the number of such groups in Kenya increased, the fear of preemption by a rival became a potent impetus for expansion. Such anxieties gave rise, especially in Kikuyuland, to a veritable mission scramble analogous in its atmosphere of urgency and even panic to the partition of Africa in the 1890s. Largely defensive in nature, each mission intended to secure an adequate recruiting base for its future church. A doctrine of effective occupation also developed in which the establishment of a small school or church or the posting of a catechist to an area was an accepted sign of possession. Moreover, the threat of rivals became a standard means for local missionaries to prod resources of men and money out of perpetually over-taxed home authorities. 'The Roman Catholics are possessing the land. They come in batches of from six to twenty', wrote one anxious CMS missionary to his Parent Committee justifying a request for reinforcements.[13]

While the missionary movement did have an ideological and structural dynamic of its own, its expansion into the African interior was greatly facilitated through association with the official agencies of European colonial policy – first the Company and after 1895 the fledgling administration of the British East Africa Protectorate. British authorities in East Africa regarded missionaries as integral to the process of 'opening up' Africa. Sir Arthur Hardinge, first commissioner of the East African Protectorate, praised the CMS missionary A. G. Smith for voluntarily and unofficially performing the duties of an assistant district commissioner at Rabai.[14] His successor, Sir Charles Eliot, commented more generally: 'The opening of a new missionary station has seemed to me to be generally as efficacious for the extension of European influence as the opening of a government station.'[15] Missionaries for the most part regarded British power and prosperity as a 'blessing for fidelity to the true faith' and thus saw nothing insidious or artificial about taking advantage of their association with British economic or political expansion to further the kingdom of God. In fact Rebmann, who worked for almost thirty frustrating years without the benefit of European political influence, came to the conclusion that 'where the power of a Christian nation ceased to be felt, there is also the boundary, set by Providence, to missionary labour'.[16] As a result CMS missionaries were not reluctant to identify actively with the political aspirations of their government. Unlike the pre-1874 era in which virtually all CMS representatives in East Africa were Germans, the period of the scramble saw the growth of an increasingly nationalist missionary consciousness. The CMS, for example, readily sent missionaries to Chagga country on the slopes of Mount Kilimanjaro in 1885 at the direct request of Sir John Kirk, British consul-general at Zanzibar, who was attempting to counter German incursions into this area.[17] In short, to English missionaries patriotism was an instrument of Providence.

There was, however, an important element of ambivalence, even tension, in the relationship between mission and state. Krapf thought that a European presence would obstruct as much as assist the missionary enterprise and warned his readers to 'banish the thought that Europe must spread her protecting wings over Eastern Africa if missionary work is to prosper. . . .'[18] If Krapf's ambivalence derived from a reluctance to rely on human agencies to further the kingdom of God, that of W. S. Price had more practical roots. While he was anxious to cooperate with the Company, he also wanted to preserve the separate identity of the mission by avoiding 'any action or cooperation such as would give the idea that the BEAC and CMS are only different names for the same thing'.[19] The colonial government was also aware of these separate interests and soon discovered, for example, that uncontrolled mission expansion did not serve the ends of orderly administration. Consequently it took measures to regulate mission expansion which included a rule requiring a minimum of ten miles (sixteen kilometres) between stations of different societies and limits on the amount of land missions could acquire. The missions bitterly resented some of these measures as, in the words of one outraged Anglican, a 'monstrous violation of British liberties'.[20] In brief, the interaction of the missionary movement with British colonial power conditioned the process of mission expansion generally by expediting it in the era of conquest and by constraining it once the period of settled administration had begun.

Finally, the attitudes and policies of those African societies which found themselves on the receiving end of the Christian gospel also significantly influenced the process of mission expansion. Missionaries, after all, could be useful to African societies in a variety of ways. They were, for example, sometimes seen as a potential element in the developing trade networks of those nineteenth-century East African societies which were in the process of shifting from a subsistence to a market trading economy. Thus in the middle of the century the CMS missionary and explorer J. L. Krapf was warmly welcomed by Kivoi, a Kamba 'merchant prince' who was developing trading connexions with the coast. Kivoi told Krapf of his desire to conduct this trade via the Tana River in order to bypass the peoples of the coastal hinterland who frequently molested his caravans.[21] He doubtless hoped that Krapf's contacts with the Arab authorities in Mombasa and with the coastal peoples would further these economic interests. Later in the century when a group of Giriama villages north of Rabai requested the CMS to send them a teacher, the missionaries observed that 'their predominant motive may be (as almost confessed by themselves) the desire that traders in cloth, knives, etc. may settle among them'.[22] In 1880 several Taita traders selling skins in the vicinity of Rabai expressed to the CMS a desire for a European to live among them.[23]

The positive reception of the CMS at Taveta also owed much to the commercial interests of this fascinating but little studied group. In its forest sanctuary along the Lumi River, Taveta became during the nineteenth century an important link in Arab–Swahili commercial penetration of the interior by acting as both a trading centre and a rest and supply station for caravans about to cross Masailand. Both its physical security and its commercial importance made many Europeans view it as an island of stability – 'the very heart of paradise' according to von Höhnel – in a sea of economic and political rivalry. A certain cosmopolitanism informed its culture as Swahili and Masai were widely understood languages and representatives of fifteen to twenty other East African peoples were to be found there in the late nineteenth century.[24] Although the CMS first actively considered establishing a centre in Taveta in the mid-1880s owing to Kirk's urging the mission towards Kilimanjaro, it was not until 1890 that negotiations for a site were concluded. In a formal ceremony at which the Taveta representatives made clear that no outright sale was involved, the CMS was granted land for a station.[25] This was by now a familiar procedure for the Taveta people as similar arrangements had been made with Swahili caravans and with the explorer and botanist Harry Johnson. In view of Taveta's traditional and commercially lucrative 'open door' policy, and given the growing number of Europeans passing through the area, the decision to admit the CMS was hardly surprising. Not until 1892, however, when the mission was ousted from its Chagga work by the Germans, who accused them of political interference, did the CMS fall back on Taveta in British territory and begin a successful station there.

If missionaries were often expected to play an economic role, their failure or inability to do so could provoke hostility or intransigence among Africans and thus prevent the mission's expansion. J. A. Wray, founder of the initially unsuccessful Taita station, quoted the people of Sagalla as telling him, 'White man, you are living in our country, but you don't buy our ivory, cattle or slaves; neither do you pay our children for coming to school. We feel we are not getting the profit out of you we had hoped for'.[26] A prominent Giriama elder, Tuvu Ki Gunda, echoed this sentiment when he observed that CMS missionaries 'did not trade and therefore were useless'.[27]

Performing economic functions could lead, however, to political involvement as missionaries were frequently persuaded to play the role of broker in disputes among various African groups. For example, the complex economic relations among the Swahili of Mombasa, the hinterland Rabai and those Kamba who had settled in the area frequently gave rise to conflicts in which missionaries were urged to mediate. The Swahili had often performed this function in various Mijikenda disputes, but as they gained the political and economic upper hand in their relations with the coastal people, their interests frequently came into conflict with those of the Mijikenda and new people were needed to perform the role of broker.[28] As the Giriama told the CMS missionary Hooper, 'If we have a case against a Swahili, are we going to let another Swahili judge it?'[29] Thus in 1879 a number of Kamba elders asked the CMS missionary Binns to help them make peace with the Swahili. While he refused to do so, he did suggest that if they 'joined the book' and were 'under a European', the Swahili would not dare fight them. The following year both Kamba and Rabai elders requested Binns to help resolve a dispute between them. His most successful effort occurred when he persuaded the *wali* or governor of Mombasa to oust a group of offensive Swahili, probably traders, living among the Rabai. His action in this case led directly to the establishment of a CMS outstation at the Rabai village or *kaya* called Fimboni.[30] The mission's reputation for influence with Mombasa and Zanzibar authorities soon spread and was largely responsible for securing for the CMS the cooperation of Digo elders of the Shimba hills. When approached in 1882 about land for a station, they made clear that their most pressing concern was protection from the ravages of Mbaruk, a Mazrui rebel against the authority of the Sultan of Zanzibar. With this in mind, they agreed to a missionary presence in their country.[31] In such ways did European missionaries, themselves powerless but with useful contacts and influence, take part in the resolution of conflicts among inter-acting African societies.

After the advent of British rule in 1895, it was of course mission links to the colonial government that most often secured for them the cooperation of Africans with political authority. For example in 1908 when trying to organize a station at Vitengeni in central Giriamaland, the CMS encountered considerable opposition from local elders who feared that the presence of the missionaries would provide an opportunity for their wives to flee if they felt mistreated at home. The missionary in charge of the project reported that 'with the assistance of the Government Commissioner at Malindi, I was able to assure them that the sole object of my mission was to teach them the things of God', and he soon found that those who had been his greatest opponents 'now were loud in their profession of friendship'.[32]

While tensions existed in the relationship between missions and the colonial establishment, Africans on the whole saw missionaries as an integral though clearly differentiated part of the European presence. Insofar as they sought some positive relationship with the intruders, they were frequently prepared to facilitate the establishment of missions and to use them as brokers or intermediaries between themselves and the colonial government. On the other hand, overt hostility to the new order often involved a definite reluctance to permit the penetration of mission agencies as well.

It was, then, the inter-action of mission, colonial and African interests that determined the direction and pace of CMS expansion in Kenya. The following illustrations exemplify this process in two major areas of Anglican concentration. The first analyses CMS expansion into Giriama country before the imposition of colonial rule, while the second examines the mission's penetration of Kikuyuland during the early years of British control.

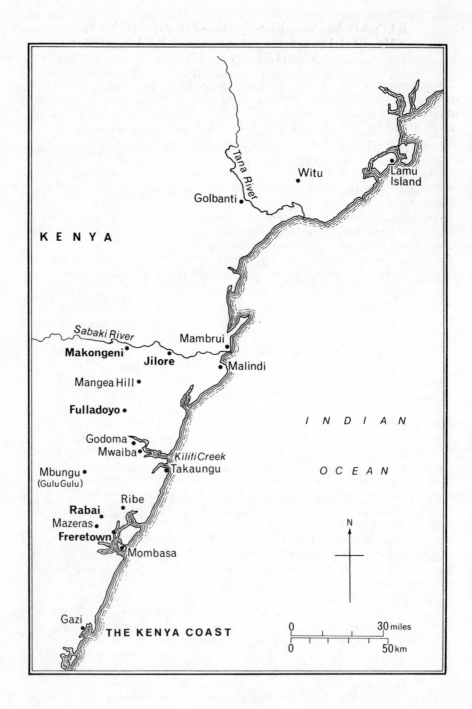

KENYA

Tana River

Witu

Golbanti

Lamu
Island

Sabaki River

Makongeni   Jilore   Mambrui

Malindi

Mangea Hill

Fulladoyo

Godoma
Mwaiba   Kilifi Creek
Takaungu

Mbungu
(Gulu Gulu)

Ribe

Rabai
Mazeras
Freretown
Mombasa

Gazi   THE KENYA COAST

INDIAN

OCEAN

N

0   30 miles

0   50 km

RUNAWAY SLAVES AND THE COMPANY: THE POLITICS OF MISSION EXPANSION IN GIRIAMALAND

The expansion of the Church Missionary Society into Giriamaland occurred in the context of revolutionary changes taking place along the East African coast during the last quarter of the nineteenth century. British attempts to end the slave trade, the decline of Arab power and threats to an Arab plantation economy based on slavery, intensification of mission activity, the coming of the IBEAC – these were factors affecting the mission's operations. The question of CMS expansion in this area occurred in the course of the mission's relations with two groups marginal to Giriama society itself. One included several communities of runaway slaves, known as *watoro*, fugitives from Arab plantations as well as from the slave-holding Giriama themselves. The other was a small community of Giriama Christians which had grown out of the CMS's earlier work in the area. By 1876 about thirty such individuals lived at Godoma under the leadership of Abe Sidi. Since the mission had failed for thirty years to make much headway among the Mijikenda, they were anxious to take up work among these receptive groups. They were, however, prevented from doing so largely by Arab–Swahili hostility and not until the Company's influence was felt on the coast was the CMS able to establish its first permanent resident station in Giriamaland.

Runaway slave communities were nothing new on the East African coast. Krapf was aware of one called Koromio a the end of Kilifi Creek as early as 1848 and speculated that they would be receptive to missionary overtures.[33] Another *watoro* settlement had been established along the southern bank of the Sabaki River and it was from this group that the initiative came for a connexion with the CMS. These fugitives from Arab plantations had established themselves initially near Lake Jilore, but Arab pressure drove them further west and by the 1880s they had created a series of sizeable well-armed and organized villages at Makongeni on both sides of the Sabaki. These *watoro* had first put themselves under the protection of the local Galla population in return for which they provided the latter with tribute, often in the form of labour. They soon found, however, that their liberty was still in jeopardy, for the Galla proved hard task-masters and were inclined to sell them into slavery again.[34] Since the early 1870s there had been contacts between these *watoro* communities and the Giriama Christians at Godoma and in 1872 the Jilore people, under the leadership of one Abdallah, expressed interest in a closer association with Godoma and Rebmann's mission at Rabai. One of Rebmann's African associates analysed their motives: '(H)e seeing Abe Sidi and his friends learning the Book took them to be under British government and he wished for the same. Thinking that if a European came and dwell(ed) among them, they would be well-protected from the Swahilis who wish to enslave them again.'[35] At Abe Sidi's invitation, Abdallah formally associated himself with the mission 'with the view of embracing the Book and being under British protection' and sent one of his number to study at Godoma. Five years later the Jilore *watoro* again invited a CMS missionary to live among them, although this time it was to shield them from Galla tyranny which had become as oppressive as coastal slavery.[36]

Other requests for mission assistance came from the small Giriama Christian community at Godoma. 'Do you not know,' they asked, 'that a sheep without a shepherd cannot be without being lost?'[37] Such requests took on a less religious flavour when in 1878 a small section of this settlement broke away and established itself at Fulladoyo about twenty miles (thirty kilometres) north-west of Kilifi. There it soon took on a wider significance as it very rapidly became a major centre of refuge for runaway slaves. Under the firm Christian leadership of Abe Sidi and his Giriama associates, Fulladoyo became a comfortably settled small town of perhaps five hundred people, with houses neatly built and well constructed, shambas (farm plots) well cultivated and people meeting morning and evening for prayers in their own church. 'So much evidence of energy and public spirit I have seen nowhere else in Africa', wrote one missionary visitor.[38]

The development of Fulladoyo may be seen as part of certain more general trends in nineteenth-century Mijikenda history. Recent studies have pointed to the emergence of new individualistic bases of organization and authority as people increasingly moved away from the traditional fortified kayas or villages and as new commercial opportunities became available. The consequent decline of such corporate institutions as the kambi or council of elders opened the way for new men such as Ngonyo of Marafa or Mwakikongo to create highly personal political units based largely on wealth derived from trade. Most strikingly similar to Abe Sidi's experience was that of Mua Wa Ngombe, a Digo trader who in the middle of the century established his own kaya, populated mainly by runaway slaves, and managed to control the trade route to Usambara.[39] Fulladoyo in this context can be seen as a new kaya and Abe Sidi as one of the new men able to create order out of the changed circumstances of the late nineteenth century.

The position of this new kaya was precarious indeed and its strategies for dealing with the insecurity were both military and diplomatic. Binns reported that it was armed to the teeth against possible Arab or Swahili attacks and Price indicated that it was sufficiently strong to compel the respect of its immediate neighbours. On the diplomatic front, Abe Sidi made an agreement with the neighbouring Giriama not to accept any of their slaves if his people were given freedom of movement, but this arrangement had broken down by 1881. A final element in its defensive strategy involved a link with the CMS and resulted in persistent requests for a European missionary to live with them, particularly as they contemplated a move to a more defensible location at Mount Mangea.[40]

The reasons behind these various requests for mission assistance are fairly clear. While not discounting the genuine religious needs of those who had only recently found their way to a new faith, it is evident that the watoro elements at Jilore and Fulladoyo desperately hoped that the presence of British missionaries would somehow afford them an element of protection against their present or former master. It was, after all, well known that many watoro had found refuge at the Rabai station of the CMS and that the mission was sympathetically disposed towards them. Furthermore, the remaining Giriama Christians at Godoma – those who had not moved to Fulladoyo – fervently sought a missionary for organizational purposes to regulate affairs and resolve disputes among this small, leaderless, and factious group. They sincerely feared the break-up of their small community and the loss of their newly found faith unless help were forthcoming.[41]

The mission responded to these invitations far more cautiously than might have been expected. Moral encouragement, periodic missionary visits and the posting of occasional schoolboys to Fulladoyo and Godoma was the extent of the mission's commitment. While several Europeans were anxious to take up permanent work in the area, none was assigned the task.

The fundamental reason for the hesitant CMS approach lay in Arab–Swahili hostility. On a political level, the *wali* or governor of Mombasa clearly disliked the CMS presence as it tended to usurp his power, for individual missionaries could and did go over his head to the Sultan in Zanzibar.[42] Furthermore, the need to protect the mission from Arab or Swahili attacks could involve him in serious trouble with his own people. More basic, however, was the mission's threat to the slave economy of the coast. Since at least 1878 the CMS station at Rabai had been accepting runaway slaves with few questions asked, and by the early 1880s, relations with both Arab and Giriama slave-owners hovered on the brink of violence.[43] It was natural for these groups to see the CMS connexion with Fulladoyo in the same light (a mission device to draw away their slaves) and to consider a violent solution to the problem. In 1881 the Arabs at Takaungu tried to persuade the neighbouring Giriama to attack Fulladoyo, but they refused.[44] What made the presence of Fulladoyo even more menacing to the Arabs was the clear and likely possibility of an alliance between the Fulladoyo *watoro* and the rebel Mbaruk who renewed his periodic revolts against the Sultan in 1882. The runaways at Rabai had been restrained from such an alliance only by the greatest exertions of the CMS agent William Jones.[45] A final dimension of Arab hostility to the CMS lay in its impact on British colonial authorities. While the British government and its consul-general at Zanzibar were determined to end the slave trade, they were not inclined to risk their already tense relations with the Arabs by supporting an ill-timed missionary campaign for abolition of slavery and certainly disapproved of the CMS receiving runaway slaves who were, after all, still the legal property of their masters. CMS authorities came to fear that further provocation of the Arabs might make it impossible for the British consul to support and protect them.[46]

By 1882 the CMS had realized the precariousness of its situation and the depth and implications of Arab animosity. Thereafter it followed an essentially threefold strategy, the first element of which was the abandonment of all ties with Fulladoyo. W. S. Price, head of the mission, came to the conclusion that it was 'positively wrong' to jeopardize more immediate CMS interests at Freretown and Rabai by further provoking the Arabs.[47] The aftermath, if not the result, of this decision was the sacking of Fulladoyo by a large Arab–Swahili force in October of 1883. Abe Sidi, though no longer living there, was caught up in the events and killed. When the settlement was subsequently rebuilt, it was without Christian leadership, though elements of mission culture such as monogamy and Sabbath observance were apparently retained.[48]

The second element in the CMS strategy involved an attempt to separate the Giriama Christians from the *watoro* and thus break the alliance which had been forged at Fulladoyo. A district settlement at Mwaiba was established for this former group, although soon it also became a refuge for fugitive slaves on a smaller scale than Fulladoyo.[49] A final strand in CMS policy was an attempt to eliminate Mbaruk as a thorn in the Arabs' flesh in the hope that the CMS might then be able to reoccupy Fulladoyo. To this end Bishop Hannington tried unsuccessfully to get the rebel leader personally to seek the Queen's protection.[50] In brief, what seemed like a promising opportunity for expansion in Giriamaland had to be abandoned. In the absence of British support, the mission was unable to overcome the opposition of entrenched but threatened Arab interests.

The establishment of a permanent CMS presence in Giriamaland was delayed until mission expansion in that area could be carried on under the umbrella of the Imperial British East Africa Company. The arrival of the Company on the coast in 1888 defused the tense political situation which had previously prevented CMS expansion, primarily by its deft offer of financial compensation to Arab owners of runaway slaves, part of which was subscribed by CMS supporters.[51] With this fundamental antagonism at least temporarily allayed, the CMS could more readily undertake expansion in the coastal hinterland. The Company's initiatives largely determined the direction of this thrust as the CMS sought to take advantage of the opportunities opened up through the IBEAC's efforts.

In November 1888 the IBEAC's chief administrator, George MacKenzie, invited the CMS to ally with the company and to follow it into the interior. The reasons for this invitation are not altogether clear. Perhaps MacKenzie wanted to check the mission's anti-slavery activities, for he clearly warned the CMS to abstain from all political involvement. Perhaps also the company wanted to avail itself of the mission's educational and other facilities and felt the need to offer a *quid pro quo*. In any event Price, acting without authorization from CMS headquarters in London, jumped at the chance, seeing in this opportunity 'the first link in dear old Krapf's chain'. He later justified his decision to the Parent Committee by suggesting that the Methodists or Roman Catholics would have taken up the offer had he declined it.[52]

With this alliance firmly established, the CMS sent a missionary to Gulu Gulu, one of the IBEAC's stations about twenty miles (thirty kilometres) north-west of Rabai. Within a year, however, the company had abandoned this southern Ukambani route to the interior and both the Company and the mission withdrew,[53] thus terminating one of the false starts that comprised the process of mission expansion. At the same time the Company was preparing to investigate the Sabaki River route inland from Malindi and thus in November of 1889 asked the CMS to occupy Malindi.[54] This invitation touched off an important debate with the CMS over the merits of a coastal versus an up-country policy of expansion. Those favouring Malindi cited the possibility of French Catholics settling there, while the advocates of interior expansion reflected the common mission preference for working among up-country 'pagan' peoples beyond the reach of coastal Islamic influence. The supporters of an interior policy won the day and the CMS declined to establish itself at Malindi.[55] In this case, the mission's own priorities and prejudices took precedence over the alliance with the Company.

This did not mean, however, abandoning Price's agreement with MacKenzie, for in February of 1890 Frederick Lugard, now exploring the Sabaki River route for the Company, invited Binns to establish a station in the vicinity of Makongeni, where the Company was constructing a stockade. Lugard's interest in the mission was probably associated with his scheme for encouraging fugitive slaves at Fulladoyo and Makongeni to purchase their legal freedom by working for the Company, a plan which would not only free the slaves but also provide much needed labour for the IBEAC. The mission's long history of contact with these settlements would certainly be useful to Lugard. More specifically, he needed CMS cooperation in refusing to accept the runaways who were trickling into Rabai from Fulladoyo and Makongeni, hoping to obtain their legal freedom without work as in the case of those redeemed earlier in the Mombasa area.[56]

On its part the mission quickly accepted the company's offer and sent Binns to establish a station at Jilore, twenty-four miles (forty kilometres) west of

Malindi. The CMS felt that Jilore was strategically located and that conditions now favoured beginning permanent work there. In particular, there had been for some years a general northward movement of Giriama people in search of better land and better supplies of water; the company had encouraged this migration by giving food and seed to those who would settle along their route to the interior. Binns reported that such actions had contributed greatly to the popularity of the English and that many were anxious to join the mission.[57] From the CMS viewpoint, the move to Jilore was designed to profit from the favourable situation, which the Company had partially created.

By 1891 buildings had been erected and both day and night schools established. Cordial relations with the IBEAC continued. During 1892, for example, Company officials assisted the mission in removing from the station coastal people, runaway slaves, and others 'repeatedly breaking rules or committing gross sins', as the CMS had decided that Jilore was to be kept exclusively for the Giriama and others relatively uninfluenced by Swahili culture.[58]

The founding of Jilore marked the first significant CMS work among the Giriama. In spite of numerous requests for mission assistance, it had taken the CMS fifteen years to establish itself among one of its nearest neighbours. This delay supports the observation that in the pre-colonial period mission expansion was largely at the mercy of local indigenous politics. Yet within two years of the IBEAC's arrival, the CMS had secured a firm foothold in Giriama country, largely through close association with the Company, thus anticipating the new conditions under which mission expansion would be pursued in the colonial era.

THE SCRAMBLE FOR KIKUYULAND

It was a full decade after the founding of Jilore before any new CMS stations were established. But between 1900 and 1914 the mission undertook its most ambitious programme of expansion in the highlands of central Kenya, an effort that resulted in the creation of six Anglican outposts among the Kikuyu and two in neighbouring Embuland. Given the failure of the mission to expand significantly in the last quarter of the nineteenth century, how can one explain its relative success in the first decade of the twentieth?

One answer to this question seems to lie in a greatly intensified missionary effort, which grew in part out of an almost desperate need to expand. By 1900 the CMS had grown substantially in numbers of missionaries and was in fact heavily over-staffed along the coast, with close to forty missionaries assigned within a fifteen-mile (twenty-five kilometres) radius of Mombasa. Binns reported that Freretown was 'cramped and congested' with an excess of missionaries, while the Anglican bishop W. G. Peel expressed amazement at their concentration and urged an immediate policy of expansion.[59] Furthermore, eight Europeans were assigned to Taveta, a small station near Mount Kilimanjaro serving an estimated four thousand people. The senior missionary there observed that his group felt a little ashamed at their numbers and added 'We must find means of expanding or surely we will damage ourselves.'[60] There was thus no lack of volunteers willing to forgo the comforts of established positions for the honour of 'opening up' an untouched part of Africa.

The primary target area was Kikuyuland. The building of the Uganda Railroad by 1900 had solved the most pressing logistical problems and cleared the

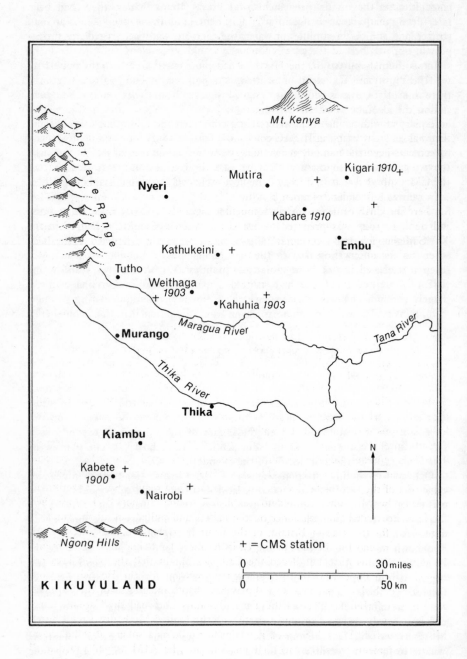

Mt. Kenya

Aberdare Range

Nyeri

Mutira ●   +   Kigari 1910 +

                                +

Kabare 1910

Kathukeini ● +   Embu

Tutho ●

Weithaga
1903 ● +
    ● Kahuhia 1903
Maragua River

● Murango   Tana River

Thika River

Thika ●

Kiambu ●

Kabete +
1900 ●
    ● Nairobi +

N

Ngong Hills   + = CMS station

                    0   30 miles
KIKUYULAND   0   50 km

way for extensive up-country missionary penetration. But if this created opportunities for the CMS, it did so also for Presbyterians, Methodists, American inter-denominational groups and also Catholics, and thus gave rise to an intemperate missionary scramble for the area. Severe competition was the most important impetus behind the greatly intensified CMS efforts.

In southern Kikuyuland, the first area occupied, the CMS's major competitor was the Presbyterian Church of Scotland Mission, which had begun operations there in 1898, two years before the CMS arrival. The location of a major Anglican station called Kabete within five miles (eight kilometres) of the Presbyterians' headquarters was bound to produce friction between the two groups. This conflict was at least temporarily resolved by the first of many 'spheres of influence' agreements negotiated among the various Protestant missions involved. In this case the two parties drew an imaginary line between the Ngong hills and Mount Kenya; the CMS sphere was to the east of the line, the Scottish mission to the west.[61]

In central Kikuyuland, known as Murang'a, this precedent was not applicable, for there the CMS came into direct competition with the Italian Consolata Fathers and neither group was prepared to negotiate 'spheres of influence' agreements. The Catholics achieved a certain initial advantage, for by 1903 they had established seven stations among the Kikuyu while the CMS had managed only two. The CMS reaction consisted in part of a substantial propaganda campaign to persuade the Parent Committee to support local efforts at expansion. A. W. McGregor, a CMS pioneer in Kikuyuland, wrote home appealing to the patriotism of his superiors:

> To me it seems a serious matter that such a district should be overrun with an influence so distinctly un-English.... I ask what must be the effect on the loyalty of these people as part of the British Empire to have the country so overrun with an alien influence, if we, who stand for all that is true, straightforward and loyal to God and country, do so little.[62]

So serious did this competition become that a local British official had to settle the dispute, which ended with an agreement that the two societies should not locate stations within one hour's walk of each other.[63]

Embuland was the last area of the highlands to be opened to mission work. The decisive military conflict occurred in 1906 but not until 1909 did the government permit mission penetration. The initial Anglican concern was to prevent the expansion of the Consolata Fathers into the trans-Tana region. Since government permission was by now required to establish a station, Bishop Peel approached the local Provincial Commissioner on the matter and pulled out all the stops. 'I urged that for the sake of Britain, of the Church of England, and the cause of Protestantism and for the sake of the CMS no more land should be given them.' In support of his plea, he alleged the Catholics taught that the whole area belonged to the Pope who in turn granted permission for the English to work there.[64] The bishop's patriotic appeal may have had some effect, for the Catholics were in fact forbidden to cross the Tana. But no sooner had the Catholic question been resolved than a serious dispute with the United Methodist Free Church Mission erupted. The CMS based its claim to Embu as a sphere of influence on earlier agreements with the Scottish mission and the AIM which awarded all territory east of the Ngong-Mount Kenya line, including Embu, to the CMS. The Methodists, not unnaturally, did not feel bound by an agreement to which they were not a party. Furthermore they resented too the way the CMS used their connexion with the Land Commissioner, Colonel J. A. L. Montgomery, to get official permission to settle in Embu, since Montgomery was also a member of the local governing body of the Anglican mission. This conflict, which resulted in a local deadlock, delayed the missionary occupation of Embu for almost a year and was finally resolved in favour of the CMS only by the home authorities of the two societies.[65] The CMS position as the missionary arm of the established church provided it with social contacts, political influence and a certain leverage in argument that were advantageous in dealing with the government.

Clearly, then, the very competitiveness of the missionary scramble for central Kenya intensified the CMS's determination to expand and hastened the establishment of Anglican stations in the area. Their success was reflected not only in the number of stations founded but also in the many requests by other missions for territorial concessions. CMS authorities admitted that they had acquired more territory than they could effectively work, but considered it 'imperative that we should retain what we have undertaken'.[66] While the missionary scramble for Kikuyuland was virtually complete by 1910, the following decade saw an amazing spate of proposals for the redistribution and rationalization of mission spheres of influence, any one of which could have substantially altered the educational and denominational boundaries of central Kenya. There is no record of African opinion, even within the mission, being sought regarding any of those proposed changes, none of which in any event succeeded. European missionaries negotiated their religious boundaries with as little regard for the wishes of Africans as did their diplomatic counterparts when deciding questions of political borders.

It was the establishment of the British East Africa Protectorate in 1895 that enabled the CMS to put its increased efforts into the successful founding of stations, for active government encouragement of mission advance soon followed. As early as 1897, John Ainsworth, one of the early Protectorate officials, was urging the CMS to settle among the Kikuyu.[67] And in 1900, after the railroad had successfully skirted the southern edge of Kikuyuland, Sir Arthur Hardinge, Commissioner of the Protectorate, suggested that the Anglicans begin work among the Kikuyu, indicating that such efforts would assist in the area's 'pacification'. At Hardinge's suggestion, the first CMS missionary in Kikuyuland, A. W. McGregor, settled at Fort Smith, the IBEAC's major administrative post in the area since its foundation in 1893.[68] McGregor started a school in the fort and was soon conducting services there as well as in nearby Nairobi. More than one missionary subsequently had the opportunity to thank some administrative official 'who placed his influence and knowledge of the country at our disposal'.[69]

From the very beginning, therefore, it was clear that the CMS was entering Kikuyu country in the wake of British political control. The realization of this certainly conditioned the attitude of many African leaders towards the arrival of the mission in their areas and measurably expedited the process of founding CMS stations. Nowhere was this better illustrated than in Murang'a where the major figure to be reckoned with was Karuri wa Gakuri. In the decade or so before European conquest, Karuri had established his military and political prominence in the area by drawing on both traditional and 'modern' sources of authority. In the former category lay his reputation as an expert in local poisons, a mediator of some repute and a skilled warrior. To these strengths he added great wealth derived from his considerable trading connexions with Kiambu and a military–commercial alliance with a free-lance European trader, John Boyes. Through this latter contact Karuri had been sufficiently impressed with the value of cooperation with intruding white men readily to enter into an alliance with protectorate officials in 1900, enabling the British to bring Murang'a under their control without the extensive use of punitive expeditions.[70] Since the CMS and other missions were attempting to establish themselves in Kikuyuland at this time, it was not unreasonable for Karuri to pursue a friendly policy towards them as a means of consolidating his alliance with the British. Thus in 1901 he invited McGregor to visit his residence at Tutho and subsequently assisted him in finding several suitable locations for mission stations, including Weithaga and Kahuhia.[71] Karuri did not limit his mission connexions to the CMS but also assisted the Consolata Fathers, arch-rivals of the Anglicans, in settling in Murang'a.[72]

In Embu a minor but ambitious chief named Kabuthi likewise actively encouraged the establishment of a CMS station at Kigari by providing the mission with twenty-five acres of land. Like Karuri, Kabuthi was one of the 'new men' thrown up by the changes of the nineteenth century. His father Kathathura had established Kigari as an important commercial centre where Arab and Swahili traders gathered in large numbers.[73] Though many such individuals later came into serious conflict with the mission, in this early period they evidently felt that a favourable response to the CMS would enhance their position in the eyes of the colonial government.

While the establishment of colonial rule did facilitate the founding of the CMS stations, it did not give the mission carte blanche to settle when and where they pleased. African authorities who had an already established relationship with the British or who had a particularly strong local power base sometimes refused or were reluctant to permit the creation of a mission station. In Kiambu, for example, long exposure to coastal caravans and close to a decade's experience with Company and Protectorate officials had created a group of people with solid links with the government by the time of the mission's arrival. One such individual, named Karanja wa Mariti, who had been station headmaster at Fort Smith since 1895, firmly rejected McGregor's request in 1900 to establish a station in the immediate vicinity of the fort. While his reasons for refusal are not altogether clear, it is certainly possible that, already enjoying the confidence of the administration, he felt himself in a sufficiently strong position not to need this additional indication of his loyalty.[74] Similarly, the wealthy and powerful Gutu wa Kibetu, regarded by the British as the 'only possible candidate' for the position of paramount chief in Embu, was decidedly reluctant to see the CMS establish itself in his area, fearing – correctly – that missionaries would act as spies for the colonial government. While unable to prevent the mission from obtaining land in Embu, he did manage to have it located at Kabare, a considerable distance from his own residence, unlike Karuri and Kabuthi who had invited the CMS to settle near their own headquarters.[75] Such cases make it necessary to qualify the assumption of 'the near-identity, in African eyes, of missionaries and white men of other professions'.[76] Some Africans at least were well aware of the separate role of missionaries and regarded their presence as a threat rather than an advantage to working out a satisfactory relationship with those 'other whites' in the colonial government. In such cases, mission expansion was hindered or delayed.

The colonial government was no less ambivalent in its attitude towards mission expansion in Kikuyuland than were some African leaders. While encouraging the establishment of mission stations, many officials were equally anxious to control that expansion. Thus mission penetration in 'unpacified areas' was strictly monitored. McGregor, for example, was initially forbidden to begin work in Murang'a. The official in charge feared that the impending imposition of a hut tax would 'unsettle' the Kikuyu and felt that the permanent presence of missionaries in the area constituted an undue risk to them and an unacceptable increase in his own responsibilities.[77] The government also acted to dampen the excesses of mission competition. In the context of the Anglican–Methodist dispute over Embu, the governor called the heads of all missions together to demand an end to quarrelling over spheres, a move which prompted the Protestant societies to create their own Board of Arbitration to resolve such conflicts and thus avoid external control.[78] Furthermore, the government was concerned that mission activity should not provide occasion for politically explosive African grievances. Thus government officials frequently complained that too many missions were acquiring too much land and doing too little with it, and after 1914 European residence was made a condition of all mission land leases. The government further required missions to obtain the permission of the chief or headman before appointing an African catechist or teacher in his area.[79] All of these measures served to inhibit mission expansion by checking the almost perpetual forward policy advocated by local missionaries.

A final constraint on mission expansion, even under otherwise favourable conditions, lay in the lack of material resources and manpower. In the CMS structure, initiatives for expansion always came from local authorities but all such requests were carefully scrutinized by the Parent Committee, largely in terms of their financial implications. A perpetually strained treasury as well as a certain belief that India and China should take precedence over East Africa resulted in frequent demands for retrenchment, thus forcing the local mission to trim its expansive designs to fit the resources available.[80]

In a number of respects the process of mission expansion can be fruitfully compared with the larger partition of Africa with which it in part overlapped. Recent research on the scramble for Africa, for example, has stressed the importance of local as opposed to metropolitan initiatives in determining the timing and character of European advance. British traders, French military officers, local crises in Egypt and South Africa are seen as having forced unwelcome decisions on frequently reluctant home governments.[81] Similarly, the roots of mission expansion were often local in origin, growing out of missionaries' desire for increased status and acute competition among rival groups. Such efforts, in fact, often ran ahead of the intentions of home authorities and on occasion presented them with an embarrassing *fait accompli*.

The highly competitive nature of the political partition of Africa found its counterpart in, and was perhaps even surpassed in intensity by, the rivalries of the missionary scramble. The divisions within Christendom, particularly if they coincided with national divisions within Europe, imparted to the process of mission expansion a preemptive character not unlike that of the diplomacy of imperialism in the 1880s and 1890s.[82] Both were concerned to occupy or dominate certain spheres of influence, more often to guarantee the future against a competitor than to secure the present for immediate exploitation.

Finally, recent studies demonstrate that Africans were not merely the passive observers of their own subjugation. A number of scholars have shown that African attempts to resist or utilize the European intruders significantly affected the timing and nature of conquest as well as the conditions under which alien rule was exercised.[83] Likewise, the policies of African societies, whether of resistance or accommodation, influenced the pattern of mission expansion. Before the imposition of European rule local opposition could effectively block a forward mission policy, while the establishment of a colonial regime often provided new and compelling incentives for cooperation with missionaries. At this point, however, the comparison between mission and political expansion breaks down, for in reacting to mission overtures, particularly after 1900, Africans were in effect responding to the emerging reality of European power. The mission contest for Kikuyuland, unlike European competition for Africa, occurred under the aegis of a larger authority which by its very existence as well as by its specific policies served variously to encourage, constrain, and direct the process.

In short, mission expansion was a complex political process, characterized by a pattern of shifting alliances among various mission, government and African groups and individuals. Its immediate significance lay in its determination of when, where and under whose auspices the making of mission communities would occur.

FOOTNOTES

1. J. F. A. Ajayi, *Christian Missions in Nigeria 1841-1891* (London, 1965); E. A. Ayandele, *The Missionary Impact on Modern Nigeria* (London, 1966); E. A. Ayandele, 'Traditional Rulers and Missionaries in Pre-Colonial West Africa', *Tarikh*, III:1, pp. 23-37; Marcia Wright, *German Missions in Tanganyika, 1891-1941* (Oxford, 1971); Felix Ekechi, *Missionary Enterprise and Rivalry in Igboland, 1857-1914* (London, 1972).

2. D. Langergren, *Mission and State in the Congo* (Uppsala, 1970), pp. 231-3, 267-9, 342-6; Wright, *German Missions*, op. cit.

3. Ken Post, *The New States of West Africa* (Baltimore, 1968), p. 51; L. H. Gann and P. Duignan, *Burden of Empire* (New York, 1967), p. 275.

4. F. B. Welbourn, *Religion and Politics in Uganda 1952-1962* (Nairobi, 1965).

5. The huge Anglican Diocese of Eastern Equatorial Africa, established in 1884, was divided into the Dioceses of Uganda and Mombasa in 1898. Since western Kenya was part of the Uganda Protectorate until 1902, the Diocese of Mombasa included Kenya east of the Rift Valley together with a CMS area in central Tanganyika. Not until 1921 was it enlarged to embrace the whole of Kenya.

6. J. C. Pollock, *A Cambridge Movement* (London, 1953), p. 132.

7. CMS/M1, Krapf to Venn, 28 February 1849; L1, Wright to Missionaries going out, 8 December 1875.

8. CMS/M2, Krapf to Venn, 10 April 1851; 1882/58, W. S. Price Journal, 9 May 1882; 1882/71, Binns to Stock, 4 September 1882.

9. CMS/1909/122, McGregor to Baylis, 29 September 1909; 1908/123, Maynard to Baylis, 21 November 1908.

10. CMS/1905/116, Peel to Baylis, 1 October 1905; 1905/117, Binns to Baylis, 11 November 1905. For other examples, see CMS/03, Binns to CMS, 5 October 1879; 1883/108, Binns to Lang, 31 August 1883.

11. CMS/1906/122, Binns to Baylis, 9 November 1906.

12. For a recent exposition of this hypothesis with reference to the French empire, see W. B. Cohen, 'Lure of Empire', *Journal of Contemporary History*, IV, (1969), pp. 103–16.
13. CMS/1903/163, Burt to Baylis, 28 October 1903.
14. Great Britain, *Parliamentary Papers*, 1897, LX, c. 8683, *Report by Sir Arthur Hardinge on the Condition and Progress of the East African Protectorate From its Establishment to the 20th July, 1897*.
15. Sir Charles Eliot, *The East Africa Protectorate* (London, 1905), p. 241.
16. CMS/M3, Rebmann to Venn, 28 April 1856.
17. CMS/1885/63, 81, Hannington to Wigram, 21 April 1885, 6 June 1885.
18. J. L. Krapf, *Travels, Researches and Missionary Labours* (London, 1968), p. 513.
19. CMS/1888/360, Price to Smith, 15 September 1888.
20. KNA: DC/EBU/9/1, John Ainsworth: Memorandum on Missions in Native Reserves, November 1918; CMS/1910/71, Wray to Baylis, 2 April 1910.
21. John Lamphear, 'The Kamba and the Northern Mrima Trade', *Pre-Colonial African Trade*, eds Richard Gray and David Birmingham (London, 1970), pp. 75–102; Krapf, *Travels*, op. cit., pp. 238–42.
22. *Proceedings*, 1874–75, p. 39.
23. Binns Journals, 8 February 1880.
24. On Taveta in the late nineteenth century, see H. H. Johnson, *The Kilimanjaro Expedition* (London, 1886), pp. 74–7, 208–15, 436; Ludwig von Höhnel, *Discovery of Lakes Rudolf and Stefanie* (London, 1894), I, pp. 91–5; John C. Willoughby, *East Africa and Its Big Game* (London, 1889), pp. 80–6.
25. CMS/1885/31, Hannington to Wigram, 14 February 1885; 1890/104, Memorandum on Meeting at Taveta, 17 March 1890.
26. J. A. Wray, *Kenya, Our Newest Colony* (London, n.d.), p. 26.
27. CMS/1887/11, Parker to Lang, 21 December 1886.
28. Thomas T. Spear, 'The Mijikenda, ca. 1550–1900', in *Pre-Colonial Kenya*, forthcoming; Krapf, *Travels*, op. cit., pp. 138–9.
29. W. W. A. Fitzgerald, *Travels in the Coastland of British East Africa and the Islands of Zanzibar and Pemba* (London, 1970), p. 202.
30. Binns Journals, 2, 20 December 1878; 24, 25 June 1879; 11 August 1879; 19 August 1880; CMS/1881/54, Binns to Hutchinson, n.d.; CMS/03, Binns to CMS, 7 August 1879.
31. CMS/1882/58, Price Journal, 16 May 1882; 1882/47, Notes of a Tour in Shimba Country.
32. CMS, *Extracts*, K. St A. Rogers, 26 January 1909.
33. CMS/M1, Krapf to Venn, 16 November 1848.
34. On these runaway communities, see CMS/017, Lamb to CMS, 19 May 1877; 03, H. K. Binns: Report on Visit to Jilore, February 1877; Margery Perham, *The Diaries of Lord Lugard* (London, 1959), I, pp. 105–6; Arthur Champion, *The Agiriama of Kenya* (London, 1967), p. 6; Fitzgerald, *Travels*, op. cit., pp. 117, 121–5, 165.
35. CMS/017, David and Nyondo to Lamb, 27 February 1877.
36. CMS/1888/394, Binns to Lang, 15 November 1888; 017, Lamb to CMS, 19 May 1877.
37. CMS/06, (Godoma Christians to CMS), 17 May 1880.
38. The initial plan of the Godoma settlers was to join the runaway slaves at Jilore but when this proved impossible owing to Galla hostility, they moved to Fulladoyo. On Fulladoyo, see CMS/1882/32, W. S. Price, Notes on Visit to Fulladoyo and Godoma, February 1882; 1881/58, Binns to CMS, 6 April 1881; *Proceedings*, 1878–79, p. 36.
39. Cynthia Brantley, 'The Giriama in the 20th Century', an unpublished paper presented to the Historical Association of Kenya, 1971; Spear, 'The Mijikenda', op. cit.
40. CMS/1881/58, Binns to CMS, 6 April 1881; 1882/32, W. S. Price, Notes on Visit to Fulladoyo and Godoma, February 1882; 1887/11, Parker to Lang, 21 December 1886.

41. CMS/1881/58, Binns to Hutchinson, 6 April 1881; 1883/17, G. David to CMS, 27 December 1882.
42. CMS/1881/61, Streeter to Governor of Mombasa, 13 June 1881.
43. Binns Journal, 25 September 1879; CMS/P1/1881/19, Binns to CMS, 18 January 1881; CMS/03, Binns to CMS, 5 October 1879. See also Norman R. Bennett, 'The Church Missionary Society at Mombasa, 1874–1894' in *Boston University Papers in African History* (Boston, 1964), I, pp. 159–94.
44. T. H. R. Cashmore, 'Sheikh Mbaruk bin Rashid bin Salim el Mazrui', *Leadership in Eastern Africa*, ed. Norman Bennett (Boston, 1968), p. 119. This article also contains an account of Mbaruk's career.
45. CMS/1882/40, Price to Miles, 7 March 1882; 1882/67, Binns to Lang, 10 August 1882.
46. Bennett, 'The Church Missionary Society', op. cit., pp. 173–82; CMS/1882/22, Price to Miles, 23 January 1882; 1882/51, Price to CMS, 19 June 1882.
47. CMS/1882/51, Price to CMS, 19 June 1882; 1882/57, Minutes of Finance Committee, 5 July 1882.
48. CMS/1883/138, Binns to Lang, 27 November 1883; 1887/11, Parker to Lang, 21 December 1886; 1885/67, Hannington to CMS, 7 May 1885.
49. CMS/1882/65, Report on the East African Mission, 6 October 1882; 1889/154, Pruen to Lang, 7 May 1889.
50. E. C. Dawson, *James Hannington: First Bishop of Eastern Equatorial Africa* (London, 1887), p. 327; CMS/1885/67, Hannington to CMS, 7 May 1885.
51. Bennett, 'The Church Missionary Society', op. cit., pp. 189–91; John S. Gailbraith, *MacKinnon and East Africa* (Cambridge, 1972), p. 150.
52. CMS/1888/424, MacKenzie to Price, 13 November 1888; 1888/425, Price to MacKenzie, 14 November 1888; 1889/9, W. S. Price, Memorandum on Opening of Mbungu, n.d.; W. S. Price *My Third Campaign in East Africa* (London, 1890), p. 254.
53. CMS/1890/22, Binns to Lang, 13 January 1890.
54. CMS/1889/348, Piggot to CMS, n.d.; 1890/6, Binns to Lang, 18 December 1889.
55. CMS/1889/283, Smith to Lang, 25 September 1889; 1889/311, Smith to Lang, 22 October 1889; 1890/6, Binns to Lang, 18 December 1889; P3/1889/lx, 10 October 1889.
56. Perham, *Diaries*, op. cit., I, pp. 98, 207, 214; Fitzgerald, *Travels*, op. cit., p. 121.
57. Champion, *The Agiriama*, op. cit., p. 5; CMS/1890/33, Binns to Lang, 28 January 1890; 1891/61, Smith to Lang, 24 January 1891.
58. CMS, *Extracts*, D. A. L. Hooper, 25 October 1892. For further evidence of CMS–IBEAC cooperation, see Fitzgerald, *Travels*, op. cit., pp. 97–8, 162, 174–83, 271.
59. CMS/1898/63, Binns to Baylis, 25 March 1898; 1901/1, Peel to Baylis, 1 January 1901; *Proceedings*, 1899–1900, pp. xxix–xxxi.
60. CMS/1896/127, Steggall to Baylis, 12 March 1896.
61. CMS/1902/111, Minutes of Executive Committee, 6–7 August 1902; 1909/134, Peel to Baylis, 8 November 1909.
62. CMS, *Extracts*, A. W. McGregor, 5 December 1903.
63. See extensive correspondence in KNA: CMS/1/689. Also KNA: CMS/1/625, Weithaga Log Book.
64. CMS/1909/68, Peel to Baylis, 23 February 1909. There is later evidence of clear anti-Catholic feeling on the part of some administrative officers which resulted in decisions on mission locations favourable to Protestants. See PCEA: B/1, Arthur to Rogers, 13 November 1913.
65. CMS/1909/131, Memorandum of an Interview between Representative of the UMFC and Baylis, 5 November 1909; 1910/13, Chapman to Baylis, 12 January 1910; 1909/130, Peel to Baylis, 4 September 1909.
66. CMS/1914/19, Buxton to Manley, 28 March 1914. There was, however, some criticism within the mission that the CMS had played an all too successful 'game of grab'. CMS/1911/110, Leakey to Baylis, 6 October 1911.

67. CMS/1897/236, Hubbard to Baylis, 6 November 1897.
68. CMS/1900/31, Peel to Baylis, 1 March 1900; 1911/24, Leakey to Scott, 3 November 1910.
69. CMS/1910/17, Annual Letter: K. St A. Rogers, 21 December 1909.
70. University of Nairobi: Research Project Archives, B/2/2(2), 'Biography of Karuri' by Charles M. Mucuha; William R. Ochieng, 'Colonial African Chiefs', a paper presented to the Historical Association, Kenya, 1971; Godfrey Muriuki, 'A History of the Kikuyu to 1904', Ph.D. Thesis, University of London, 1970, p. 204; John Boyes, *A White King in East Africa* (New York, 1912); KNA: DC/FH. 6/1, History of Fort Hall.
71. KNA: CMS/1/625, Weithaga Log Book; CMS/1903/167, McGregor to Baylis, 22 October 1903; 1906/3, McGregor to England, 8 December 1905; *Mombasa Diocesan Magazine*, April 1908.
72. Fr. C. Cagnolo, *The Akikuyu* (Nyeri, 1933), pp. 268–80.
73. CMS/1909/70, Rogers to Baylis, 27 March 1909; KNA: PC/CP.1/5/1, Embu District Record Book; EBU/45A III, Embu Political Records, Missions.
74. Interview with Chief Josiah Njonjo, 28 January 1970; KNA: DC/MKS/1/5/1, Ukamba Province Quarterly and Special Report, December 1909; KBU/109; Scott to Tate, 7 April 1909; Muriuki, 'A History of the Kikuyu', op. cit., p. 111.
75. KNA: PC/CP.1/5/1, Office of PC (Provincial Commissioner), Nyeri to Chief Secretary, 19 January 1917; PC/CP.1/1/1, Central Province Political Record Book; Daudi N. Petero, *Jubilee A. C. Kigari and A. C. Kabare (1910–1960)*, n.d., p. 21.
76. For a recent illustration of this assumption, see F. B. Welbourn, 'Missionary Stimulus and African Response', in *Colonialism in Africa, 1870–1960*, ed. Victor Turner (Cambridge, 1971), III, p. 311.
77. CMS/1903/167, McGregor to Baylis, 22 October 1903; KNA: CMS/1/689, McGregor to Burt, 2 August 1903.
78. CMS/1910/3, Rogers to Baylis, 18 December 1909; 1910/69, The Agreement of the Board of Arbitration, n.d.
79. KNA: DC/MKS/10A/1/4, ———— to H.M. Commissioner, 31 March 1906; Coast Province 9/272 and 40/715; CMS/1915/66, Rogers to Manley, 8 September 1915.
80. See, for example, CMS/L10, Baylis to Peel, 7 December 1908; 1911/3, Annual Letter: K. St A. Rogers, 3 December 1910. In 1913 the bishop wrote that the mission was threatened with 'collapse' owing to reductions in manpower and budget. CMS/1913/92, Peel to Manley, 10 November 1913.
81. John Hargreaves, who has detailed the pattern of local initiatives and limited government response in his *Prelude to the Partition of West Africa* (London, 1963), has more recently suggested that this *leitmotif* largely persisted until the mid-1890s. See his 'British and French Imperialism in West Africa, 1885–1898', in *France and Britain in Africa*, eds P. Gifford and W. R. Louis (New Haven, 1971), pp. 261–82. The local dynamics of military expansion are examined in A. S. Kanya-Forstner, 'Military Expansion in the Western Sudan – French and British Styles', in Gifford and Louis, op. cit., p. 409–41, while R. Robinson and J. Gallagher argue that the impetus for British expansion in Africa derived more from the collapse of informal empires than from any positive desire to create formal ones. See their *Africa and the Victorians* (London, 1961).
82. Bismarck's imperialism, for example, has been re-interpreted by one recent scholar who sees his primary motivation as a 'mounting concern about the possible adverse consequences of continued abstention'. Henry A. Turner, Jr, 'Bismarck's Imperial Venture: Anti-German in Origin?', in *Britain and Germany in Africa*, eds R. Louis, P. Gifford and A. Smith (New Haven, 1967), pp. 47–82.
83. See, for example, John D. Hargreaves, 'West African States and the European Conquest' and T. O. Ranger, 'African Reactions to the Imposition of Colonial Rule in East and Central Africa' in *Colonialism in Africa, 1870–1960*, eds L. H. Gann and

Peter Duignan (Cambridge, 1969), I, pp. 199–216, 293–321; Michael Crowder, *West African Resistance* (New York, 1970); Boniface I. Obichere, 'The African Factor in the Establishment of French Authority in West Africa, 1880–1990', in Gifford and Louis, *France and Britain*, op. cit., pp. 443–90.

CHAPTER IV

❊❊❊❊❊❊❊❊❊❊❊❊❊❊❊❊❊❊❊❊❊❊❊❊❊❊❊❊❊❊❊❊❊❊❊

The Making of Mission Communities

The transformation of mission stations into mission communities represents a significant social as well as religious change in modern African history, for in the course of twenty to thirty years isolated outposts of European religious propaganda became focal points for new associations of Africans and new networks of interaction between Africans and Europeans. The first three decades of the new century saw the emergence of these social institutions – often the earliest of the new voluntary associations – in most of non-Moslem Africa. In central and eastern Kenya the number of people formally associated in some way with the CMS grew from under 2,000 at the turn of the century to over 33,000 by the mid 1930s.[1] These figures also disclose a progressive shift in the distribution of the missions from the older coastal stations of Freretown and Rabai to the newer interior centres, particularly in Kikuyuland.

THE PRE-COLONIAL ENCOUNTER

While the making of mission communities was predominantly a phenomenon of the colonial era, the process was under way in many places well before alien rule became effective. Though Buganda represents the most dramatic East African example, Kenya too had its pre-colonial mission communities centred around the CMS stations at Jilore, Taveta and Sagalla in addition to those at Freretown, Rabai and Fulladoyo. Interpretations of such early mission efforts have usually stressed the marginal character of those who were attracted to the mission. Gann and Duignan, for example, have argued that

> In 'stateless societies' or among people with weakly defined political authority, the missionaries would often make their first converts among outcasts, runaway slaves, exiles or old women without relatives, the *déracinés* of tribal society.[2]

While this view is by no means wholly inaccurate, the members of early mission communities were not merely social misfits. Nineteenth-century missionaries, after all, frequently encountered eastern African societies during a particularly dynamic, fluid and sometimes painful period in their history and in fact became minor participants in the ongoing social processes of disintegration, change and reformation. The growth of Fulladoyo had important links with processes of dispersal and regrouping in post-1850 Mijikenda history as well as with the tensions of the coastal slave economy. Further south the dislocations associated with Ngoni and Yao raiding persuaded many to seek in various mission stations a 'substitute corporate life'.[3] The formation of heterogeneous communities and new identities has been a pervasive theme in nineteenth-century African history; the mission station simply provided an additional centre around which such communities could cohere.

Another weakness in many interpretations of these early mission communities as well as those established during the colonial era involves a neglect or mis-understanding of the religious element in the mission–African encounter. Some have denied that any religious exchange could occur without some ulterior motive to stimulate it. Others have seen religious inter-action largely in terms of con-version or backsliding, an ethnocentric view which unduly narrows the range of people participating in the process and both oversimplifies and distorts the nature of the encounter itself.[4] Recent research has tended to show that African religions allowed or even encouraged inter-action with missionaries on a genuinely religious plane as well as in political and economic ways. One indication of this religious inter-action lies simply in the range of questions with which early missionaries found themselves confronted. If God was love, why did He not send rain? Why is it wrong to have dances to drive away evil spirits? If all men rise again, whose will be the land which we now cultivate?[5] While one hesitates to generalize about African religion as a whole, there do seem to be several features of these systems of belief and practice that have represented points of contact with mission Christianity and have thus served to attract people into the orbit of the mission community.

First, most African religions assume that suprahuman forces or beings underlie all the events of this world and that a wide variety of ritual means may be effective in invoking or controlling their powers.[6] It was this eclectic or pragmatic – almost experimental – character of African religious rituals which opened the way to inter-action with mission Christianity. CMS missionaries observed un-happily that many Africans felt the mere possession of the Bible or acquisition of the skills of literacy to be effective in warding off misfortune or promoting temporal success.[7] It has been suggested that the failure of traditional religious practitioners to prevent the terrible famines of 1898–1900 predisposed some Kikuyu to a sympathetic hearing of a possibly more potent religious technique.[8] Tapping the power of the alien intruders frequently involved the giving up or destruction of old paraphernalia or charms which were sometimes turned over to baffled but pleased missionaries. Such behaviour occurred, for example, in the context of efforts to control witchcraft where the missionary message of sin and damnation must often have sounded like a description of the effects of witchcraft and the invitation to salvation like an alternative to the cleansing rituals designed to rid the community of this blight. A probable example of such an identification occurred in the mid-1880s on the lower Congo where Swedish missionaries found themselves receiving and destroying the *nkissi* or charms of what became a con-gregation of over one thousand people in an area where others were burning their charms in the process of adopting a new indigenous anti-witchcraft cult.[9] Mission communities, in brief, represented a potential ritual source in the flexible spiritual economy of African societies.

A second point of religious contact lay in the prophetic element of some African religions, for missionaries on occasion found their advent foretold. When the African teachers of the CMS discovered that certain communities among the Digo had long expected white men who would provide them with work and teaching, they were not slow to point out the fulfilment of that prophecy in the European estates springing up in the area as well as in the written words of

53

scripture introduced by the missionaries. Similarly the acceptance of Christianity among the Malawi Ngoni was facilitated by the injunction, shortly before the arrival of the Scottish missionaries, 'Something great is coming from the sea. Receive them courteously.'[10] In such ways did African prophecy ease the acceptance of new religious ideas without seeming altogether to abandon the old.

A final element of possible conjuncture between African religion and Christianity lay in the realm of theology or religious belief. The preaching of the life, death and resurrection of Christ by the early Baptist missionary, Richards, struck a particularly resonant chord among the Bakongo whose mythology of cyclical regeneration made them receptive to these themes.[11] It has also been argued recently that the idea of a High God, present in the beliefs of many African societies, achieved a heightened development and significance during the nineteenth and twentieth centuries as the impact of the wider world impinged on previously more isolated cultures. Evidence for such an adaptation within indigenous African beliefs can be found for the Kalabari, Tswana and Tonga peoples, for example, though it is primarily twentieth-century in focus. Given this development, Christian monotheism and Christian means of approach to God, it is suggested, might well seem religiously and intellectually attractive to people confronted with a need to explain, predict and control a new and larger world.[12] Religious inter-action and social reintegration, then, were among the processes that went into the making of the early CMS communities at Jilore, Taveta and Sagalla.

The earliest of the mission's pre-colonial efforts in the interior occurred at Sagalla in the Taita hills and was seen as the first link in the westward chain towards Buganda. Although this effort was in most respects a failure, the multiple inter-actions between the resident missionary and his Taita neighbours effectively illustrates the dynamics of European–African encounter at this early stage of contact. J. A. Wray, a twenty-five-year-old lay missionary and former mechanic posted to Sagalla in 1883, was certainly not ignored by the Taita, who saw his presence alternately as a threat and an opportunity.

Wray's initially favourable reception in Sagalla probably reflected the hope that he would act as a commercial link with the coast, for several years earlier another CMS missionary had visited the Taita hills, escorted by a group of Taita traders, and subsequently received an invitation to settle among them.[13] But Wray's relationship with the people of Sagalla was almost immediately conditioned by the fact that his arrival coincided with the advent of a severe drought and famine. Some apparently felt that Wray could be of material or religious assistance and the missionary soon found himself at the centre of a small community of one to two hundred people. 'You shall be our chief, our king, our father or whatever you want to call yourself', they told him. Most of Sagalla, however, saw in Wray the cause of their misfortune and felt that his mirror, thermometer, harmonium and bell were the instruments of his malevolent withholding of rain. Only the protection of his followers saved Wray from the hostility of his enemies.[14] The decreasing population of Sagalla (owing to the famine) and the expense of provisioning Wray and his supporters led to the temporary abandonment of the station in 1885. The major outcome of this initial period of inter-action, then, had been the introduction of a new cleavage into Sagalla society.

When Wray returned in mid-1886, he attempted to assert complete political control over his followers, arguing that according to African custom they were his 'slaves' since he had rescued them from famine. Those who had earlier fled the famine began to return and sought to heal the breach in their community introduced by Wray. With argument, ridicule and threats of violence, they succeeded in drawing away a number of Wray's following, reducing him in the process to a state of impotent rage. He wrote to CMS authorities asking for a dozen men from Fulladoyo to 'strike a little terror into them' and to the British Consul in Zanzibar requesting imprisonment for the opposition leaders. His racial and cultural consciousness was fully engaged as he argued that Taita should be 'told plainly that they cannot rob and threaten a European with impunity'.[15] Serious tension persisted over a number of issues including the missionaries' continued prevention of rainfall and their failure to provide employment opportunities, and the station was closed again in 1890.

Six years later Sagalla was opened for a third time, though under very different conditions. There had been a sharp military encounter with the IBEAC in 1890; the Protectorate had been declared in 1895; and the Taita hills lay very close to the route of the Uganda Railroad, resulting in a substantial demand for porters. All of this combined to produce for Wray a kind of reception and response that he had never known before, for he was now clearly linked in the minds of the Taita with potent forces in a rapidly impinging wider world. At Wray's request the people of Sagalla donated to the CMS a hill of great political and religious significance and by 1901 the Bishop estimated that some five hundred people there could be classed as 'adherents'. Invitations to settle in other areas in the Taita hills arrived and weekly services involving 1,200 people were soon being held in Mbale.[16] That there was an evident religious dimension to this new attitude was reflected particularly in the old question of rainfall. While the missionaries were no longer accused of preventing rain, they were seen as an alternative religious source for producing it. During the widespread famines of 1898–1900, a number of men met nightly in Wray's house to pray for rain. When in 1903 rain fell at Mbale, where the CMS was located, but not at the *kaya* or village on the other end of the mountain, the chief of the *kaya* came to the missionary Maynard in great distress and the two men invoked God for rain. Church and school attendance in several places demonstrably fluctuated in rhythm with the success or failure of mission rituals in producing precipitation.[17]

Though no baptisms occurred until 1900, the previous seventeen years had witnessed an intense cultural and religious encounter between the CMS and elements of the Taita. This inter-action had induced a small group of people to associate closely with Wray during the 1880s and gave rise to the beginnings of a much larger mission community during the last five years of the nineteenth century.

A second early CMS community grew up on the banks of Lake Jilore where a CMS station had been established in 1890 in an area of fairly dense Giriama settlement, the product of their general northward migration since mid-century. This dispersal from the *kaya* gave rise to the homestead as a new form of social organization in which solidarity was the product of economic success and personal attachment rather than kinship, and in which leadership did not depend on the traditional criteria of age-set position. Located directly on the IBEAC's route to the interior, Jilore station seemed to attract people in much the same way as surrounding homesteads or villages and thus the mission participated in the process of Giriama adaptation following the collapse of the *kaya* system. The remnant of Giriama Christians from Mwaiba and a handful of individuals from a half-dozen East African ethnic groups were also represented in the settlement, though people from the coast and runaway slaves were rigidly excluded.[18]

Within a decade a flourishing community of over a hundred persons had developed with perhaps another hundred sympathizers in surrounding homesteads. For most of this time, Jilore was under the stern and austere leadership of D. A. L. Hooper, a Cambridge man who had experienced a dramatic change in his life through the Moody–Sankey revivals held there in 1882.[19] Hooper's African employees were paid at half the regular CMS scale lest they be moved by 'mercenary motives', while Hooper himself lived in a wattle and daub hut to set an appropriate example for others. Corporal punishment for moral offences was not unknown and the missionary directed that 'filthiness, foolish talking, jesting and all that is frivolous' were to be given up, while girls were forbidden to wear corsets, use beads or plait their hair.[20] Despite this strict regime there seemed ironically to be more opportunity for and evidence of African initiative in Jilore than in any other early CMS community. A Church Council of five members was organized which on its own drew up rules for the settlement including one that no European contribution would be allowed for the upkeep of the church. Hooper intensively trained a small group of Giriama teacher–catechists, who, it was said, 'can manage excellently without Europeans'. Mission authorities were much impressed with the religious tone of Jilore, which was imbued with a certain 'revival' atmosphere complete with frequent and public confession of sin. This was perhaps not surprising given the probable tensions growing out of a new and socially heterogeneous community. 'We are having a new Gospel,' declared one Jilore resident, 'and we had better try it.'[21] Jilore became essentially an autonomous Christian community independent of the regular CMS structure, for Hooper, an independently wealthy man, relieved the mission of all expenses associated with Jilore and so expected and generally received permission to run things in his own somewhat eccentric way.[22]

The other unique feature about Jilore was the surprisingly favourable response in villages on both sides of the Sabaki to the Christian preaching of Hooper and his band of itinerant Giriama evangelists. Numerous Giriama villages and five Kamba settlements asked that a Jilore teacher be posted among them, and accounts of people willingly destroying their 'charms' punctuate mission reports of the period. For example, in 1896, Hooper wrote about two villages on the north side of the Sabaki:

> All their fetish worship has stopped. We were commissioned to destroy every sign of it, e.g. small grass houses, pots, sticks etc.... The people have stopped wearing charms. All of the men and some of the women attend morning and evening worship – many learning to read.[23]

In at least four cases, entire villages 'joined the Book', while in others only a section of the community began to make extensive use of Christian symbols and rituals, thus introducing new cleavages and generating new conflicts.[24] Some of this behaviour clearly represented an alternative religious response to the famine which began in 1898, the worst in Giriama memory, but evidence of similar activity well before the famine suggests the presence of other strains or tensions calling for more potent religious resources or techniques. One can only speculate as to what these may have been: perhaps tensions associated with the making of new and largely non-kin-oriented communities, where ancestor cults may have declined and witchcraft accusations increased; possibly religious crises provoked by the entry of mission, company and protectorate; perhaps also a very practical attempt to persuade the British of their neutrality in Anglo–Mazrui hostilities and thus avoid British suspicion and possible punishment.[25] In any event, it seems clear that some Giriama looked to the mission as a religious means for resolving pressing problems.

Much of this was clearly ephemeral, the product of temporary religious needs. As the famine passed and the old order seemed relatively stable, a number of villages abandoned their earlier interest in new religious forms. The mission community at Jilore likewise suffered decline. The station was staffed only intermittently after 1902 and a number of the most promising converts and catechists, apparently feeling the need for some reconciliation with Giriama ways, opted for a second wife or committed some other 'grievous sin', thus at least partially severing their ties with the mission.[26] While Jilore remained officially a CMS station for some time, its heyday had clearly lain in the 1890s and the new century, normally associated with the growth of mission communities, saw it recede into the backwater of CMS affairs.

If the making of Jilore was associated with the larger process of Giriama dispersal and regrouping, the growth of the early CMS community at Taveta was linked to the more general themes of ethnic intermixing which had long been characteristic of the area. Taveta society itself was the product of an extended and complex series of migrations into the protected forest region along the Lumi River. The nineteenth-century civil wars among the Masai, political conflict among and within the Kilimanjaro states, as well as various natural disasters made Taveta a place of continuing attraction for a variety of displaced people.[27] There they could find either temporary physical security or the possibility of assimilation into a new social order. A large number of *Wakwavi* or agricultural Masai, for example, were settled separately at the southern end of Taveta, while the Rombo, another Masai group, had apparently been more closely integrated into Taveta society.[28]

When the CMS began work there in 1892, it quickly attracted to its settlement at Mahoo or Happy Land a clientele as rich in ethnic diversity as the larger Taveta society. A census taken in 1899 revealed the following ethnic distribution among Mahoo's 312 residents:[29]

Masai	– 89
Taveta	– 72
Chagga	– 58
Taita	– 29
Ugweno	– 24
Kamba	– 21
Kahe	– 9
various ethnic groups	– 10

By 1901 there had gathered around the mission station a community of almost four hundred people, organized into seventy-five separate homesteads, most of whom came to Mahoo because of famine or political dislocation in their home regions – all of this in spite of the determined opposition of the Parent Committee to further mission settlements, which they regarded as both expensive and spiritually unproductive.[30] Even more people could have been recruited had not the mission's rules against admitting polygamists intervened. The case of Justin

Lemenye was not untypical. Born in Usambara about 1877, he was taken prisoner in a Masai raid and lived with his captors as a goat herder until his mid-teens. Ill treatment caused him to run away to Moshi where he came into contact with the CMS and followed the mission when it moved to Taveta in 1892. In baptism, training in the Freretown divinity school and his position as a teacher in Taveta, the young man apparently found a more secure and satisfying world than he had known before.[31] In both function and composition, Mahoo had come to resemble the larger society of which it was a part.

The reception given to Christian teaching outside the settlement operated according to a different rhythm. Though the missionaries had access to all of Taveta, there was little apparent interest in their message for several years. A partial famine in 1893 and a severe locust invasion in early 1894 changed all that as the Taveta collectively began to search for an appropriate explanation for and response to these calamities. Their first effort consisted of planting protective medicine on all roads leading into Taveta. When they offered this help to Mahoo, the CMS missionary McGregor found the opportunity to point them to the alternative religious resource of 'Him who alone was able and longing to help them'. The failure of the medicine led to more drastic measures as a specialist from Useri was imported to conduct an anti-witchcraft cleansing ceremony. All were required to drink his medicine in the belief that anyone using witchcraft against another would die. The experimental nature of African religion could hardly be more clear. It was in the context of these measures that the Taveta turned a more receptive ear to Christian teaching. They invited the mission to hold services in the political centre of their community and these were attended by as many as 400 to 500 elders and warriors. McGregor confessed himself astonished at how welcome he was made to feel and how willing were the people to listen to his teaching.[32]

Having used protective magic and anti-witchcraft cleansing rituals, it was not unnatural for the people of Taveta to invoke also the power of God through whatever rituals the missionaries might use. An early study of Taveta religion has indicated that rituals designed to tap the power of the Creator or High God were employed only in time of special stress of a large-scale nature.[33] And the missionaries at Taveta were not slow to suggest that God, when approached appropriately, both could and would respond to their temporal crisis. The distinction recently drawn between Christianity as a religion of communion and African religions as basically concerned with explanation, prediction and control of this world's phenomena is not wholly accurate if applied to evangelical missionaries of the late nineteenth century.[34] McGregor clearly believed and preached that God had sent both famine and locusts to Taveta for His own high purposes and could be induced to withdraw them. Wray and others in the Taita hills had done likewise. Binns flatly told inquiring Kamba that Britain's temporal power and prosperity grew directly out of its acceptance of the Book. And missionaries informed the Rabai that their 'charms' were ineffective as only God could protect them from sickness and danger.[35] Both mission Christianity and African religions saw personal purpose behind natural events and rejected the notion of random causes. The difference between them lay in the agency of causation (God alone rather than in conjunction with ancestor spirits or witches) and in the means of approach to God (church attendance, Bible reading, 'accepting Christ' as opposed to sacrifice). Nothing the missionaries taught made it unreasonable for the people of Taveta to look to mission rituals as a possibly more effective means of invoking the power of God for the resolution of their collective misfortune.

But this level of religious inter-action lasted only so long as the need for it persisted. As famine and locusts receded, a new wave of opposition arose based largely on a realization of the extent of cultural transformation being demanded by the missionaries. Drinking, polygamy and ancestor veneration were among the major issues involved.[36] When the people of Taveta once again evinced a greater interest in the mission during 1896 and 1897, it was based now on the new pressures of the colonial situation.

Despite the lack of many 'conversions', the pre-colonial encounter of missionaries and Africans in Kenya represented more than strangers passing in the night. Mission stations after all had served at least temporarily as centres of social reintegration in very fluid and changing circumstances. For some individuals, experience in these communities provided them with a significant head start in meeting the demands of the colonial age.[37] On a religious level, there had been sufficient points of contact between mission Christianity and African religions to allow a measure of inter-action to take place though it was generally a one-sided affair with Africans seeking to utilize elements of Christian belief and practice. But the functions which mission communities could perform in pre-colonial African societies were neither many nor exclusive, for there were, of course, other centres of social cohesion and other religious resources available. Herein lay the limits of mission growth before the pressures of a new social order were felt. It was the colonial situation that created many more functions for mission communities to perform and ensured that some of those functions would be the almost exclusive domain of these new social units.

COLONIAL PRESSURES AND THE GROWTH OF MISSION COMMUNITIES

During the early colonial era it was the specific and direct pressures of alien rule that channelled a relatively small number of people into mission communities. For example, the coinciding of mission expansion with the political adjustments accompanying European conquest meant that a number of prominent individuals or recently appointed chiefs could use their friendship with the missions as a way of demonstrating loyalty to the new regime. Thus, prominent among the first people associated with the new CMS stations in Kikuyuland were a number of young men deliberately sent to the mission by local chiefs. Most of those baptized during the first decade of mission occupation had been sent by these chiefs or other prominent individuals.[38] The chiefs, however, seldom sent many of their own sons but rather dispatched the children of their more distant relatives or social inferiors, though these individuals frequently claimed direct kinship to the chief himself and were often believed by the missionaries. An even more direct connexion between the new political order and the growth of mission communities occurred in Taveta, where in 1896 the assembled elders approached CMS missionaries in a futile attempt to persuade them to prevent the British from sending an administrative officer to their country. As an indication of their friendship with the mission they 'proclaimed religious liberty' and urged everyone to attend school and church. When the unwanted official, Captain Temple Maxstead, nevertheless arrived, he summarily ordered parents to send their children to school on pain of a fine.[39]

With the creation of a settler economy, the demand for labour from settlers, chiefs and the administration itself was the form in which many people most directly experienced the constraints of the new regime. Recognized association with mission schools often served to shield individuals from these demands as missionaries were able to negotiate arrangements with district officers whereby properly registered students were excused from most or all of these requests for labour.[40] Association with a mission was also a means of avoiding service in the Carrier Corps during the First World War, surely the most radical demand of the colonial regime. Between 1914 and the end of 1917 over 160,000 men were recruited, many of them by force, of whom over 46,000 did not return alive. Since missions were largely exempt from this military draft until 1917, enrolments in CMS schools jumped dramatically from 1,332 in 1913 to 3,304 in 1916. In the end, however, mission adherents did not escape the war. Rumours of a massive call-up which would include mission students prompted the major Protestant missions to create a mission Carrier Corps of some 2,000 men. Officered largely by missionaries, it was intended to show the government that mission schools were not simply the 'refuge of able-bodied loafers' and to maintain Christian influence over their students and adherents. From the Murang'a area alone, the CMS quickly recruited 820 'volunteers', though H. D. Hooper admitted that many regarded the mission battalion as but a lesser evil than serving directly with the government.[41]

Mission communities could also be viewed and used as economic resources. Some of the CMS's staunchest adherents – Levi Gacanja of Kahuhia and Petero Gacewa of Kigari for example – had been among the earliest porters sent to fetch the baggage of the newcomers. Employment opportunities constructing mission roads, bridges and buildings attracted others, while sewing classes allowed women access to material at a far lower price than Indian or European shops. Over and over again, missionaries found themselves confronted by demands for wages from their early students. At Kigari, about fifty such students went on strike when they discovered that they were not to be paid for thus obliging the Europeans. Though the missionaries understandably felt that 'the obligation was the other way round', it was hardly unreasonable for Africans to regard education as employment since many missionaries had enticed people to school or church with gifts of cloth, salt, beads or even money. Moreover, as McGregor admitted, students were economic assets to their families who considered it only just to be compensated for the loss of their children's labour.[42]

There are indications of a more complex economic dynamic which operated at least in Kikuyuland to pressurize some individuals into mission communities. Evidence from Kikuyu informants suggests that most of the early students in CMS village or station schools were children of poorer families. These were probably *ahoi* or tenant families who under normal circumstances might have hoped to find land for themselves on the expanding frontier of Kikuyu settlement, but who now found themselves substantially blocked in that ambition by European farms. Some of these frustrated individuals found an alternative means of improving their position in becoming squatters on European farms, while others saw the mission community as a possible avenue of social and economic mobility. For a time, in fact, sending one's children to school was an admission of poverty shunned by those more fortunate.[43]

Many of these early attractions of mission communities represented either the possibility of escaping the demands of the colonial situation or of achieving status or wealth within the traditional social setting. Increasingly, however, people began to see the mission community as a means of mobility within the new and larger social order created by British rule. The realization that African society and white society were inextricably connected was fundamentally a function of a heavily state-assisted settler economy which, through tax policy, manipulation of reserves and limited coercion, forced large numbers of Africans on to the labour market.[44] It was rapidly apparent that those who could enter this market at the level of subordinate clerical service for the government were far better off than the ordinary farm labourer. In fact, CMS schools at the coast, particularly Freretown, produced the great bulk of these employees during the first two decades of the colonial regime.[45] The war too helped to produce a heightened awareness of the emerging social order. Missionaries who served in the Carrier Corps spoke of a new intimacy between Europeans and Africans born of 'very close and prolonged contact', and testified that many young men began to see missions as a 'key to the wider horizon' exposed by this new experience.[46]

The outcome of these conditions was a quickened response to mission activity generally and more specifically a growing enrolment in mission schools. Hostility to mission adherents declined as the connexion between education and new employment opportunities became apparent, while baptism, a Christian name and a church wedding became popular symbols of entrance into the new society. Missionaries grew increasingly concerned about the motives of their new adherents and worried lest the social pressure for baptism allowed some 'unworthy' persons to slip unprepared into church membership.[47] These were the 'improvers', those who accepted the colonial framework, if not its particular policies or structures, sought to enhance their position and that of their people within that framework, and regarded the missions and especially their schools as a major agency for the achievement of these aspirations.[48]

This new movement for association with mission communities was unevenly distributed in both time and space, with the earliest results to be found in the growing urban centres of colonial Kenya where the opportunities of the new order were most apparent. It was in Mombasa, the early commercial and political capital of British East Africa, that the CMS first encountered these new conditions which gave rise not to a community of professing Christians but to an institution, Buxton High School, which stood at the apex of the CMS education system.

Efforts to establish mission work in Mombasa did not begin until the late 1880s owing partly to concentration on Freretown and Rabai and partly to intense anti-mission sentiment among Arabs over the runaway slave issue. When medical and evangelistic work was begun, religious results were non-existent and missionaries were driven to despair at their first attempt to penetrate a predominantly Moslem culture. 'Some people think Mohammedanism is a good preparation for Christianity. Give me the unsophisticated heathen – for I have tried both', mourned W. E. Taylor, head of the small mission team in Mombasa.[49] In fact the direction of religious change was more often from Christianity to Islam as mission adherents from the mainland sought to take advantage of the economic opportunities available in Mombasa and found Christianity a clear liability, particularly for positions as domestic servants. The missionary F. Burt described the problem:

> The European, owing perhaps to having got hold of some bad mission boys, or owing perhaps largely to prejudice, often refused to engage mission boys as servants; consequently some Christian boys change their name and call themselves by a Mohammedan name in order to get work. The work in the house

on Sunday is heavier than on any other day. The 'Boy' gets no time for church or class and so sometimes lapses altogether.[50]

It soon became the consensus of mission opinion that only a first-rate educational facility stood even a remote chance of gaining a hearing for the Gospel in Mombasa. The strategic consideration of pre-empting potential educational competitors, whether Arab, Indian, Roman Catholic or government, added urgency to expediency, as did an exaggerated mission fear about the imminent spread of Islam. 'I pray to God', wrote the Anglican Bishop Peel, 'to bring it about that CMS shall have charge of education in Mombasa, the gate of East Africa, for, if Islam becomes strong and educated there, we shall have, I fear, fierce struggles later on in the interior.'[51] After 1897 trained schoolmasters were recruited, new buildings erected, the curriculum upgraded and in 1904 the institution was inaugurated as Buxton High School. This investment of resources had the desired effect, for average attendance rose from forty-six in 1904 to over 170 by 1911. But while the school was intended to make inroads into 'African Mohammedanism', about seventy per cent of its pupils were drawn from the Indian community of Mombasa, owing probably to the relatively greater employment opportunities available to Indians both in the subordinate ranks of the administration and in the commercial sector of the colonial economy.[52]

The CMS relationship with its student clientele was extremely fragile and was based on two conditions which subsequently proved difficult to maintain. The first was the continuation of the mission monopoly on secular education in Mombasa, for not until after 1910 were alternative opportunities available. The second involved the willingness of the mission to offer instruction in English, in sharp contrast to the language policy elsewhere in the CMS educational system at that time. The practical basis for this exception lay in the inability otherwise to attract any students whose sole desire was 'to learn enough English to be able to obtain some subordinate position in the government'. It was therefore all the more convenient that it was a common belief that Arabs, Swahilis and Indians ranked higher on the 'scale of civilization' than Africans and were thus possessed of greater ability to benefit from advanced instruction in English. In urging a programme of advanced education, the schoolmaster W. E. Parker observed, 'I do not see how it is possible to keep the boys together if we only teach on mission lines.... (I)t is good for the simple tribes etc. who have never heard of anything else and probably could not rise to a higher level except in rare cases.' There was also a concern that missionaries of 'intellectual capacity' be found for dealing with Moslem peoples in Mombasa.[53] There developed a kind of tacit understanding between the mission and its students whereby the CMS would provide an education in English in return for the opportunity of offering religious instruction in the school. Scripture in fact was one of the examination subjects, while the English Bible was an important textbook, an arrangement which the students 'did not quite appreciate'.[54] But if a measure of cultural compromise was the price of progress, many were willing to pay it, at least until more palatable alternatives became available.

The CMS effort in Nairobi, begun in 1906, gave rise to a rather different relationship. In the first place far more people were involved. Over one thousand students were enrolled in CMS schools there by 1920, a number which reflected the growing importance of Nairobi as the administrative and economic centre of the colony. Further, the mission's educational system in Nairobi operated at a much lower level than that of Mombasa and at least initially served primarily to produce domestic servants for the European population of the capital. Morning classes in the Nairobi school were devoted to unemployed persons as well as small children living permanently in the city, while afternoons were taken up with domestic servants, and evening school catered to those who worked in offices and shops during the day.[55] Finally the mission's Nairobi efforts were far more productive of religious change than had been the case in predominantly Moslem Mombasa, for associated with the school work was an active African church congregation of 1,500 persons by 1917, of whom seventy-five per cent were young men between the ages of fifteen and thirty. At the heart of the process of improvement many of these people actively sought recognition as Christians in order to legitimize and reinforce their new social roles. In 1913, for example, one hundred Christian young men wrote to the CMS asking that they be provided with suitable and separate accommodation in the city. Baptism, wrote one Nairobi missionary, is 'sadly too popular', complaining about African pressure for the Christian rite after certain basic literacy requirements had been met.[56]

Not for long was the awareness of a new social order limited to the cities, for by the 1920s consciousness of new opportunities had penetrated into large areas of the urban hinterland as well, resulting in substantially increased enrolments in CMS schools and churches. By the mid 1930s, the CMS station at Kabete boasted a Christian community of over 7,000 people with some 2,000 students attached to its schools, while corresponding figures at Dabida in Taita country were 2,666 and 1,699, to mention only two examples.[57] But for many of these people, the agency which provided education, diffused new religious ideas and attracted them into the mission community involved neither missionary initiative nor the central stations of the CMS. Rather these functions were performed through an informal, local and undirected process of which the institutional product was the 'outschool'.

The proliferation of outschools offering rudimentary education and religious training was the outward sign of the 'awakening' which missionaries professed to see in many areas of colonial Kenya during the inter-war period and sometimes even earlier. In the highland areas alone the CMS boasted some sixty-three outschools by the mid 1920s while before the war there had been only a handful. With their unimposing buildings and ill-prepared teacher-catechists, these institutions were for many the agency of recruitment into some association with the mission community. For example, of the 1,712 students attending schools connected with the CMS centre at Kabete in 1934, 1,232 or seventy-two per cent were enrolled in the station's twelve outschools.[58] Yet these were by no means the direct result of European evangelistic efforts. On the contrary, missionary influence followed and tried to control an outschool movement that possessed a dynamism of its own.

One pattern of outschool development followed the lines of labour migration as people employed away from home sought opportunities for both teaching and learning. For example, Petero Kigondu, a CMS agent dismissed for getting his fiancée pregnant, took up government work in Fort Hall where he founded in 1912 a small school and church which subsequently became a CMS outstation.[59] In other cases labour migrants approached the mission either directly or indirectly for assistance in establishing a school. CMS adherents working for the railroad in Nakuru, where they had on their own initiative begun a regular night school, repeatedly asked the mission to supply them with a teacher, promising to pay his salary and build him a house and school. The CMS responded favourably to the request and by the mid 1930s Nakuru appeared on the books as a CMS station serving a Christian community of 1,400 people and a student population of 144.[60] In other instances European employers of African labour initiated contact with the CMS in an effort to tap the educational resources of the mission. Sympathetic Christian officers in the King's African Rifles camp outside Nairobi paved the way for a mission school among the African enlisted men though not without objections from others that Islam instilled a more vigorous martial spirit. The manager of a large soda works also hoped for a mission school for his workers though there were no teachers available at the time.[61]

Since much labour migration in Kenya was to European farms or estates, it is hardly surprising that the outschool movement was strongest in these places. Farm labourers often started their own schools, made contacts with the missions or urged their employers to do so. Acute labour shortages, particularly after the war, persuaded many employers to agree in the hope of attracting or maintaining a sufficient and contented labour force. Even some Arab and Swahili plantation owners, anxious to revive their declining fortunes by attracting Mijikenda labour, 'begged' the CMS to send them teachers. European agricultural employers in the highlands, with varying degrees of enthusiasm, made similar requests, though some, such as Lord Delamere, refused to do so on principle.[62] The general mission response involved sending a usually untrained teacher-catechist to open a school, but by 1928 the number of these outschools had grown so much that the CMS felt the need for 'inspection by a white man' and so posted a missionary to Nakuru to oversee the work on European estates.

If the establishment of outschools followed patterns of labour migration outside the African reserves, within them the development of these institutions proceeded along different lines. Here the catalysts were usually people in some association with a central station who actually lived some distance away. After training in a large mission school, young men often returned to their home areas to found an outschool. Or individuals growing tired of the distance between their homes and the mission station would start a church school closer to their place of residence. A kind of chain reaction was generated in which central stations gave rise to outschools which in turn spawned further outschools. The encouragement of a friendly chief, elements of local rivalry or the assistance of local people employed in Nairobi all served to facilitate the growth of outschools in the reserves. The initiative in these developments was almost wholly local, as small groups gathered materials, provided labour and raised money for their own schools and churches, with the mission usually supplying only the teacher.[63] In subsequent years, these people would recount with great pride the evolution of their churches from ones constructed in mud and thatch to those built with iron sheeting and finally to the erection of a stone building.

In its attempt to guide and control the outschool movement, the CMS encountered a variety of difficulties, the first of which involved the colonial government. By 1919 the administration felt the need to control the rapid proliferation of schools and so imposed a series of conditions for the founding of an outschool including the requirement to obtain the permission of the district officer and the chief or headman of the area where the school was to be located. This required the missionaries to engage in a great deal of 'wearisome bargaining' with frequently suspicious or hostile African chiefs and led them to talk of 'persecution' in numerous quarters.[64] The outschool question also exacerbated the frequently suspicious relations between the CMS and other mission bodies, both Protestant and Catholic, for the Africans who initiated these institutions were unconcerned with the policy of spheres which so agitated the missionaries.[65]

Conflict between the outschools and the mission itself was another potential outcome of the movement. Though they were largely independent in origin, the CMS did attempt to exercise a degree of control over these satellite centres through missionary touring and meetings of outschool elders at the central stations, but the distances involved and the shortage of European personnel made close supervision difficult. Missionaries, in fact, often complained of their inability to oversee the work adequately. The outschool communities for their part were increasingly likely to resent the intrusion of arbitrary European authority into their affairs, and missionaries soon noticed a 'spirit of independence' among the councils of elders which operated the schools. When a CMS missionary refused to pay an outschool teacher because he had not been informed of the man's departure for another job, the aggrieved instructor pointed to what had become the common relationship of outschool to mission:

> It is the custom at those schools, teachers are sought and employed by the Chairman and his elders and that it is only his 'kipande' (official registration certificates for Africans) which is sent to the European principle (sic) for endorsement, otherwise the teacher is laid down on the custody of the Elders.[66]

Nonetheless missionary intervention in outschool matters did not occasion the kind of conflict experienced by the African Inland Mission which saw twenty-two out of thirty outschools surrounding its Githumu station closed by 1926 in protest against a variety of AIM policies which threatened local autonomy.[67] In fact, at least one CMS outschool severed its connexion with the mission owing to the inability of European missionaries to resolve a factional dispute within the outschool community, though they indicated that they wished to continue attending CMS religious classes.[68] Outschools, then, saw certain advantages in retaining a CMS connexion. Such a link functioned to legitimize their new religious faith, served as a channel through which government financial aid was funnelled to these schools and allowed missionaries to act as third-party arbitrators in certain kinds of internal disputes. The outschool–mission relationship was delicate but not necessarily antagonistic.

If potential outschool–missionary conflict represented one process of differentiation within the mission community arising from the outschool movement, another involved the relationship between younger and older adherents. It is possible to distinguish a central core of individuals, usually among the earliest 'converts', whose lives had come to be substantially integrated with the mission community and whose new values had been confirmed through the alienation from their own societies which an early mission connexion almost necessitated. Many of these people have testified to being hated and despised by family and friends for their connexion with the mission and many built their homes as close to the mission station as possible, for 'whoever started education did not live with his family'. Johana Muturi, one of the first Christians in the Weithaga area, observed that in the early days association with the mission meant that one was regarded as 'lost'. The same feeling was prevalent among the Giriama. 'The cry among these people is that if their children become Christians they are lost to them,' wrote a local missionary. Among the Kikuyu, girls who attended the mission were liable to be called prostitutes, while young men who did so were labelled *Ihii cia Bwana*, the uncircumcised boys of the missionaries, for the wearing of trousers made it impossible to tell who was circumcised and who was not.[69] The people who comprised the nucleus of those communities attached to the various CMS stations have been described by the Kikuyu novelist Ngugi wa Thiong'o:

> Joshua . . . was then a young man who ran from the hills and went to live with the white man in the newly established Mission. He feared the revenge of the hills; the anger of his friends, betrayed. In Siriana he found a sanctuary and the white man's power and magic. He learned to read and write. The new faith worked in him till it came to possess him wholly. He renounced his tribe's magic, power and ritual. He turned to and felt the deep presence of the one God. Had he not given the white man power over all? . . . He realized the ignorance of his people. He felt the depth of the darkness in which they lived.[70]

In contrast to these first-generation Christians were those whose association with a mission community occurred later and often through an outschool rather than in direct contact with a European missionary. Such individuals were not called upon to make such a clear break with the past as had the earlier adherents, for the outschools had frequently become symbols of pride and progress in the local community, while education and elements of Christian belief and ritual had become widely associated with individual mobility and social improvement in the new order. These people were to some extent on the periphery of the mission community in that their network of social relations extended well beyond the community. The frequently utilitarian motives of such people, as well as the cultural demands of the missionaries, ensured considerable movement back and forth across the physical and cultural boundaries of the mission communities. The ubiquity of the backsliding problem and the high rate of attrition even among the employees of the mission reflected both the strains which could attend association with the mission and the lack of absolute dependence on the mission such as was experienced by first-generation Christians.

The possibility of conflict between the two groups was reflected over the issue of teachers for outschools. The older stalwarts, generally supported by the missionaries, insisted on men of proven and steadfast Christian character, while the younger men were more concerned with the educational qualifications of the teacher. Since the newer adherents, many of whom were employed in Nairobi, largely financed the outschools, they felt they should have a decisive voice in determining school policies. When the members of the Kathukeine outschool at Uthaya who were living in Nairobi demanded to know how the elders at home were spending their money, they were accused by the missionaries of merely stirring up trouble and in return subtly threatened to withhold money for rebuilding the Uthaya church.[71] Thus, while the outschool movement served to recruit large numbers of people into the mission community, it also gave rise to several potential lines of conflict which subsequently found their most dramatic expression in the context of political awakening and cultural crisis.

FROM MISSION COMMUNITY TO AFRICAN CHURCH

'Essentially the African in Kenya desires, passionately, to be free to manage his own church affairs without what he thinks undue interference. He is dragooned in civil life by alien laws which he is not allowed to have a voice in forming. He wants to keep that dominance out of the church.'[72] So wrote the CMS missionary W. E. Owen in 1938, pointing to what had become a major issue in the making of mission communities – the distribution of power. To what extent were these communities dominated by their European founders? How successful had missionaries been in realizing their proclaimed goal of creating self-supporting, self-governing and self-propagating churches?

There were at least three institutional arenas within the CMS communities in which Africans might potentially have had a voice: the mission organization, the central organs of the embryonic African church, and the local pastorate or congregational councils associated with particular mission stations. Within the structure of the mission itself there was never any formal African representation whatever. When this possibility was broached by the Parent Committee in 1913, Bishop Peel replied that while it would be useful to have non-missionary Europeans on the local policy-making organs of the CMS, an African presence would not be useful 'for some time to come'. A few years later Africans specifically asked to be represented on the mission's Women's Council and were informed that the matter was 'difficult' but would be arranged 'when possible'.[73] Africans officially connected with the CMS were employees or, as they were usually called, 'agents', of whom there were about 170 by 1918. Divided into an elaborately ranked hierarchy including pastors, junior and senior catechists, junior and senior readers, and four grades of schoolmasters, the mission's employees were reviewed for promotion by the local all-European Executive Committee. After 1907 all such agents were required to sign a 'conditions of service' agreement which brought them even more thoroughly under the control of the mission, for under its terms they could be dismissed at twelve hours' notice for improper conduct or could lose up to a month's wages for lack of punctuality or insubordination.[74] The pattern of exclusion from and subordination to mission policy-making bodies which had earlier provoked the revolt of the Bombay Africans and spawned the African Workers Council continued unabated into the new century. But since African employees were now scattered on a variety of interior stations rather than concentrated at the coast, they were apparently unable to maintain their earlier unity. Expressed through missionaries in charge of particular stations, their demands and grievances were dealt with individually and through official channels.

What was new in the early years of the twentieth century was a more energetic mission effort to create an African church organization distinct from the mission. Little had been done along these lines during the previous twenty-five years though CMS policy, since Venn's famous Minute of 1851, had looked forward to the progressive withering away of the mission as an independent African church in communion with the parent body took over the mission's evangelistic, pastoral and educational functions along with financial responsibility for these operations. By 1900 conditions were ripe for an initial effort in this direction.[75] East Africa had been ecclesiastically sub-divided and a new Diocese of Mombasa established with Bishop W. G. Peel, an enthusiastic advocate of African church development, at its head. Furthermore, the years just before Peel's appointment had seen a major crisis among the mission's African employees which revealed discontent with their limited role. Church building initiatives then, were both politically and ecclesiastically expedient.

In his efforts to create new institutions of church government, Peel reorganized the financial arrangements of local congregations to stimulate a greater degree of self-support, founded Bishop's Local Councils to deal with matters of church discipline and, most important, established an African Church Council (ACC), which in Anglican ecclesiastical practice was a first step towards the eventual creation of a diocesan authority with its own constitution and ultimately the formation of an ecclesiastical province independent of Canterbury. This latter step provided at least in theory for a certain African voice in the affairs of the church. On the parish or station level the unit of government was the Pastorate Committee consisting of the pastor, the resident missionary and five lay communicants, whose powers included collection and distribution of certain church funds, arranging for regular services and care of church property. At the central level was the African Church Council itself, composed of two representatives of each pastorate committee, all African clergy and a number of missionaries. The chairman of the ACC was appointed by the CMS Parent Committee and was invariably the bishop.[76]

During the first fifteen or twenty years of its operation the ACC was essentially a failure. By the end of the First World War it was contributing to the support of only eighteen 'agents', while the mission financed almost ten times that number. Even this small group could be maintained only with a CMS subsidy to the ACC amounting to Rs. 1,944 out of a total budget of Rs. 6,577.[77] Moreover, only five of these men were ordained pastors or deacons of whom three had been commissioned since the inception of the ACC. The Council was therefore unable to assume a major role in the evangelistic, pastoral or educational work of the mission even after some forty years' CMS work was renewed on the coast. With the exception of Nairobi, African congregations seemed unable to generate sufficient funds to pay their own pastors. And in spite of persistent missionary urgings that British East Africa was very different from Uganda, where Bishop Tucker refused to commission lay or clerical agents unless they were supported by the church, the Parent Committee of the CMS proved unwilling to increase its grants to the ACC in order to finance the ordination of additional clerics. By 1915 there were in fact four prepared men whose ordination and employment with the ACC had to be delayed owing to the refusal of the CMS to pay their salaries.[78] The principle of self-support thus cut both ways. If adhered to, it could delay the growth of an African church organization, while if suspended it could result in a financially dependent church. During these early years, it appears that the ACC in Kenya got the worst of both worlds, for it relied on the mission for about thirty per cent of its budget, but even this was insufficient to permit substantial growth. To the extent that financial constraints were at the heart of ACC failure, the CMS cannot be criticized for a policy of deliberate delay.

If the ACC was unable to become self-supporting, it was not allowed to become self-governing and no genuine sharing of power emerged in these early years of church growth in Kenya. 'The system works best', wrote the Secretary of the Parent Committee in 1910, 'when the Church Council is always led to realize that it is a subordinate body' reporting to the mission until the establishment of a diocesan authority.[79] But custom as well as policy worked to erode a sense of cooperation where it was probably most important, for the ACC's ordained African pastors were treated in a clearly second-class manner. There was little confidence in the judgement of these men, especially in the critical matter of baptism where they tended to be more inclusive and less demanding than their European counterparts. This cultural difference was not to be tolerated and in 1900 Peel organized a special sequence of church classes for 'inquirers' and 'catechumens' in order 'to avoid hasty baptisms' by African pastors. James Deimler, a freed slave ordained in 1896, was transferred to Rabai from an independent charge in 1912 'to be under more direct supervision'. Such attempts to limit the independence of African pastors sometimes assumed extreme dimensions. In 1906, for example, Binns suggested giving up the CMS station at Taveta to a Lutheran mission rather than entrusting it to an African pastor in the absence of a resident missionary.[80] Finally there is reason to question the extent of active missionary commitment to the development of the ACC. George Wright complained that many of his colleagues had little interest in the Council, while Burns of Nairobi observed that most missionaries were 'keen on preaching' and implied that they were less concerned about the 'African church growing up in our midst'.[81] Nor were Africans involved in the embryonic church organization unaware of their position within it. In August of 1900, only six months after the formation of the Bishop's Local Council at Rabai, its members threatened to resign as a group unless larger powers were granted to them. Some missionaries and Parent Committee representatives were of the opinion that the position of African clergymen in the mission, including their possible subordination to women missionaries, was in part responsible for the reluctance of African agents to come forward for divinity training and ordination.[82]

If the pre-war period saw little in the way of church growth, ecclesiastical development picked up markedly during the 1920s and 1930s. The pace of ordinations increased as recruitment into mission communities, many of whose members were employed in the modern sector of the colonial economy, surged ahead, and by 1939 thirty-three Africans from central and eastern Kenya had been ordained as pastors or deacons. The ratio of African clergy to church members, however, rose from 1:479 in 1915 to 1:708 twenty years later, indicating that ordination by no means kept pace with the growth of mission communities. The financial picture also improved and by 1938 the CMS had phased out its grants to the ACC, though many of its pastors were still in part supported by donations from outside their congregations. Furthermore the ACC had assumed certain new functions including responsibility for evangelistic work along the coast, complete charge of Freretown and Rabai schools and financial contributions to other elementary schools. In fact the growing involvement of missionaries in the institutional side of mission work ensured that most evangelistic efforts, within both the mission and the ACC, were conducted by Africans. Structurally, the ACC was brought closer to its constituent congregations through a policy of decentralization which led to the creation of four district councils in addition to the central council.[83]

But if the ACC was developing in terms of personnel, finances and functions, the problem of authority had hardly been touched. Handley Hooper, African Secretary of the CMS after ten years at Kahuhia, pointed in 1929 to the central difficulty from the European viewpoint: 'This is the paradox. . . . [W]e want to see the beginning of a genuinely indigenous church, but we do not believe that Africans are yet ready to carry out many of the essentials of indigenous life in a corporate religious sense.' Really to release Africans from tutelage, Hooper added,

Europeans must prepare themselves for a 'general lowering of standards'.[84] Most missionaries agreed with Hooper's analysis but were unwilling to accept its implications. If it came to a choice, they clearly preferred European 'standards' to African independence. Thus throughout the 1930s government grants to mission schools continued to be funnelled through the mission rather than the Council since, as one missionary put it, 'The Government expects to have some responsible party to refer to when it comes to administration both financially and educationally and the ACC is not yet competent to do this.'[85]

Such policies resulted in an underlying tension over the question of representation and periodic demands for a more genuine sharing of authority. Thus the ACC in 1934 asked for permission to nominate all candidates for Divinity School training and requested that certain of the larger mission schools be placed under African boards of governors. There was also concern for greater African authority in the financial affairs of the church. 'We are very desirous to keep the money we receive from church collections on Sundays . . .' wrote a number of CMS clergy, teachers and adherents from the Fort Hall area in 1937. They also wanted 'some African representative' present when gifts from abroad were being allocated. The fundamental issue involved in all of these grievances was perhaps best expressed when the ACC complained that no Africans were included on a mission committee charged with changing Kikuyu orthography:

> May we request that in future when matters concerned with African peoples come before you, you consent of your great goodness first of all to consult with the people concerned in the matter.[86]

Nor were the old coastal stations spared the tensions born of African assertion in the inter-war period. When the CMS decided to sell a large portion of their old estate at Freretown, the descendants of the original freed slaves strongly protested at the mission's right to do so, deeply resented being required to resettle at a new village and left the mission community in large numbers. A similar questioning of mission authority occurred at Mombasa when the CMS arbitrarily removed two well liked African agents who were serving the local congregation. This action provoked a 'very antagonistic' reaction among the mission's adherents and came very close to sparking the formation of a rival and independent church.[87]

Younger missionaries in particular felt the new African rejection of missionary paternalism. Harvey Cantrell, for example, who came out as a twenty-five-year-old man in 1931 to replace a much older person at Weithaga, was told in no uncertain terms that he was only *manake* or a young man and that 'you can't put it over us like old daddy Crawford – we're not having it'. Furthermore the withdrawal of many missionaries into their institutional responsibilities reduced the face-to-face contact with Africans which had been the basis of the earlier paternalism.[88] The evident willingness among Africans to dispute the authority of Europeans did not represent a demand for serious structural change in the mission community, but, like the protests of the Bombay Africans some fifty years earlier, was rather an insistence on participation based on a premise of gradualism, on the expectation of missionary respect, and on a large residue of affection and gratitude for individual missionaries. Like much inter-war political expression, these protests did not so much challenge the fact of European leadership as object to the unwillingness of those leaders seriously to consider African participation in the policy-making process. Disappointed 'collaborators' rather than frustrated 'resisters', they had hoped for better things from their missionary mentors.

If both the mission organization and the central organs of the ACC severely restricted African authority, opportunities to exercise initiative were more frequent at the level of local 'pastorate committees' which were generally associated with a particular station and represented the basic unit of church government within the mission community. This enhanced ability to act independently derived from three sources. At the level of the outschools, which were represented on the pastorate committees, financial independence was the key to the large measure of self-government which these institutions enjoyed. But the withdrawal of European missionaries for military service during the war, furloughs, retirement or retrenchment also allowed Africans to assume degrees of responsibility which they might otherwise have been denied. When the CMS removed all European staff and support from Rabai in 1922, thus throwing a larger burden on the local church, the African staff members voluntarily reduced their salaries, while the whole congregation welcomed the new independence which had been forced upon them.[89] The departure of missionary leadership could also allow the incorporation of more traditional modes of organization and decision making into the mission community. When Hooper left Kahuhia for eighteen months during 1920–21, he appointed the senior teacher in charge with a number of elected elders to assist him. Upon his return, however, he discovered that they had replaced the representative principle with a consensus mode of operation by convening monthly assemblies of all confirmed Christians to discuss matters of local policy.[90] But it was not contingency alone that afforded Africans greater opportunity for leadership and expression in pastorate committees, for at this level at least the mission encouraged a policy of devolution and expressed a concern to 'wean' Africans from their dependence on the missionary. At Weithaga and Kabare, for example, African committees were responsible for the collection and distribution of all local funds by the mid-1920s.[91]

'[W]e have only now begun to organize the African Church', confessed the CMS Kenya secretary in 1937.[92] Nevertheless, the transformation from mission station to mission community to African church was under way, though it was a process that reflected the strains of social change under colonial conditions. Some of these strains, such as the outschool–central station cleavage and the tension between younger and older adherents, arose from the process of growth and differentiation itself. But these communities did not escape confrontation with the central issue of colonial societies – the unequal distribution of power among racially defined groups. Political conflict, however, was often associated with a clash of cultures, for mission communities were important arenas in the struggle over values as well as power.

FOOTNOTES

1. *Proceedings*, 1901, p. 122; H. R. A. Philp, *A New Day in Kenya* (London, 1936), Appendix IV. Mission statistics are always suspect, especially after the First World War, when the proliferation of outschools, many of them seldom visited by missionaries, made the collection of statistics difficult. They can be used, however, to indicate relative growth or decline over time.

2. L. H. Gann and Peter Duignan, *Burden of Empire* (New York, 1967), p. 276.

3. Marcia Wright, *German Missions in Tanganyika 1891–1941* (Oxford, 1971), pp. 85–6; Roland Oliver, *The Missionary Factor in East Africa* (London, 1952), pp. 56–9.

4. Aiden Southall, *Social Change in Modern Africa* (London, 1961), p. 3; H. A. C. Cairns, *Prelude to Imperialism* (London, 1965), pp. 10–11; Geoffrey Moorhouse, *The Missionaries* (London, 1973). A. G. Temu, *British Protestant Missions* (London, 1972), p. 41, in referring directly to East Africa suggests that Africans saw missionaries only as 'allies' or as a source of 'material wealth'.

5. CMS/1901/1, Annual Letter, V. V. Verbi, December 1909; 1913/25, Wright to friends, 10 February 1913; CMS, *Extracts*, Mr Pratley, 20 November 1889.

6. See, for example, Robin Horton, 'African Conversion', *Africa*, XLI (April 1971), pp. 85–109; Elizabeth Isichei, 'Seven Varieties of Ambiguity: Some Patterns of Igbo Response to Christian Mission', *Journal of Religion in Africa*, III (1970), pp. 215–6; Paul Bohannan and Philip Curtin, *Africa and Africans* (Garden City, 1971), p. 174.

7. The Giriama phrase for becoming a Christian was '*kugwira chow*', which meant 'to embrace the book', while the alphabet scroll which was used in basic literary classes became on occasion something of a charm or amulet. A similar phenomenon has been noted in West Africa where Islam and literacy in Arabic have been introduced. CMS/1888/258, Diary of Itineration in Giriama, 9 November 1887; 1903/160, *Mombasa Diocesan Magazine*, October 1903; 1885/139, Taylor to Lang, 28 September 1885; Jack Goody, ed. *Literacy in Traditional Societies* (London, 1968).

8. William B. Anderson, 'The Experience and Meaning of Conversion for Early Christian Converts in Kenya', an unpublished paper.

9. Jocelyn Murray, 'Interrelationships Between Witchcraft Eradication Movements and Christianity in Central Africa', an unpublished paper; Sigbert Axelson, *Cultural Confrontation in the Lower Congo* (Falkoping, 1970), pp. 271, 281, 285–6; Jan Vansina, Review of Axelson's *Cultural Confrontation* in *Africa*, XLII (January 1973), pp. 85–6.

10. Margaret Read, 'The Ngoni and Western Education', *Colonialism in Africa*, ed. Victor Turner (Cambridge, 1971), III, p. 357; CMS/1913/64, Wright to Manley, 5 September 1913.

11. Terence Ranger, 'The New Mission Historiography in Eastern Africa', an unpublished paper delivered at the American Historical Association, 1973, p. 8.

12. Robin Horton, 'African Conversion', op. cit., pp. 85–108; Robin Horton, 'A 100 Years of Change in Kalabari Religion', *Black Africa*, ed. John Middleton (London, 1970), pp. 192–211; B. A. Pauw, *Religion in a Tswana Chiefdom* (New York, 1960) pp. 212–17; Elizabeth Colson, 'Converts and Tradition: The Impact of Christianity on Valley Tonga Religion', *Southwest Journal of Anthropology* (1970), pp. 144–55.

13. J. A. Wray, *Kenya, Our Newest Colony* (London, n.d.), p. 26; Binns Journals, 18, 20 August 1879, 8 February 1880; CMS/o3, Binns to CMS, 29 September 1879.

14. Wray, *Kenya*, op. cit., pp. 16–60; CMS/1884/70, Wray to Lang, 23 May 1884; 1885/46, Hannington to CMS, 9 March 1885.

15. CMS/1886/338, Wray to Lang, September 1886; 1887/356, Wray to Shaw, 8 September 1887; 1887/375, Wray to Lang, 15 October 1887; 1887/404, Wray to Lang, 10 November 1887; 1882/222, Wray to Price, 20 May 1888. The only solution, he argued, was to 'absolutely possess the village'.

16. CMS/1896/208, Wray to Baylis, 6 June 1896; 1901/72, Report by Bishop of Mombasa, 26 March 1901; 1901/46, Maynard to Baylis, January 1901.

17. CMS/1899/38, Wray to Baylis, 12 January 1899; 1904/7, Maynard to Baylis, 24 November 1903; 1912/113, Annual Letter: V. V. Verbi, 30 November 1912. Traditional rituals for generating rain were by no means abandoned. See CMS, *Extracts*, R. A. Maynard, 30 November 1908.

18. On Giriama expansion see Cynthia Brantley Smith, 'The Giriama Rising, 1914', Ph.D. dissertation, UCLA, 1973, esp. pp. 321–2. CMS/1891/61, Smith to Lang, 24 January

1891; W. W. A. Fitzgerald, *Travels in the Coastland of British East Africa and the Islands of Zanzibar and Pemba* (London, 1970), p. 98; CMS, *Extracts*, D. A. L. Hooper, 25 October 1892.

19. J. C. Pollock, *A Cambridge Movement* (London, 1953), p. 71.

20. CMS/Acc. 85, 5 May 1892; Acc. 85, Wyatt to Baldey, 9 October 1893; CMS, *Extracts*, D. A. L. Hooper, 25 October 1892; *Proceedings*, 1894, pp. 41–3; CMS/1896/394, Hooper to CMS, 29 October 1896.

21. CMS, *Extracts*, D. A. L. Hooper, 4 December 1893; E. A. Wyatt, 11 October 1894; *Proceedings*, 1894, pp. 41–3; Alfred R. Tucker, *Eighteen Years in Uganda and East Africa* (London, 1907), I, pp. 140, 168, 291–2.

22. There is extensive correspondence regarding Hooper's numerous quarrels with the local governing body of the CMS over a variety of minor mission policy matters. See, for example, CMS/1901/172/, Peel to Baylis, 19 October 1901; 1902/79, Hooper to Baylis, 14 June 1902.

23. CMS/1897/45, Hooper to Baylis, 19 December 1896; 1898/203, Hooper to CMS, 14 November 1898; 1899/182, Burness to Baylis, 2 November 1899; *Proceedings*, 1892, p. 42.

24. CMS/1899/182, Burness to Baylis, 2 November 1899; 1903/76, Burt to Baylis, 28 April 1903; 1904/66, Deimler to CMS, 16 May 1904; 1908/20, *Mombasa Diocesan Magazine*, January 1908.

25. Smith, 'The Giriama Rising', op. cit., pp. 116–27. While the Giriama initially allied with the Mazrui Arabs in their conflict with the British in 1895–6, they progressively shifted sides as they perceived the strength of the British.

26. *Proceedings*, 1902, p. 103; 1903, p. 93; 1898, p. 106.

27. On the history of Taveta, see the reference in footnote 24 in Chapter III.

28. H. H. Johnston, *The Kilimanjaro Expedition* (London, 1886), p. 210; CMS/1896/63, *Taveta Chronicle*, Christmas 1895.

29. CMS/1900/25, *Taveta Chronicle*, January 1900.

30. CMS/1901/183, *Taveta Chronicle*, November 1901; 1897/xli–xlii, 6–20 July 1897; 1897/77, Memo re Taveta Colony, 26 November 1896.

31. CMS/1899/128, *Taveta Chronicle*, June 1899.

32. CMS/1894/128, McGregor to Committee, 26 April 1894; 1894/129, Steggal to Baylis, 19 May 1894; 1893/267, Smith to Baylis, 29 September 1893; *Proceedings*, 1895, p. 85.

33. CMS/1900/47, A. C. Hollis, 'Taveta Totems and Religion', *Taveta Chronicle*, April 1900.

34. See Horton, 'African Conversion', op. cit., for the distinction and Humphrey J. Fisher, 'Conversion Reconsidered: Some Historical Aspects of Religious Conversion in Black Africa', *Africa*, XLIII (January 1973), p. 28, for a critique.

35. CMS/1894/128, McGregor to Committee, 26 April 1894; 1881/58, Binns to Hutchinson, 6 April 1881; 1895/331, Ackerman Journal, 4 August 1895.

36. CMS, *Extracts*, A. W. McGregor, 15 October 1896, V. V. Verbi, 10 November 1897 and A. R. Steggall, 1 November 1895; CMS/1896/63, *Taveta Chronicle*, Christmas 1895.

37. A number of Freretown or Rabai men, for example, had good positions in the early colonial bureaucracy. See Harry Thuku, *An Autobiography* (Nairobi, 1970), p. 15.

38. CMS/1906/3, McGregor to England, 8 December 1905; 1908/58, *Mombasa Diocesan Magazine*, April 1908; KNA: CMS/1/625, Weithaga Log Book; Interview 9.

39. CMS/1898/141, Steggall to FC, 7 July 1898; 1896/302, *Taveta Chronicle*, October 1896.

40. Numerous administrators complained bitterly about this problem. KNA: NYI/10, Nyeri Political Records, 11 December 1916; KBU/9, Dagoretti Annual Report, 1915–16; Interview 20.

41. KNA: Coast Province 20/136, Giriama Handing Over Report, 14 May 1918; *Proceedings*, 1913, p. 62; 1916–17, p. vi; CMS/1918/12, Hooper to Manley, 25 October 1917; Hooper Papers, Carrier Corps Diary.

42. Interview 20; Daudi N. Petero, *Jubilee A. C. Kigari and A. C. Kabare (1910–1960)*, n.d. E. May Crawford, *By the Equator's Snowy Peaks* (London, 1913), p. 128; CMS, *Extracts*, A. W. McGregor, 27 November 1901; CMS, Annual Letters, H. D. Hooper, 29 October 1922; CMS/1910/6 Annual Letter, Miss F. Deed, 27 November 1909.

43. Interviews 20, 21, 25, 27, 29, 33; Godfrey Muriuki, 'A History of the Kikuyu to 1904', Ph.D. Thesis, University of London, 1970, p. 202; Rebmann M. Wambaa, 'The Political Economy of the Rift Valley', an unpublished paper; RH: Coryndon Papers, 17/3/19, 'In Appreciation of Rev. Canon Leakey and his Wife', 2 March 1932.

44. For a recent discussion of Kenya's economic development between the wars, see E. A. Brett, *Colonialism and Underdevelopment in East Africa* (London, 1973), pp. 165–216.

45. Harry Thuku, *An Autobiography*, op. cit., p. 15; CMS/1910/34, Binns to Baylis, 27 January 1910.

46. Hooper Papers, 'Native Issues in Kenya Colony'.

47. CMS/1919/53, McGregor to Manley, 10 June 1919; CMS, Annual Letters, A. W. McGregor, 1 November 1923; E. Lockett, 22 October 1923.

48. For a further discussion of the concept of 'improvement', see John Iliffe, *Tanganyika Under German Rule, 1905–1912* (Nairobi, 1969), p. 166; John Keith Rennie, 'Christianity, Colonialism and the Origins of Nationalism among the Ndau of Southern Rhodesia, 1890–1935', Ph.D. Dissertation, Northwestern University, 1973, pp. 459, 499–561.

49. CMS, *Extracts*, W. E. Taylor, 25 November 1893.

50. *Proceedings*, 1903, p. 91.

51. CMS/1909/110, Peel to Greg, 27 July 1909; 1901/81, Peel to Baylis, 12 April 1901; 1897/313, Parker to Binns, 30 October 1897; 1898/1, Taylor to Baylis, 6 January 1898.

52. CMS, *Extracts*, T. S. England, 27 December 1904; CMS/1911/52, Martin to Baylis, 11 March 1911; J. S. Mangat, *A History of the Asians in East Africa* (London, 1969), pp. 71–7.

53. CMS, *Extracts*, K. St A. Rogers, 1 December 1900; CMS/1897/313, Parker to Binns, 30 October 1897; 1895/44, Tucker to Baylis, 8 January 1895; CMS, Annual Letters, W. H. Good, 8 November 1922.

54. *Proceedings*, 1904, p. 81; CMS, *Extracts*, Miss M. Bazett, 24 November 1893.

55. *Proceedings*, 1920–1, p. xxvi; CMS/1917/47, Burns to Manley, 10 May 1917; KNA: PC/CP.4/2/1, Ukamba Province Annual Report, 1914/15.

56. CMS/1917/31, Memo of Mission Work in Nairobi; 1913/45, Minutes of Missionary Conference, 24 June – 1 July 1913; CMS, Annual Letters, Miss E. Lockett, 22 October 1923. For an examination of the role of cultural borrowing in facilitating role change, see David Parkin, 'The Politics of Syncretism: Islam Among the Non-Muslim Giriama of Kenya', *Africa*, XL (1970), pp. 217–33.

57. H. R. A. Philp, *A New Day in Kenya*, op. cit., Appendix IV.

58. Thomas Jesse Jones, *Education in East Africa*, (London, 1924), p. 122; KNA: CMS/1/334.

59. SPDC, 2/Petero Kigondu.

60. CMS/1918/37, Burns to Manley, 23 May 1918; 1917/53, Hamshere to Manley, 10 July 1917; Philp, *A New Day*, op. cit., Appendix IV.

61. Diary of Rev. George Wright, 1913; CMS/1919/43, Burns to Manley, 29 April 1919; CMS, Annual Letters, George Burns, November 1919.

62. Diary of Rev. George Wright, 13 January 1913; CMS, Annual Letters, J. E. Hamshere, 4 November 1921, Interview 29; CMS/1919/78, W. P. Low, n.d.; KNA: CMS/1/182, Minutes of Executive Committee, 29 May – 2 June 1928; Wambaa, 'The Political Economy', op. cit., p. 3.

63. Interviews 17, 20, 22, 25, 27, 29; CMS, Annual Letters, H. T. Harris, November 1921; CMS/1917/10, Clarke to Manley, 11 December 1916; St Stephen's Church, Njumbi,

Jubilee 1968; 'A Short History of St Stephen's Church, Thimbigwa'; H. D. Hooper, *Leading Strings* (London, 1921), pp. 25–31.

64. Hooper Papers, H. D. Hooper's letter home, 31 October 1923; CMS, 'Historical Records', 1928–9, p. 75; KNA: CMS/1/639, Kabare Log Book; CMS/1921/8, DC to All Missionaries, 7 March 1919.

65. KNA: Ed./1/117, Rampley to Italian Mission, 12 June 1928; CMS/1/270, Downing to Secretary, CMS, 6 February 1936; PCEA: B/1, Leakey to Arthur, 6 June 1913; CMS/1921/6, Rogers to Manley, 22 December 1920.

66. KNA: CMS/1/270, Elija to Secretary, CMS, 17 August 1937; Interviews 3, 4; EHA: Box 247, H. Hooper, 'The Limits of Missionary Education'.

67. David P. Sandgren, 'Kikuyu Society and the African Inland Mission,' an unpublished paper presented at the American Historical Association Conference, 1973, pp. 7–9.

68. KNA: CMS/1/270, Kariuki to CMS, 28 December 1937.

69. SPDC, 3/Johanna Muturi, August 1965; 'St Stephen's Church, Njumbi, Jubilee 1968'; CMS, *Extracts*, Miss Florence Deed, November 1904; CMS/1910/158, Annual Letter, W. E. Crawford, 23 November 1910; Interviews 8, 20, 21, 29; Wambaa, 'The Political Economy', op. cit.

70. James Ngugi wa Thiong'o, *The River Between* (Nairobi, 1965), p. 33.

71. Interviews 3, 4, 7; KNA: CMS/1/270, Mallanger to Secretary, CMS, 30 November 1937; Bewes to Smith, 10 September 1937.

72. KNA: CMS/1/104, Owen to Smith, 4 February 1938.

73. CMS/1914/8, Peel to Manley, 22 January 1914; 1920/42, Minutes of Women's Council, 28 July 1920.

74. CMS/1907/45, Draft Agreement with Mission Teachers, 1 March 1907.

75. For a consideration of the Anglican theory of ecclesiastical development in mission churches, see Eugene Stock, *History of the Church Missionary Society* (London, 1916), IV, chs 39, 40.

76. CMS/1900/20, Minutes of Finance Committee, 16 January 1900; 1900/34, Minutes of Finance Committee, 27–28 February 1900; CMS/P6, Regulations for Church Council, 4 December 1900.

77. CMS/1918/42, Minutes of ACC, 6–7 June 1918.

78. CMS/1915/59, Rogers to Manley, 18 August 1915; 1915/56, Manley to Rogers, 28 October 1915; Roland Oliver, *The Missionary Factor in East Africa*, op. cit., p. 220.

79. CMS/L10, Baylis to Rogers, 6 October 1910.

80. KNA: CMS/1/634, Rabai Log Book, 13 December 1912; CMS/1901/164, Peel to Baylis, 11 October 1901; 1906/97, Binns to Baylis, 24 August 1906.

81. CMS/1915/81, Memo of Interview with Wright, 20 December 1915; 1915/71, Burns to Manley, 23 October 1915.

82. KNA: CMS/1/634, Rabai Log Book, 14 August 1900; CMS/1913/61, Kenyon to Manley, n.d.

83. KNA: CMS/1/50, Secretary to Turton, 30 December 1937; CMS, 'Historical Records', 1927–8; CMS/1923/9, Minutes of ACC, 17 November 1922; CMS/1925, Garfield Williams Report, 14 April 1925.

84. CMS, Acc. 85, Hooper to Sandy, 6 September 1929.

85. KNA: CMS/1/50, Secretary to Turton, 30 December 1937.

86. KNA: CMS/1/103, Minutes of ACC, 30 July – 2 August 1934; Nguru to Secretary, KMC, n.d.; CMS, Acc. 85, H. D. Hooper, typescript.

87. See correspondence in KNA: Ed./1/2069 and CMS/1/599.

88. Interview 3; E. S. Atieno-Odhiambo, 'A Portrait of the Missionaries in Kenya Before 1939', *Kenya Historical Review*, I: 1 (1973), p. 11.

89. CMS, Annual Letters, H. T. Harris, November 1922, October 1923; F. T. Austin, 6 December 1922.

90. EHA: Box 236, Hooper letter, 5 January 1922.

91. CMS, 'Historical Records', 1924–5, p. 44; KNA: CMS/1/625, Weithaga Log Book, 22 August 1927. Hooper, *Leading Strings*, op. cit., p. 26.
92. KNA: CMS/1/50, Secretary to Turton, 30 December 1937.

CHAPTER V

∜∜∜∜∜∜∜∜∜∜∜∜∜∜∜∜∜∜∜∜∜∜∜∜∜∜∜∜∜∜∜∜∜∜

The Making of Mission Culture

'Missionaries felt it right that the African must receive the Western culture with his Christianity.'[1] Such has been the common understanding of missionary attempts to guide the process of cultural change among members of their communities, for their often severe denunciation of African culture has been viewed as evidence of their insistence on wholesale 'westernization'. Indeed both critics and defenders of the missionary enterprise have viewed it as a major and deliberate agent for change in colonial society. African nationalists and their European supporters have damned missions for indiscriminately undermining African cultural self-confidence, while secular champions of mission activity have seen it as an important agency of social mobilization and as a mechanism for easing the transition to the modern world.[2]

Some recent scholarship suggests, however, that it may be necessary to question the equation of missions with change. In the first place, the extent to which missions acted as an independent motor of social and cultural change needs to be re-examined. Robin Horton has reduced the role of missionaries even in the process of religious transformation to that of a catalyst for other changes already in the air. Many have observed that missions seldom made much headway until other political and economic changes had been imposed. While missions may, for example, have shaped the character of the 'new elite', they can hardly be credited with the unaided creation of this important social group. Several recent studies from Malawi have in fact suggested that certain missions, Roman Catholic and Dutch Reformed Church for instance, simply did not generate anything akin to a modernizing elite at all and their authors have been critical of African historians generally for an over-emphasis on the modernizing outcome of the colonial encounter.[3]

If we, with hindsight, need to be careful about equating missions with change, we should be no less critical of common assumptions about missionary consciousness of themselves as agents of modernizing or westernizing change. In an examination of Catholic missions in Zaire, Markowitz has commented perceptively on the issue:

> Their own anti-intellectualism and anti-cosmopolitanism also led many missionaries to become exponents and supporters of African provincialism. They idealized African village life and rejected such aspects of modernity as urbanization and industrialization. To them rural life was the epitome of virtue while the city was filled with evil and atheism. In its extreme form this rural romanticism led to rejection of the accoutrements of Western civilization and to cultural asceticism.[4]

In a similar vein, it seems clear that the development of mission culture within the Anglican communities of Kenya was not simply imposed by an uncritically westernizing missionary leadership, for CMS missionaries harboured important elements of ambivalence in their attitudes towards both African and western culture. Nor did African Christians uncritically accept the cultural prescriptions of their mentors. The process of cultural change within the mission communities was informed rather by a large measure of conflict over values which derived as much or more from African opposition to missionary limits on their access to western culture as from missionary attacks on customary ways of life.

MISSIONS AND AFRICAN CULTURE

There is, of course, no denying that late nineteenth- and early twentieth-century missionaries were culturally arrogant in the extreme and as a consequence possessed negative views towards unfamiliar African ways of life. Judgements such as that of R. A. Maynard on the Taita – 'almost all the customs of the people are bad, very bad' – are too numerous to need much documentation.[5] From such attitudes derived the missionary impulse to establish – both institutionally and symbolically – clear boundaries between their communities and neighbouring African societies. There was little in the way of reaching out to establish points of cultural contact. Particularly before the First World War CMS efforts were devoted almost entirely to saving individuals from 'their heathen surroundings' with little or no real attempt to redeem African culture. The creation of boarding schools at most CMS centres both reflected this sentiment and represented the major institutional means of achieving the desired separation. Yet it was one thing to condemn African culture generally and quite another to devise policies to cope with specific offending institutions and practices, for African adherents could not, after all, check their culture at the gate to the mission compound. Three areas in particular – drink, family structure and religion – will serve to indicate the nature of the missionary encounter with those elements of African culture with which they most strongly disagreed.

Abstinence from intoxicating beverages became for the missionaries a symbol of genuine conversion and a relatively easy means of identifying those who were solidly committed to the mission community. Recognizing the social functions of drinking, missionaries feared that participation would lead to 'the many evil things the heathen do' and saw abstinence as a means of effectively separating mission adherents from much of traditional society. The campaign against drink took a variety of forms. The Women's Conference proposed in 1900 a temperance crusade, while the government was petitioned to restrict the sale of *tembo* (locally brewed beer). Nor did the mission shrink from more direct action, for when illicit distilleries were discovered on mission land at Taveta, missionaries and schoolboys sallied forth in the tradition of the church militant and chopped down the plants used in the brewing process. Regulations forbidding all 'agents' and members of pastorate committees from drinking was the mission's strongest stand on the matter.[6] There were, however, limits to CMS action on the question of alcohol, for the mission itself never imposed total abstinence as a condition for baptism. The product of a more tolerant Anglican tradition, this decision represented in fact a major point of conflict between the CMS on the one hand and the African Inland Mission and the Presbyterians on the other, and was in part responsible for the failure of the Kikuyu movement for Protestant unity in Kenya.[7]

Certain groups of African Christians, apparently seeing in the issue of drink a potent symbol of their new identity and religious commitment, sometimes took matters in their own hands and went further than the missionaries themselves. At Mbale in the Taita hills, for example, church elders, without consulting the resident missionaries, decided that drinkers could not be baptized nor have their children baptized and that offenders were to be 'boycotted as much as possible'. Likewise at Kabare, African Christians resolved to forbid drinking among 'readers' and imposed a fine of one month's work (Sh. 5) on those who transgressed this prohibition. In other matters as well Africans took the initiative in defining the cultural imperatives of the mission community. They discouraged the use of drums and mixed singing during Christmas celebrations at Kabare, much to the disappointment of the missionaries, while at Kahuhia church elders virtually forbade curious missionaries from seeing certain traditional dances and ceremonies.[8]

A second aspect of African culture that elicited strong criticism from missionaries concerned family organization and the role of women and involved the issues of polygyny, dowry, inheritance of wives and sexual morality. While polygamy certainly ranked high on most missionaries' list of 'native customs to be deprecated', the CMS encounter with the reality of the situation produced an early and startlingly flexible response. In the first place, many missionaries were genuinely concerned about the fate of those wives who had to be discarded when their husbands sought church membership. In 1909 in fact the CMS was a party to a joint Protestant resolution to 'in no case urge heathen men to put away their wives with a view to baptism'. There was also a very practical realization that the mission ban on polygyny was the source of much hostility, especially among women, and a probable cause of the slow growth of mission communities in the early years of the twentieth century.[9] Despite these reservations, it is more than a little surprising to find local CMS missionaries in 1907 formally indicating a desire for the Lambeth Conference of Anglican bishops to reconsider the whole question of polygamy. The Mission Conference expressed the view that baptism should not be denied to a man having more than one wife though any church member subsequently taking a second or additional wife would be subject to church discipline. Now in 1907 this was a very progressive view indeed and the Parent Committee lost no time in making the missionaries in Kenya aware of their error. Indicating that great embarrassment would follow if the resolution permitting baptism of polygamists were made public, they clearly ordered the local mission authorities not to express any such opinion to the Lambeth Conference and in fact suggested that persons holding such views would never have been appointed missionaries in the first place. Following this sharp rebuke, the local mission promptly backed down and no more was heard of such dangerous notions.[10] A promising opportunity for 'adapting' Christianity to African culture had been lost and the initiatives permitted to 'men on the spot' proved to have very definite limits.

On the question of dowry or bride wealth, mission opinion was even more complex and conditioned by circumstances. Believing that it made of marriage a 'mere mercantile transaction', the mission resolved in 1907 to discourage the practice among baptized Christians 'as far as possible'. In this effort, however, they were never very successful, for Christians continued to give and receive bride-wealth and some even approached individual missionaries about loans for this purpose.[11]

Beyond this problem of enforcement, there was the more theoretical question of what standards of behaviour to expect from inquirers and catechumens, people at an earlier stage of Christian profession than those who had gone on to the third step of baptism and church membership. The issue took on an especially acute form in the many situations in which Christian partners of whatever standing were simply unavailable. In such cases the CMS apparently decided to make a virtue of necessity, for in 1911 the mission established a policy for 'mixed' marriages whereby the parents of a 'heathen' girl had to agree to put their daughter under Christian instruction before receiving payment from the Christian young man whom she planned to marry. Since a church wedding was thus impossible and traditional marriage ceremonies were in all cases forbidden to Christians, the mission recommended a civil ceremony in such instances of 'mixed' marriages.[12] This compromise did not, however, satisfy everyone and disputes over Christian–non-Christian marriages continued to unsettle the mission. Bishop Peel in particular was strongly opposed to such unions as they required him to deny the Christian partner access to communion and a Christian burial. Binns, on the other hand, felt they should be tolerated lest Christian girls, unable to find a mate, be driven into prostitution; in fact he threatened to resign if the bishop's policy prevailed.[13] Mission policy on marriage – 'the bugbear of my life out in Africa' according to Binns – generated heated debate within the mission and demonstrated the difficulty of agreeing on a cultural policy that both reasonably conformed to accepted Christian doctrine and allowed some chance of practical success.

If a certain flexibility born of experience was evident on the question of dowry and mixed marriages, no such tolerance was extended to the practice that the missionaries called 'inheritance of wives' whereby a widow would be taken as a wife by another male member of her husband's family, often his brother. This custom not only suggested to the missionaries a view of women as moveable property but also represented a means by which a Christian woman and her children could 'pass into heathenism' and thus be lost to the mission community. The practical alternatives open to the CMS in such cases were limited and generally involved attempting both to strengthen the resolve of the widow in resisting incorporation into her husband's brother's family and to enlist the support of local district officers in ensuring the rights of Christian widows 'with due regard to English law'. Despite persistent missionary prodding, it was not until 1931 that the government of Kenya passed a Native Christian Marriage Ordinance which provided that African women reached the age of majority upon widowhood and were thus no longer subject to the authority of their husband's family.[14]

Similarly the mission was adamant on the issue of sexual morality. The 'grievous sins' for which many were subjected to church discipline or dismissed from mission employment most often involved breaches of the mission code of behaviour which limited sexual activity to the monogamous marriage relationship. In 1909 the CMS decided to expel from mission land for at least six months all non-Christians who were proved guilty of 'fornication', while Christians who so indulged were to be dealt with at the discretion of the resident missionary.[15] The sharp and persistent condemnation of both African and European dancing derived from a fear that such behaviour stimulated sexual activity.

Polygyny, bride wealth and levirate marriages combined to persuade missionaries that women in African societies were regarded as 'mere chattels, the worth of so many goats and cows'. Another and more practical spur to mission action on behalf of African women lay in the general lack of suitable Christian wives for converted young men, for the 'backwardness' of women compared with the men was widely regarded as a serious danger for the embryonic African church. The solution to both problems was generally seen to lie in greater educational opportunities for girls. There had long been a boarding school at the coast; another opened at Kahuhia in 1923, while at Kabete there was established a refuge for runaway girls. Yet efforts to improve the status of women encountered serious obstacles largely because of the male dominance of the missionary structure. Nowhere was this more evident than in the attempts of Mrs M. C. Hooper to encourage educational reform in mission schools in Kenya.[16]

The enthusiastic young wife of the CMS missionary Handley Hooper, she had come to Kenya in 1916 with a well developed sense of women's rights. As a consequence she was appalled by the position of women in African society and published her views in a pamphlet entitled *Property in the Highlands of East Africa*. There she set forth a fairly typical notion of African women as 'a piece of property', denounced female circumcision as 'a disgusting ceremony', and pleaded for Europeans to atone for their exploitation of Africa by working for the welfare of its women. She soon discovered, however, that the male dominance of African society was matched by that of the CMS itself. 'The men on the mission do not show women any say even in the arrangements of their own work', she complained, and insisted that her goal was nothing less than the 'abolition of sex disqualifications'. Furthermore, she argued, male missionaries showed little concern for work among African women and as a result she felt that 'the work among girls is being ruined'.

Mrs Hooper's view of the direction that women's work should take focused on the creation of a system of boarding schools and dormitories culminating in an inter-mission college designed to produce teachers, nurses and other trained women. Temporary immersion in the Christian atmosphere of such an institution would, she felt, 'give them something to take back into their village lives that wasn't there before'. When proposals to this effect were presented to the Kikuyu Conference of Protestant missions in 1918, Mrs Hooper took the lead in defending them, albeit unsuccessfully. The major objections from the male side suggested that such schools unnecessarily Europeanized African girls and broke up families, and that young men in any event preferred village to dormitory girls as wives. In her 'cheeky' reply, Mrs Hooper criticized men's training for not engendering an appreciation for educated girls, observed that boys' boarding schools were not regarded as destructive to family life and insisted that her purpose was to 'Christianize' village life rather than to Europeanize African girls. The opposition of the male leadership and the inability of Protestant missionaries to work effectively together doomed Mrs Hooper's proposals, though a milder resolution encouraging the establishment of boarding schools for girls 'where necessary' was passed by the Conference.

The issue of mandatory representation of women on African church councils also came before the conference, and Mrs Hooper again took an active role in supporting the measure. When Archdeacon Owen proposed separate men's and women's councils, with the former having the final say, she countered with the observation that the 'mother church . . . was an entirely masculine organization' and asked why, if women's resolutions had to go through the men's council for modification, the reverse should not also apply. Not unpredictably her proposal failed. There was thus within the CMS a measure of vigorous female leadership committed to improving the position of African women, though this element found itself often frustrated by male control of the mission establishment and by the priority assigned to 'men's work' in a context of scarce resources. While issues concerning family structure and the role of women provided occasion for much missionary condemnation of African culture, mission policy on such matters was not simply imposed ready-made from Europe but rather had to be hammered out in Africa and implemented under local conditions. Some of these conditions set definite limits on the ability and desire of the mission to induce fundamental changes in this area of African life.

Religion was a third aspect of African culture to which missionaries took strong exception, for even apart from their lack of the Christian revelation, African religions offended missionary values and beliefs in a variety of ways. While missionaries were pleasantly surprised to learn that Africans generally had a concept of a High God, they were dismayed at their apparent lack of love for and communion with the Supreme Being. The 'nearness of the evil spirits', wrote one, surpassed even the sense of God's presence. Furthermore, Africans did not limit their spiritual universe to God, but rather populated it with a variety of subordinate beings, particularly ancestor spirits, whose worship was strongly condemned by missionaries and staunch mission adherents.[17] Likewise the sacrifices which were an important part of African religious practice were regarded by missionaries as a denial of the efficacy of the 'Great Sacrifice'. This concern was reflected in the strong opposition of several missionaries to the payment by Christians of certain goats during the ceremonies associated with the change of generation sets among the Kikuyu and Embu peoples. During the 1920s this issue caused a considerable stir within the mission community at Kabare in particular on the grounds that the goats in question were used for 'pagan sacrifices'. The missionary insistence on separating the religious and social functions of the ceremony led to extensive negotiations among mission adherents, traditional elders and local government officials. A compromise was finally arranged whereby the goats of Christians from the *mwangi* or incoming generation were killed and eaten in the presence of a missionary to ensure that no sacrifice occurred.[18]

African attempts to explain and control evil or misfortune by reference to witchcraft beliefs were regarded as rank and baseless superstition which should be 'banished'. 'Evil spirits' on the other hand, where they were distinguished from witchcraft beliefs, possessed a spiritual reality in much missionary thinking. As a result missionaries lamented the 'bondage' of Africans to 'Satan's satellites', but did not deny their existence.[19] Such bondage was in a sense a measure of African spiritual depravity that went beyond mere religious ignorance. A further indication to many of such deficiencies lay in the absence of a sense of sin and guilt among Africans and as a consequence their lack of a felt 'need for a saviour'. The vigour with which Africans denied that they had 'sin in their heart' – probably to protect themselves from witchcraft accusations – came as a surprise to missionaries, many of whom were acutely conscious in their own lives of falling short of the imperatives of Christian morality.[20] A final element in the missionary critique of African religious thinking lay in its alleged 'dim view of an hereafter'. The notion of the resurrection, according to the missionary Verbi in 1909, was still a stumbling block to the Taita, while according to McGregor the Masai had no concept of an afterlife whatever. That African religions did not conceive of history as moving towards a future goal was in sharp contrast to the highly eschatological emphasis of mission Christianity.[21] To many missionaries in fact their own enterprise was a major element in bringing closer the denouement of history, for not until all peoples had heard the Gospel would Christ return to earth. Missionary condemnation of African religion, then, was based not only on misunderstanding – though there was much of that – but also on profoundly different conceptions of time, the nature of spiritual reality, God's role in the world, the sources of evil and other important cosmological questions.

Nonetheless most missionaries believed with McGregor that 'God has not left Himself without witness' in Africa. Thus they took positive notice of certain elements in African religious life that might be 'developed', including the concept of God, the practice of sacrifice, the existence of rest days, and among the Kikuyu, the custom of the 'new birth'. In 1909, in fact, the Protestant missions jointly resolved to 'sympathetically respect' African religious customs and use them as a basis for teaching where possible. Despite such good intentions CMS missionaries never conducted any formal or extended investigations of traditional religion nor were they studied in the mission's Divinity School where Islam and Hinduism represented the African student's only exposure to non-Christian religions.[22] Thus the CMS made no consistent or systematic attempt to present the new religion in terms of the old.

The consequences of these attitudes for the religious culture of the CMS communities are difficult to estimate, for a considerable range of religious behaviour was practised within them. On the one hand there were among the core group of mission adherents those who, like Ngugi's Joshua, 'had renounced his tribe's magic, power and ritual. He turned to and felt the deep presence of the one God.' Leakey pointed to this conscious transfer of religious allegiance when he described how the 'fear of evil spirits' was replaced by a 'feeling after God' among many mission supporters. African Christians themselves on occasion defined both verbally and in action those aspects of traditional religious practice that had to be rejected. A group of Kikuyu Christians in 1929 listed the customs which the gospel 'drove away' and included the worship of and sacrifice to 'departed spirits', 'witch doctors and their business' and 'charms'. At other times, early converts took the religious offensive and deliberately desecrated sacred places or flaunted the prescriptions of traditional religious practitioners.[23] Such behaviour suggests that conversion represented an experimental search for religious power rather than a psychological crisis of guilt and forgiveness. 'Moody,' wrote a recent student of early Christian history in Kenya, 'would have been disappointed.' Nor did conversion necessarily alter the basic conceptual framework of religious thinking, for as Handley Hooper perceptively observed, acts of repudiation could become 'an indirect tribute' to those subordinate spiritual beings or forces that pervaded the African religious universe.[24] The act of faith, then, was a calculated shift of religious allegiance within the structure of already familiar categories.

It is not therefore surprising that many mission adherents retained multiple religious loyalties which became a source of serious strain only when the exclusivity of mission Christianity was enforced. The use of traditional charms and medicine among those associated with the CMS communities was a widespread phenomenon. It is said that the Reverend Simeon Kalume, the first African minister in Nairobi, wore protective charms while many others sought the assistance of traditional diviners or medicine men in cases of illness or other personal crises. A great many mission people also kept an open mind as to the powers of ancestral spirits. Perhaps the most dramatic example involved Yohana Nene, the first ordained African from Taveta, who was suspended from the diaconate in 1907 in part for allegedly consenting to the removal of his mother's skull from her grave according to Taveta custom.[25] Nor were many Christians altogether immune to fears of witchcraft. The heterogeneous mission communities at Jilore and Taveta experienced considerable difficulty in this regard. Ibrahim Mwambonu, a promising CMS agent among the Taita, was discovered in 1911 manufacturing and dispensing an anti-witchcraft medicine not, he argued, because he believed in its power, but because the people demanded something. With no Christian resources to draw upon, he apparently felt no serious conflict in accepting the role of a traditional medicine man to meet the needs of his people. His suspension from CMS employment, however, provoked a sharp reaction at Wusi, including the holding of 'opposition services' and the temporary disaffection of many mission adherents, though within a year the crisis had passed and Mwambonu had returned to mission service. The CMS outschool at Iyego near Weithaga was the scene of serious witchcraft accusations in 1933 when local Christians suspected a nearby 'excommunicated bigamist' and three of his friends of bewitching them. Much to the disappointment of the missionaries, they took matters into their own hands and brutally beat the four men who had aroused their suspicion.[26] Many African Christians apparently found it both possible and desirable to incorporate elements of traditional practice into their new religious life or to shuttle among several systems of belief and ritual. All of this represented a movement away from the dogmatic mission view of Christianity as a religion of exclusive validity towards a pragmatic or experimental position more in keeping with traditional African religious practice. In such subtle ways did the Africanization of Christianity take place within the confines of mission communites as well as more obviously in independent churches.

The generally negative attitude of CMS missionaries towards much of African culture had a variety of consequences. It was in the first place largely responsible for the external antagonism generated by these new social units. In fact, what gave mission communities their unique identity and cohesion, at least in the early years, was not so much the motives of their members as the animosity of their neighbours. The exasperation of parents over their loss of opportunity to socialize their children appropriately could provoke the use of force to remove them from the mission. Around 1913, for example, a number of boys slightly under the age for circumcision were captured from the Kigari station and prematurely circumcised to make certain they would be properly initiated. Though missionaries frequently performed circumcision on boys, such an operation in no way satisfied the initiation requirements of the Embu.[27] Popular hostility among elders to mission communities was not, however, necessarily based on a total opposition to change nor on a rejection of formal education but rather grew out of a determination to resist the substantial cultural changes demanded by the missionaries. 'We wish to be taught', declared a group of Taveta elders in 1904,

> but we do not wish to be compelled to give up the things we are accustomed to, such as drinking beer, having several wives, and so on, but to be taught little by little so that afterwards we may come to understand ourselves about these things.[28]

A similar selectivity informed the attitude of a number of Kikuyu elders who discussed the status of mission adherents with administrative officials in 1912. While indicating a preference for government schools, they stated that they would encourage their children to go to the mission for education and denied that becoming a Christian would prejudice anyone's access to land in the reserves. But they became adamant when matters touching the integrity of the family were at stake. In particular they refused to consider giving up the children of a Christian widow to her new husband upon remarriage, an action which would mean the loss of the children to the family of the dead husband. If pressed in this matter, the elders threatened to forbid their offspring from becoming Christians. Likewise a number of Kamba chiefs informed the Director of Education that they refused to send their children to mission schools on account of mission teachings on monogamy.[29] Thus when the politicized Christian young men of the 1920s and 30s insisted on separating modern education from the cultural demands of the missionaries, they were in a sense following in the footsteps of their fathers.

Mission communities thus represented the introduction of a new cultural cleavage into African society. There is evidence, however, that most mission adherents themselves did not desire a total break with their society. During the 1912 discussions with district officers and elders, Kikuyu Christians indicated a willingness to pay and receive bride-wealth, accepted traditional patterns of inheritance, agreed that missions should not interfere in such arrangements, and consented to come under the jurisdiction of local *kiamas* or councils except for participation in sacrifices. 'We want to live with our fathers and not with the missionaries,' declared the young converts.[30] Some years later another group of staunch mission adherents drew up a list of traditional customs to be rejected and in the process indicated something of their image of themselves. 'The Gospel', they wrote, 'began to form a new nation from that of old Kikuyu.... We are at the beginning of a great building up of new customs and the forming of Christianity, the same as those who before us made ordinances for the generations after them.' Conscious of change in Kikuyu history, they felt an apparent need to assert some continuity with previous agents of change and saw themselves, not permanently alienated from their own society, but rather in the vanguard of a progressive transformation. References in the Kikuyu newspaper *Muigwithania* to the various missions as 'clans', since each had its own burying place, pointed to the cultural distinctiveness of mission communities and yet implied a sense of inclusion in the larger Kikuyu society.[31]

What was desirable, however, was not always possible, for the impulse among African Christians to retain links with their own society came into frequent collision with the cultural demands of the missionaries. The result was a consistently high rate of turnover among mission employees and the constant exercise of church discipline as missionaries sought to enforce their version of Christian culture while Africans sought to retain some social standing in their societies and access to the religious resources of their own people. The 'grievous sins' which were the occasions for dismissal and discipline generally involved drinking, breaches of mission sexual morality, consulting traditional religious practitioners or participation in 'native feasts and dances'. In 1911, to cite an example almost at random, one hundred people were excommunicated at Rabai and Jilore alone for having 'gone back to heathenism'. When Bishop Heywood arrived in Kenya in 1919, he indicated that church discipline had to be exercised 'frequently and severely' owing to the recent emergence of Africans from 'savagery'. Shortly thereafter the mission resolved to publish the names of those baptized but unconfirmed Christians who were convicted of 'grievous sin' and to forbid their further preparation for confirmation until they had publicly repented.[32] All of this represented an element of continuing tension generated within the mission community as a consequence of the clash of cultures and ensured that many people's association with CMS communities would be both brief and unpleasant.

An interesting expression of this internal conflict over values involved the role of the Old Testament within the mission. The cultural parallels between traditional African society and ancient Hebrew culture forcibly struck many mission people, though their missionary mentors were less than enthusiastic about the literalness with which Africans interpreted the Old Testament. The liberal Archdeacon W. E. Owen of CMS Nyanza went so far as to urge delaying the translation of the Old Testament into Luo against the wishes of Luo members of the ACC as he feared that it would only provide justification for 'backsliding' into the 'polygamy of the surrounding pagan society'.[33] The Scriptures, it turned out, needed considerable interpretation.

Before the circumcision crisis of 1929 the most dramatic and overt expression of protest against the cultural demands of the mission occurred in Mombasa where the CMS's Buxton High School was located. What had enabled a Christian school to persist – though not without serious tension – in a primarily Moslem community had been the willingness of the mission to offer advanced instruction in the English language and the absence of any educational alternatives. Such a situation came to an abrupt end in 1911. In that year the Indian community of Mombasa, which contributed almost seventy per cent of the school's students, organized an effective campaign against Buxton High School at the heart of which was a petition sent to the colonial government complaining about compulsory Christian teaching and the inefficiency of the school's staff. At the same time an independent Indian school was established in the hope of being subsidized or taken over by the government. It immediately attracted over half of the CMS's Indian pupils so that total attendance dropped from 150 in early 1911 to only sixty by the end of October.[34]

While the missionaries saw these actions as a sudden and unexpected movement motivated by the 'evil intentions' of the Indians, it seems more reasonable to view the events of 1911 in the context of a decade's protest by Indians against the communal or racial discrimination imposed upon them in a territory increasingly coming under the influence of European settlers. Recent studies have pointed to a new aggressiveness in Indian politics in 1910 associated with the visit to London by A. M. Jeevanjee, the first Indian representative on the Protectorate's Legislative Council, as well as protests made on behalf of Kenya's Indians by the London branch of the All India Muslim League.[35] The coincidence of this fresh upsurge in Indian political activity with cultural protests over Buxton High School was not perhaps altogether fortuitous. A further possible factor may have been the fact that in Nairobi a new government school for European children and one for Indians had been established in 1910.

When the colonial government, concerned to prevent a serious religious incident, responded positively to Indian demands for a government school, the reaction of the CMS was immediate. Without consulting their London headquarters, the local missionaries decided that Scripture teaching would no longer be compulsory and that all pupils would be admitted to the school under a conscience clause. The purpose of this move was of course to preempt for the CMS any government subsidies for education in Mombasa and thus preserve the mission's educational monopoly in the city. This tactic however proved unsuccessful. The government ultimately declined to grant subsidies to the CMS on terms that it would accept, for it became apparent that the local missionaries were unable to win the confidence of the highly suspicious Indian community. Within a few years, therefore, the government established an Indian school as well as one for the Arab and Swahili population of Mombasa. For several years, the CMS was able to compete successfully with these new institutions, but by the end of the decade improved government schools had drained off many of the mission's former students. The Indian section of Buxton High School was permanently closed in 1921 and thereafter the school catered mainly for African Christians from the interior who were living in Mombasa.[36] Thus the cultural opposition of local people when given political expression not only forced the CMS temporarily to abandon compulsory religious training but also resulted in the end of the CMS educational monopoly in Mombasa and ultimately required the mission to alter its educational policy there. This desire of local people for more and better education of a type that did not threaten their own culture foreshadowed the more widespread demands associated with the independent schools movement of the 1930s.

MISSIONS AND WESTERN CULTURE

The missionaries' condemnation of large areas of African culture by no means implied a desire to subject their adherents to a process of wholesale westernization, for they were profoundly ambivalent about modern western culture, particularly as it appeared in Kenya. Nor was this altogether surprising since the missionary movement as a whole represented a particular kind of critique of modern society and included in the pattern of missionary motivation was an important element of escape. Industrial England, based ultimately on a scientific rationalism that left increasingly little room for the supernatural, seemed to promote material over spiritual values while it destroyed those rural communities in which the church had played an important social as well as religious role. But it was higher criticism of the Bible that came to symbolize for conservative churchmen the modern assault on the faith and from this erosion of Scriptural authority, according to a recent study, missionaries escaped to Africa much as settlers fled a growing democracy and higher taxes at home. Within the CMS, Kenya remained a stronghold of an orthodox theological position though it was felt necessary periodically to reaffirm their rejection of a 'rationalistic theology'.[37]

No-one expressed the missionary critique more passionately than the CMS pioneer J. L. Krapf who from his vantage point in East Africa inveighed strenuously against the materialism, 'vain philosophy' and 'popery' of Europe. 'A civilized man who has no fear of God', he wrote, 'is indeed ten times worse off than a savage of Africa who fears his charms and leaves his neighbour's property intact.' When God's judgement falls on Europe, Krapf continued, the faithful remnant will find a 'hiding place' among Christian communities abroad.[38] As the nineteenth century drew to a close, missionaries were no longer permitted the luxury of abstract criticism but rather had to confront the practical impact of modern western society on their own enterprise. From the very beginning the dominant feeling was one of ambivalence. Although the arrival of the British East

Africa Company in 1888 had obvious political advantages for the CMS, its presence drew many mission people away from their Christian environment into a worldly cash nexus while the character of its officials left much to be desired from the viewpoint of Christian example. With similar concerns in mind, Bishop Tucker observed that the coming of the railroad would not prove an 'unmitigated blessing'. Nor were the majority of European settlers, hard-drinking, sexually permissive and irreligious, much of a comfort to missionaries in their task of building Christian culture in Kenya.[39]

But the dominant concern of CMS missionaries vis-à-vis the impact of the west lay in their fear of 'detribalization', a possible direction of cultural change that was viewed with much the same horror as 'unredeemed' African culture. This was an anxiety that became increasingly pronounced after the First World War as the social and economic impact of colonial rule became more evident and as African political movements began to make their presence felt in response. Handley Hooper conjured up the image of a

> detribalized and suspicious proletariat with no ties of home affection, no steady interests in this world, and no settled community life to balance the revolution in outlook and to lay the stable foundations of the visible church.

Fearing that Africans would be 'ruined by contact with encroaching civilization', he saw the enemy of the missionary enterprise no longer 'hidden in the fastness of heathenism' but rather as the 'dead weight of materialism'.[40] Based on a view of African culture as essentially weak and likely to disintegrate under external pressure and on a view of Africans as basically passive in the process of cultural change, detribalization was seen as profoundly inimical to the interests of mission communities in a variety of interlocking ways.

In the first place missionaries believed that 'detribalization' would render impossible the creation of a truly African church. Bishop Tucker had used this argument when he forbade the wearing of European clothes to certain CMS agents in 1895 and missionaries continued to deplore the predilection of Africans for western modes of dress. In the same vein the CMS Parent Committee deprecated the erection of large European-style churches on the grounds that they tended to 'Europeanize' the congregation and to sap its independence. Likewise the taking of European rather than biblical surnames at baptism was strongly discouraged.[41] Despite the superficiality of such measures, they do indicate a genuine concern that Africans should not experience Chrisitianity as a foreign transplant. Within at least these narrow limits, missionaries did attempt to distinguish between what was essentially Christian and what was merely European.

Secondly, missionaries argued that 'detribalization' had a markedly undesirable effect on the character of their converts. Too much education for a girl allegedly taught her to despise manual labour, 'practically unfitting her for future life of usefulness as a married woman'. Students educated out of their 'natural surroundings', according to the collective wisdom of the Parent Committee, lacked 'backbone' and proved unable to face temptation.[42] But it was towns in general and Nairobi in particular that provoked the most widespread criticism among missionaries on the grounds that urban life, largely lacking, they assumed, in mechanisms of social control, produced self-centred young people and exposed them terribly to all sorts of grave temptations. To the veteran missionary McGregor, Nairobi was 'in truth a place where Satan's seat is'. Making much the same point in a novel, *New Patches*, based on her missionary experience in Kenya, Mrs M. C. Hooper had her main character describe the effects of urban life on a young African man:

> I think he is typical Nairobi. He's a nice enough looking boy and well-dressed too, but I think he probably is mostly taken up with himself. I'm sorry when a man becomes so apart from his people that he doesn't bother about his land or home. He's given up tilling his land here, you know, and that's bad for the women too. I can't think what Wanja will do with herself in Nairobi with no gardening and no home to keep going. It's an unhealthy life for an energetic girl. It is more possible when a woman is older and has had a real tribal home life and is one with her people and when she holds a place in her own Christian community and has a real soul value as well as a physical one, but in this case I'm really afraid for the girl.

Such attitudes were neatly symbolized when missionaries opposed the building of a bridge between Freretown on the mainland and urban Mombasa island.[43] The ideal Christian community was clearly rural and any connexion with the city, associated as it was with sin, depravity and the absence of organic relationships, was a matter of deep regret among missionaries.

In the notion that Africans uprooted from their own societies were rendered more susceptible to Islam lay a third reason for mission opposition to 'detribalization'. In 1912 one missionary wrote that the 'disintegrating forces' operating in the coastal hinterland demonstrated the need for reinforcements to forestall the imminent spread of Islam. That converts from interior stations working on the coast were frequently lost to the church was viewed as evidence of this threat, while periodic proposals to move the mission's central educational institutions up-country was one of its consequences.[44]

Though it was seldom broached openly, the mission concern about 'detribalization' was certainly compatible with and served the function of maintaining the social distance between Africans and Europeans which lay at the heart of a colonial society. Canon George Burns of Nairobi, however, made the connexion explicit in the context of a debate over the merits of a more widespread teaching of English. Writing in strong opposition to such a proposal in 1919, Burns included among his reasons 'the danger in which such a course would place our white women and girls' and 'the danger of organizing against the government and Europeans along the lines of Home organizations resulting in opposition and bloodshed'.[45] The ease of social intercourse which a knowledge of English suggested and the premise of equality which it implied posed too great a threat, at least to Burns, to a now familiar pattern of black–white inter-action based on very different principles. The question of culture thus had implications for the future of colonial society as well as for the development of the African church.

Associated in some quarters with the fear of 'detribalization' was a grudging respect for certain of the general values and structures of African life, if not their specific manifestations. African religiosity compared favourably with European secularism, though not the particulars of African religious belief and practice; the 'sense of filial obligation' was approved but not polygamy and bride-wealth; the sanctions associated with the 'socialism of savage life' met with favour, but not trial by ordeal and blood feud. Some missionaries professed to find in Africa an analogy with biblical culture. 'We live in Old Testament times out here in many ways,' confided Lorna Bowden to her diary in 1925. More rhapsodically, Canon T. F.

C. Bewes defined his appreciation of African life in terms of the possibilities it offered for teaching biblical truths.

> We often used to say to each other, 'This is Gospel country.' There is no need to look further afield for analogy and parable; it is all here – the rich man gathering into the barns, the sower in the fields, the stall for the fatted calf, girls getting ready for a wedding, children playing in a market place. Sheep are always getting lost; thieves may still beset a traveller on a lonely road, the father waits for news from Nairobi of his foolish prodigal boy; there are wild and gorgeous lilies growing in the field. . . . These might be his own fields and valleys and the winding paths of Galilee where Jesus walked.

Appreciation of things African, however, often represented less a sympathetic evaluation of African society than an effort at criticism of the west by comparison, and probably owed something, as Norman Leys perceptively observed, to the 'now fashionable view that African society should be kept separate from European society'.[46]

The missionary model of a good society, then, was something quite distinct from contemporary English culture though it did of course include elements of that culture. Insofar as they looked to the western tradition for desirable cultural patterns for Africa, it was in the Middle Ages rather than the modern era that they sought inspiration. Elements of a nostalgic medievalism, including an emphasis on the wholesomeness of rural communities, the religious integration of life and the centrality of the church in the social order, informed at least some missionary thinking on cultural questions. Hooper indicated that he had been reading books on the Middle Ages and land tenure in order to gain some appreciation of African attitudes towards land. While he denied being an 'enthusiastic medievalist', he did confess it possible that 'we have sacrificed an outlook on life inherent in these earlier organizations without realizing we have lost something in the spiritual realm by their surrender'. In the mid-1930s Leonard Beecher defined the social goal of the mission as 'a contented, educated Christian peasant community', while John Comely in Embu described his aims in similar terms:

> My policy was to make Christians of the natives, to encourage them to stay in the reserves, to develop the reserves and to uphold the Tribal system.[47]

Shorn of its grossest abuses and infused with Christianity, traditional African society represented in missionary thinking a more desirable cultural alternative and a better base for future development than the increasingly secular, urban and industrial society from which they had come. As rationalism and religious modernism swept the Old World, Africa presented a chance to build anew in a more congenial, essentially pre-modern environment, the Church of Christ. Far from embracing modernity, missionaries felt called upon to resist it at numerous points and this imperative set definite limits on their role as conscious agents for change in African society.

This resistance found practical expression in a variety of mission policies which, often interpreted by Africans as attempts to limit their efforts at personal and social improvement, gave rise to continuing tension within the mission community. One such area involved the matter of salaries for mission employees. From the CMS viewpoint both financial constraints and a concern to ensure appropriate motives among their agents produced a salary scale that was consistently well below what was available elsewhere. In 1921, for example, Binns pointed out that many young men could get as much as Rs. 100 to 150 per month in government service while a veteran teacher with twenty years' experience with the CMS received only Rs. 45. Nor did the mission allow its employees to supplement their wages through trading, fearing that it would diminish their commitment to mission work, a concern that had overtones of an earlier Christian anxiety about the moral consequences of commerce.[48] Africans, however, rejected the mission policy of payment by need particularly when the CMS wanted to pay its up-country agents at a lower rate than those at the coast owing to differences in the cost of living. The salary question, in fact, contributed significantly to the high rate of turnover among mission employees and to the persistent shortage of ordained Africans. In 1912, for example, four candidates refused ordination on account of low wages, feeling that those who accepted blocked the way for others yet to come. A dozen years later, the African members of the Highlands District of the ACC unanimously rejected the mission's offer of Sh. 50 per month for deacons, insisting that such a low salary would seriously inhibit the supply of ordinands.[49]

Another arena of mission resistance to 'detribalization' lay in CMS concern for the agricultural development of the African reserves as a counter to the negative social and moral consequences of labour migration and as a means to develop the economic basis of a self-supporting Christian community. 'Home production is almost a fetish with me, for reasons of social rather than economic interest,' declared Hooper in 1924. Limited mission resources did not allow an active programme in this area, but the CMS did sponsor an annual agricultural show at Kahuhia and encouraged the cultivation of farm plots at each of its many outschools. Much grumbling and occasional strikes by students required to work on these *shambas* reflected the view of most participants that education was for very different purposes.[50] Finally, much mission activity in the political arena was motivated by a concern to protect the possibility of African agricultural development in the face of settler demands for African labour.

It was, however, within its educational system that the CMS most obviously confronted the spectre of 'detribalization'. Three issues informed much of this effort: the amount of education, the type of education and the question of language. Within the evangelical missionary movement there had long been a certain suspicion of too great an involvement in education on the grounds that it was at a tangent to the major religious goal of the entire enterprise. Missionaries in the field, particularly in the early years, could also view it as harmful to the character of their converts. Around 1906 the hours of education for girls in the mission were cut from five to three per day in the hope that such action would make the girls more willing to engage in manual labour and would reduce the time that they were withdrawn from home industries. The mission furthermore attempted to restrict the number of years that a student could attend school. Four years of elementary school were recommended for all children but entrance into the three standards of higher-grade school and the two standards of final-grade school was strictly controlled, as was entry into such specialized institutions as the Divinity School, Normal School and Buxton High School.[51] Though mission resistance to education considerably diminished after the war, there were still those who saw danger rather than opportunity in mission educational efforts. John Comely, the missionary in charge of Kigari during the 1920s and 30s, dramatically warned his superiors of its perils in 1923:

To those who would precipitously educate the natives in order to supplant the skilled Indians in this colony; I ask them to consider the danger. Unexperienced, flushed with money, surrounded by temptation and removed from restraints of their villages, is it our wisdom to rush babes in Christ into positions where the chances are against them?[52]

In keeping with his views, Comely consistently refused to accept government aid for his schools with the result that Kigari became by far the most educationally backward of the CMS areas in central Kenya.

By the 1920s, however, most had come to the position that a higher-quality educational system (though one still oriented towards rural development) was necessary if the CMS were to retain the allegiance of its adherents, desirable in the interests of 'guiding' the social changes of the post-war era, and urgent if the growing intervention of the colonial government in educational matters were not to overwhelm or bypass the mission. 'The situation seems to demand from missionaries a more serious educational provision than the haphazard elementary schools of pioneer evangelists,' concluded Hooper in 1921.[53] Government money did allow the CMS to improve its educational system by providing funds for the hiring of more trained educators, the establishment of teacher training centres at Maseno, Kahuhia and Kaloleni and the up-grading of the mission's technical educational programme.

Despite these improvements, African Christians within the mission consistently pressed for more and better educational opportunities and in the process developed a new and critical awareness of CMS policy. Such attitudes were clearly expressed in 1919 by the African Christian Educational Society, an organization representing African adherents of the CMS and Methodist missions on the coast. In submitting a statement to the government's Educational Commission, the Society argued that existing mission schools were

quite inadequate to train pupils up to anything approaching a decent standard to start life either in Government or commercial firms and that the present standard is required to be raised and fully trained teaching staff provided to cope with any improvements that may be instituted.

They concluded by advocating a system of industrial education and a 'miniature sort of University for the coast'.[54] Similar criticism in the interior was not far behind. Teachers were pressing for better training in order to increase their ability to attract students, for they and their missionary superiors observed that their most promising pupils were dissatisfied with the teaching provided in CMS schools. Petero Kigondu, an outspoken CMS adherent, in complaining directly in an African Church Council meeting that the mission 'has not given us the training adequate to fit us for carrying sole responsibility', suggested that this was one reason for the reluctance of Africans to support the church financially, and urged strongly that older untrained men be made pastors and not allowed near the schools.[55] When the mission proved unable to provide a primary post-Standard III school or a European headmaster at Kabete in the mid-1930s despite the desperate pleadings of the local Christian community, Kabete elders concluded that 'this shows us as you are not interested with our school and church which we expect would never happen to you for many years to come'. CMS pastors, teachers and elders in the Fort Hall area in fact suggested that the mission turn its educational efforts over to the government if it were unable to perform 'satisfactorily'.[56] What had been occasional and polite requests for further training by mission employees before the war became in the 1920s and 1930s more general, frequent and insistent demands, tinged now with the suspicion that missionary unwillingness, not simply incapacity, lay at the heart of their apparent reluctance to provide the desired educational facilities.

Manipulation of the curriculum as well as limits on the amount of education provided the CMS with an additional means of controlling the access of its people to what they regarded as potentially harmful or inappropriate modern opportunities. One such adjustment involved the attempt to introduce industrial or technical education, for a wholly literary or academic programme was widely regarded with considerable suspicion in missionary circles. In Kenya the medical missionary Edwards felt that 'habits of industry and manual work' represented an altogether sufficient curriculum for the great bulk of mission students and that only those few with appropriate aptitude and character should do 'book work'.[57] Industrial education on the other hand supplied a sort of antidote to detribalization by providing an alternative discipline for those for whom traditional sanctions had lost their force. It also functioned in this view to correct certain inherent, almost racially defined, disabilities which Africans were said to suffer. One spokesman for the cause of industrial training argued that it served to check conceit, train the hand and eye, develop accuracy, promote self respect and develop manual work, in all of which Africans were supposedly deficient. The much bandied-about 'natural laziness' of Africans might, it was hoped, also be remedied by such a programme.[58] Finally missionaries, no less than other Europeans, were concerned that Africans be prepared to occupy their 'proper place' in the colonial economy and that they be taught 'certain things that will make them more useful to Europeans'. That mission education should perform this function many regarded as wholly apparent, and that industrial training was the way to do it, beyond serious dispute. An AIM missionary stated the case in 1909:

> In order to take their place among the white settlers who are occupying the country, they [Africans] must be fitted to understand the work and methods of the white man. . . . It is the duty of all who have anything to do with natives who are just coming out of the darkness of heathenism, to so train them that they should not aspire beyond what they are able to do. But so that they shall be able to fill some place in the economy of the country where they dwell.[59]

Anxiety about social disintegration, a frankly racist view of African capacities, and an effort to make education functional in a colonial economy – these were among the elements of an emerging ideology of non-academic education which finally crystallized around the notion of 'adapted' education as articulated by the Phelps–Stokes reports of the 1920s.[60] But well before this occurred such ideas informed much missionary educational thinking and policy.

The history of CMS efforts in the area of industrial and technical education before the war was one of repeated initiatives and repeated frustrations, largely due to financial difficulties. Following the collapse of the various industrial training programmes at Freretown in the early 1890s, little was attempted in this direction until the arrival of Bishop Peel in 1899. Peel soon proved himself a prime mover for non-academic training, feeling that it would not only enable Africans to replace the many Hindu and Moslem Indian artisans who were then being imported into the Protectorate but also provide employment for mission adherents who would otherwise fall into 'profligate ways' and escape mission influence. 'There is the remedy . . .', he wrote to the Parent Committee, 'I mean the remedy of industries . . . all is development, development. Now is *the hour* for the starting of industries with the aid of those who renounce the view that any scheme for the improvement of the African is doomed to failure'.[61] Realizing that the CMS would be reluctant or unable to finance such programmes, Peel applied to the Industrial Missions Aid Society, an interdenominational concern formed in 1895 to start self-supporting industries in connexion with mission work, particularly in India. By 1904 the IMAS had established brick making, cotton growing and carpentering industries around Freretown, but by 1906 the entire enterprise was in deep financial trouble and as a consequence its educational function of training young men in trades proved a total failure. Hoping to salvage something from the situation, the CMS encouraged the formation of East African Industries, Ltd by 'friends of the CMS' with the new company absorbing the debts of the IMAS in return for leases of property and other favours in East Africa. EAI took up where IMAS left off and initiated several new ventures as well. However it was little more interested in the mission's industrial training programme than its predecessor, feeling that its 'first object is to make a dividend'.[62] Profit and education, it seemed, did not mix. Rather more successful in implementing the mission's concern for industrial education were the efforts undertaken at individual stations. At Kabete, for example, Leakey constructed a workshop and offered instruction in carpentry to a limited number of students with financial assistance initially from the government and later from certain of his 'settler friends'. At Wusi, Verbi trained carpenters and builders and experimented with coffee and rubber, while carpentry, blacksmithing and boot mending were taught at Taveta. The mission encouraged these individual initiatives and in 1910 resolved to incorporate an element of industrial training in all of their schools.[63] Financial constraints, however, limited their ability to do so and not until the CMS was able to receive large grants from the government during the 1920s could its desire for extensive technical training be turned into reality.

Language policy was likewise viewed as a means of managing a potentially dangerous and difficult process of social and cultural change. The mission had very early abandoned the widespread dissemination of English in favour of Swahili, while in the interior the emphasis was on local vernaculars with English reserved for the very highest standards and then only when trained teachers were available. Even in the Divinity School, an institution designed to train an African church leadership, the principal was most unwilling to teach or even address his students in English. 'I have taught in this medium [Swahili] for fifteen years', he observed in 1910, 'and they need no better.'[64] He did not choose to add that a decade earlier his reluctance to teach English had sparked a strike in the Divinity School and precipitated a major crisis in the mission. A variety of mission concerns inspired this general reluctance. Among the practical constraints were the lack of qualified teachers and the difficulty of English in comparison with Swahili. Yet for some there was more at stake. Burns argued that English would expose immature African Christians to 'oceans of doubtful and vile literature', promote a spirit of self-advancement, pose sexual dangers to European women and political dangers to the colonial state and in general 'more than anything else I know of, harm the spiritual life of the church'.[65] While such vehemence was untypical, the fear that a knowledge of English would encourage the kind of detribalization, with all its attendant hazards, that the missionaries laboured so strenuously to avoid was a potent factor in inhibiting a forward policy in this area.

Probably more than any other single item the question of English symbolized to Africans within the mission communities of the CMS the unwillingness of the mission to allow them access to the full range of western culture and modern opportunities. The demand for instruction in English has been a persistent feature of the educational history of British colonies, for it has represented a general desire for 'improvement' and social mobility, a means for a subordinate people of asserting and achieving a measure of equality with Europeans, and a recognition of the economic value of a knowledge of English. William Jones, Jr, son of a former CMS African pastor at Rabai, gave expression to such sentiments before the Education Commission of 1919:

> The mission (CMS) having kept out any useful English teaching from their schools have precluded any idea of our children's advancement. I note from the general trend of events that English is necessary, nay essential, for one's welfare in this Protectorate now and for all future time.[66]

African members of the ACC likewise pressed for further instruction in English, while a petition of complaint from CMS adherents in Fort Hall district prominently featured the language question as well. The emergence of the independent schools in central Kenya in the early 1930s, a major attraction of which was the availability of English even in the lower grades, forced the mission to look more carefully at its language policy, for the CMS in some areas lost large numbers of students to the independents.[67]

Mission communities have long been recognized as arenas of cultural conflict, though the dominant interpretation has pitted Europeans unambiguously committed to the westernization of their converts against Africans equally intent on preserving their heritage. What emerges on closer examination, however, is a more complex picture of European–African cultural encounter within mission communities. In the first place the lines of cultural conflict did not wholly coincide with those of colour, for core groups of African Christians sometimes proved more ardent in their criticism of African culture than did missionaries themselves, while missionaries on occasion proved vigorous critics of their own culture and highly suspicious of its impact in Africa. Missionary thought and action, therefore, was directed as much towards preventing the allegedly dangerous disintegration of African society as it was towards excising what they regarded as undesirable aspects of African culture. Even in the latter case, missionaries found it tempting to be more flexible in practice on such questions as polygamy, dowry and mixed marriages than they may have felt comfortable with in theory. Whatever the consequences of their action, missionaries were more concerned with creating a Christian peasantry than in generating a new elite. For their part Africans within these communities were critical of and in fact resisted mission policy on two fronts, for not only were many reluctant to accept fully missionary demands for cultural transformation, but they also demonstrated a desire for freer access to a wider range of modern cultural, educational and economic opportunities than missionaries were willing to grant. The common denominator of these dual sources of cultural tension, sometimes issuing in open conflict, lay in a rejection of absolute missionary control and in an insistence on sharing in decisions regarding the pace, extent and direction of their own cultural change. It was perhaps less a matter of accepting or rejecting change than of resisting subordination, for in a colonial society questions of culture were never far from those of control.

FOOTNOTES

1. E. S. Atieno-Odhiambo, 'A Portrait of the Missionaries in Kenya Before 1939', *Kenya Historical Review*, I: 1 (1973), p. 5.
2. See, for example, A. J. Temu, *British Protestant Missions* (London, 1972), p. 155; Raymond F. Hopkins, 'Christianity and Sociopolitical Change in Sub-Saharan Africa', *Social Forces*, XLIV:4 (June 1966), pp. 555–62.
3. Ian Linden, *Catholics, Peasants and Chewa Resistance in Nyasaland, 1888–1939* (Berkeley, 1974); M. L. Chanock, 'Development and Change in the History of Malawi', *The Early History of Malawi*, ed. B. Pachai (Evanston, 1972).
4. Marvin D. Markowitz, *Cross and Sword* (Stanford, 1973), p. 13.
5. CMS/1904/7, Maynard to Baylis, 24 November 1903.
6. CMS/1900/43, Minutes of Women's Conference, 16 February 1900; 1901/129, *Taveta Chronicle*, June 1901; 1909/87, Minutes of Mission Conference, 14–20 May 1909; 1912/85, ACC Minutes, 19 June 1912; 1915/56, ACC Minutes, 4–5 August 1915.
7. CMS/1916/7, Peel to Manley, 28 December 1915; 1923/2, Rogers to Manley, 7 December 1922.
8. CMS, Annual Letters, S. A. Dixon, 11 November 1922; KNA: CMS/1/639, Kabare Log Book, 10 May 1923, 25 December 1931; Interview 2.
9. CMS/1909/126, United Missionary Conference, 7–14 June 1909; 1909/143, Annual Letter: A. M. Barnett, 14 December 1909; 1908/20, *Mombasa Diocesan Magazine*, January 1908; 1910/55, Annual Letter, R. A. Maynard, 16 February 1910; KNA: KBU/109, Arthur to Maxwell, 14 April 1924.
10. CMS/1907/104, Minutes of Mission Conference, 24–27 June 1907; 1908/22, Minutes of Mission Conference, 10–12 December 1907; L/10, Baylis to Binns, 26 September 1907.
11. CMS/1907/104, Minutes of Mission Conference, 24–27 June 1907; Hooper Papers, 'Memorandum on Marriage for Converts'; Mockerie to Hooper, 22 February 1925.
12. CMS/1911/89, Minutes of Mission Conference, 7–13 July 1911; 1921/23, Binns to Manley, 7 February 1921; Bowden Papers, Bowden to all, 16 August 1923.
13. CMS/1921/21, Binns to Manley, 29 January 1921.
14. CMS/1913/14, Minutes of Standing Committee, 7 January 1913; 1909/126, United Missionary Conference, 7–14 June 1909. For a fictional account of the problem, see M. Cicely Hooper, *New Patches* (London, 1935). Leon Spencer, 'Defense and Protection of Converts: Kenya Missions and the Inheritance of Christian Widows', *Journal of Religion in Africa*, V:2 (1973), pp. 107–26.
15. CMS/1909/87, Minutes of Mission Conference, 14–20 May 1909.
16. The following three paragraphs derive from Hooper Papers, MCH to Mother, 5–11 August 1918, 18 September 1918, MCH to HDH, 5 November 1917; PCEA: Ed. 1912–19, Scheme for Higher Education of Native Girls; Interview 2.
17. CMS, Annual Letters, A. R. Pittway, 9 November 1923; CMS/1909/126, United Missionary Conference, 7–14 June 1909; Ephantus G. Macharia, 'Traditional Religion among the Kikuyu', an unpublished paper; William B. Anderson, 'Development of Leadership in Protestant Churches in Central Kenya', an unpublished paper.

18. Hooper Papers, 'Itwika', n.d.; KNA: CMS/1/639, Kabare Log Book, 3 November 1922, November 1924, July 1925; NYI/9, Nyeri Political Records; CMS, ACC. 85, Karimu to all Christians of Fort Hall, 22 November 1927.

19. CMS/1913/25, Wright to friends, 10 February 1913; 1903/160, *Mombasa Diocesan Magazine*, October 1903; CMS, Annual Letters, Rev. Harry Leakey, 27 October 1923.

20. Diary of Rev. George Wright, 31 May 1907; CMS/1910/9, Annual Letter, Emily Wilde, November 1909; CMS, *Extracts*, J. A. Wray, 6 December 1889.

21. Bowden Papers, Bowden to Mother, 2 March 1924; CMS/1910/1, Annual Letter, V. V. Verbi, December 1909; 1909/7, McGregor to Bailey, 24 November 1900; 1913/25, Wright to friends, 10 February 1913; John S. Mbiti, *New Testament Eschatology in an African Background* (London, 1971), p. 25.

22. *Proceedings*, 1908, pp. 53-4; CMS/1909/126, United Missionary Conference, 7-14 June 1909; RH: Coryndon Papers, 17/1, Syllabus of CMS Divinity School.

23. James Ngugi wa Thiong'o, *The River Between* (Nairobi, 1965), p. 33; CMS, Annual Letters, Rev. Harry Leakey, 27 October 1923; Anderson, 'Development of Leadership', op. cit.; UCN–RPA: D/3/2(2), H. S. K. Mwaniki, 'The Impact of British Rule in Embu, 1906-1923'; CMS, *Extracts*, F. Deed, 18 December 1905; CMS/1895/94, Ackerman Journal, 6 January 1895.

24. William B. Anderson, 'The Experience and Meaning of Conversion for Early Christian Converts in Kenya', an unpublished paper; Hooper Papers, 'Land and the African', n.d.

25. *Kenya Churches Handbook* (Kisumu, 1973), p. 34; CMS/1897/106, Ackerman Journal, 15 March 1897; 1907/48, Peel to Baylis, 12 March 1907.

26. CMS, *Extracts*, D. A. L. Hooper, 15 October 1894; CMS/1898/20, *Taveta Chronicle*, December 1897; 1912/5, Annual Letter, V. V. Verbi, 19 December 1911; 1912/42, Annual Letter, V. V. Verbi, n.d.; KNA: CMS/1/271, Crawford to Bishop, 17 March 1933.

27. Matthew Mwangi, 'History of Weithaga'; Mwaniki, 'The Impact of British Rule', op. cit.; Bowden Papers, Diary, 3 April 1925. This incident provided the name of the age-group – *Kimate* or the captured ones.

28. *Proceedings*, 1904, p. 89.

29. KNA: Coast Province 64/252A, Northcote to PC, Fort Hall, n.d.; Coast Province 32/446, Orr to Hobley, 20 September 1916; KBU/76, Dagoretti Political Record Book, 25-26 April 1912; KBU/9, Kaimbu Political Record Book.

30. KNA: KBU/76, Dagoretti Political Record Book.

31. William Anderson, 'Development of Leadership', op. cit.; *Muigwathania*, August 1928; September 1929.

32. CMS/1911/122, note on copy of Hooper to Rogers, 23 April 1911; 1919/86, Minutes of Mission Conference, 26 September – 2 October 1919; R. S. Heywood, 'First Impressions of British East Africa', *Church Missionary Review* (September 1919), p. 253.

33. Bowden Papers, Diary, 21 April 1925; Hooper Papers, Hooper to friends, 20 August 1922; CMS, 'Historical Records', 1935-6, p. 46.

34. CMS/1912/49, 'The Future of Buxton High School', n.d.; 1912/8, Rogers to Baylis, 3 January 1912.

35. J. S. Mangat, *A History of the Asians in East Africa c. 1886 to 1945* (Oxford, 1969), pp. 103-8; Robert Gregory, *India and East Africa* (London, 1971), pp. 79-95.

36. CMS/L10, Baylis to Binns, 8 May 1921; KNA: CMS/1/628, Minutes of Standing Committee, 10-14 December 1921; CMS, 'Historical Records', 1922-3, p. 32; CMS/1911/115, Minutes of Standing Committee, 12 October 1911.

37. Gavin White, 'Kikuyu, 1913: An Ecumenical Controversy', Ph.D. Thesis, University of London, 1970, p. 32; K. S. Inglis, *Churches and the Working Class in Victorian England* (London, 1963), pp. 21-4; Gordon Hewitt, *The Problems of Success: A History of the Church Missionary Society, 1910-1942* (London, 1971), pp. 409, 460; KNA: CMS/1/472, Declaration, May 1938.

38. CMS/M1–2, Krapf to Venn, 16 April 1848, 14 March 1853; Krapf to Secretaries, 20 January 1848.
39. Norman Leys, *Kenya* (London, 1925), p. 211; CMS/1898/176, *Taveta Chronicle*, September 1898; 1895/203, Tucker to Baylis, 18 June 1895.
40. H. D. Hooper 'The Expression of Christian Life in Primitive African Societies', *International Review of Missions* (January 1924), pp. 67–73; H. D. Hooper, 'Carols', *Church Missionary Review* (March 1924), p. 42; CMS, Annual Letters, H. D. Hooper, 1923; CMS/1919/61, Hooper to Manley, 20 July 1919.
41. CMS/1919/18, Minutes of Standing Committee, 18–21 January 1919; 1921/21, Binns to Manley, 29 January 1921; CMS/L11, Manley to Burns, 15 March 1917; KNA: CMS/1/634, Rabai Log Book, 7 February 1895.
42. CMS/1904/84, Minutes of Women's Conference, 21 June 1904; L9, Baylis to England, 8 February 1906.
43. Hooper, *New Patches*, op. cit.; CMS/1922/9, The Educational Policy of CMS Kenya Colony, 1921; CMS, Annual Letters, M. B. Jeffrey, 9 October 1923; A. McGregor, 1 October 1922; CMS/1904/47.
44. CMS/1912/8, Rogers to Baylis, 3 January 1912; *Proceedings*, 1903, p. 91; 1906, p. 57.
45. CMS/1919/92, Burns to Britton, 26 November 1919.
46. Leys, *Kenya*, p. 237; CMS, Acc. 85, Hooper to Gurner, 25 January 1927; CMS, Annual Letters, H. D. Hooper, 1923; Bowden Papers, Diary, 21 April 1925; T. F. C. Bewes, *Kikuyu Conflict* (London, 1953), pp. 18–19.
47. Hooper Papers, 'Native Issues in Kenya Colony', 1928; 'Land and the African', n.d.; CMS, 'Historical Records', 1935–6, p. 58; KNA: Embu Log Book, 13 July 1925.
48. CMS/1921/21, Binns to Manley, 29 January 1921; 1904/186, Binns to Baylis, 31 March 1904.
49. CMS/1912/85, Minutes of ACC, 19 June 1912; EHA: Box 247, Précis of a Discussion upon Salaries of Deacons in the Church, 27 November 1924.
50. EHA: Box 247, Hooper to Oldham, 9 January, 18 October 1924; CMS, Annual Letters, H. D. Hooper, 1923; Interview 3.
51. CMS/1906/108, Education Committee, 17 October 1906; 1904/85, Minutes of Missionary Conference, 25 June–1 July 1904.
52. CMS, Annual Letters, John Comely, 12 October 1923.
53. EHA: Box 247, H. D. Hooper, 'The Limits of Missionary Education', 1921.
54. Noah Manasseh to Education Commission in British East Africa Protectorate, *Evidence of Education Commission* (Nairobi, 1919).
55. Hooper Papers, H. D. Hooper's letter home, 31 October 1923; Hooper to 'folks', 18 April 1925; CMS, 'Historical Records', 1926–7, p. 55; EHA: Box 247, Précis of a Discussion upon Salaries, 27 November 1924.
56. KNA: CMS/1/335, Kabete Elders to CMS, 9 January 1935; CMS, Acc. 85, Hooper typescript, Mbatea to Cash and Hooper, September 1937.
57. CMS/1900/94, Burt to Baylis, 24 July 1900; World Missionary Conference, Report of Commission III, 1910, p. 169.
58. World Missionary Conference, Report of Commission III, p. 170; CMS, *Extracts*, George Burns, November 1906; 'Industrial Training in Africa', *International Review of Missions*, III (1914), pp. 343–4.
59. CMS/1909/126, Report of United Mission Conference, 7–11 June 1909; KNA: PC/CP.6/5/1, Stevenson to McClure, 17 November 1917.
60. See Kenneth King, *Pan Africanism and Education* (London, 1971).
61. CMS/1900/85, Peel to Baylis, 19 July 1900.
62. CMS/1900/55, Industrial Scheme, 27 March 1900; 1906/xxiii(a), 7 September 1906; 1907/106, Binns to Baylis, 27–8 August 1907.
63. CMS/1910/90, Minutes of Missionary Conference, 17–23 June 1910.
64. World Missionary Conference, Report of Commission III, pp. 6, 207–8; CMS/1900/90, Report of Education Sub-Committee, 9 July 1900.

65. CMS/1919/87, Rogers to Manley, 16 October 1919; 1919/92, Burns to Britton, 26 November 1919.
66. Jones to Education Commission in British East African Protectorate, *Evidence of the Education Commission* (Nairobi, 1919).
67. KNA: CMS/1/288, Beecher to Smith, 4 August 1936; CMS/1/102, Minutes of Highland District ACC, 23 May 1935, April 1936; CMS, Acc. 85, Hooper typescript.

CHAPTER VI

꒛꒛꒛꒛꒛꒛꒛꒛꒛꒛꒛꒛꒛꒛꒛꒛꒛꒛꒛꒛꒛꒛꒛꒛꒛꒛꒛꒛꒛꒛꒛꒛

Mission Communities and Colonial Society

The evolution of CMS communities was conditioned not only by the cultural encounter of their component groups – European missionaries and African Christians – but also by their inter-action with a larger social environment which can be most conveniently summarized as a colonial society. Georges Balandier has aptly described the defining characteristic of such a society as

> the domination imposed by a foreign minority, racially (or ethnically) and culturally different, acting in the name of a racial (or ethnic) and cultural superiority dogmatically affirmed, and imposing itself on an indigenous population constituting a numerical majority, but inferior to the dominant group from a material point of view....[1]

Two aspects of this social order impinged directly on the development of mission communities. One involved the ability of the colonial authority to define policy, allocate resources and create new social and economic roles, while the other concerned the reaction of Africans to their subordinate position in the society. As one of those points of intersection between rulers and subjects, mission communities were unusually sensitive to the politics of colonial societies, for they had their feet, as it were, in both camps. This chapter probes the inter-action of the CMS communities with the colonial establishment, while the next details their encounter with the challenge of African protest.

MISSIONARIES, SETTLERS AND THE COLONIAL STATE

The relationship of missions to the colonial state in Kenya has generally been regarded as close and subservient. In fact one recent study characterized missions as nothing more than an 'arm of the colonial administration'.[2] Evidence on CMS relations with the government supports elements of this view, for the mission clearly made itself available in many ways to assist in the articulation of the colonial state and became in fact part of its mechanism of communication with and control of the African population. Missionaries were asked to report on local political conditions and on occasion had to be cautioned about excessive zeal in this regard. In 1901 the CMS agreed to use its influence to encourage the payment of the government's hut tax. The missionary Leakey complained bitterly that the government had twice used him to assure the people living around Kabete that no more of their land would be alienated, only to be proved a liar on both occasions.[3] Missions were also willingly used to recruit and train the lower level of the government and commercial bureaucracies, with CMS schools at Freretown and Rabai providing most of the early African government officials in Kenya. Whatever limited social mobility was possible in colonial Kenya was provided very largely through mission schools. The socialization of Africans into colonial culture was likewise a manifest function of mission communities, for the expectation that missions would establish 'sentiments of loyalty to the crown' in their students was an unspoken assumption on all sides. The First World War provided another opportunity for missions to demonstrate their utility to the colonial authorities. The CMS offered the government unqualified use of its personnel and property on the principle that 'it is our first duty to render the Government any assistance in our power, even though it may interfere with our work'.[4] In such a crisis, the demands of the state apparently superseded those of God or, more likely, there was little sense of contradiction between the two. In all of these ways and more, mission communities functioned as mechanisms of integration in a social order which Balandier described as 'in a state of latent crisis'.

Frequently, however, the relationship was rather more complex. The obvious racial cleavage in colonial societies may on occasion blur those 'lesser inflections' or intra-group conflicts which likewise informed the politics of those societies. Among the Europeans, for example, were a large number of separate groups, agencies and institutions which had by no means identical interests. The Colonial Office, the Kenya government, district and provincial officials, the Education Department, the settler community and the various mission societies constituted the major contending parties. Though they clearly agreed on certain fundamentals, such as the continued existence of the colonial state, differences over goals, means and allocation of resources frequently provoked sharp conflict. Despite an authoritarian government and the lack of an extensive franchise, colonial Kenya was an intensely political rather than a merely administrative society and missionaries entered the arena of 'white politics' on numerous occasions to protect and enhance what they regarded as the interests of those communities which their activity had called into being. Within the confines of a racially based colonial society there developed, then, a consciousness of separate interests, antagonism and sometimes conflict between missionaries and other whites in the colonial establishment, a divergence that had important consequences for the development of mission communities.

The earliest form of this antagonism grew out of the government's attempt to control the process of mission expansion. While the permission of colonial authorities had long been necessary to open up a new mission station, it was not until 1910 that the approval of local chiefs was required for the posting of an African catechist. That mission agents could now be expelled 'at the whim of a drunken savage' was both an affront and a threat. CMS and other missions sought support locally and in England though without noticeable effect. Missionary fears, as was frequently the case, were exaggerated, for the enforcement of the regulation was spasmodic, depending as it did on the attitude of local officials. The major outcome was the necessity to negotiate endlessly with African chiefs over the opening of out-schools, an experience that proved more frustrating than inhibiting, given the growing grass-roots desire for education. A further tightening up of control occurred in 1915 when European residence was made a condition of all mission land leases in order to avoid the establishment of 'a place run by a native'. This limitation on missionary freedom also occasioned vigorous but ineffectual opposition.[5]

If the proliferation of mission centres gave rise to anxiety in government circles, it was largely because they harboured deep reservations about the social and there-fore political implications of these institutions. Concerned to maintain 'a sense of nationalism (tribalism) amongst the native tribes', the government feared that mission converts and students were beginning to 'individualize themselves', to form a separate community distinguished by its members' affinity for European dress and aversion to manual labour, no longer under the control of traditional or appointed authorities. The Director of Education, obviously concerned about the theoretically universal implications of Christianity, pointedly questioned the missions about the consequences of their efforts:

> Religiously, perhaps, all men are brethren: politically the negro will for centuries be a child and any attempt at pretending that within twenty or even fifty years he can attain the state of development reached by the white race in 3000 years . . . can only be fraught with the greatest danger. . . . (W)ill your educated pupils still consider themselves part of the tribe or will they form a new community? Are your pupils taught that all men are equal? Do you consider that natives can be prevented from adopting European dress or is it an inevitable outcome of their contact with the white man?[6]

Acting on these fears, the administration established in 1912 a committee to report on the question of 'native converts' in the Kikuyu reserves. Two approaches to the problem soon became apparent within the government. One strongly deprecated the 'detribalization' of African converts and insisted that missions be urged to teach their adherents that their real homes were in the reserves. Other officials, less con-cerned about preserving the purity of Indirect Rule and more interested in African development, held that Kikuyu Christians 'cannot retain identity with the tribe' and suggested that where missions had broken down the 'apathy' of traditional society, government should encourage rather than retard the process. To do other-wise, wrote Chief Secretary A. C. Hollis, would provoke a 'general outcry' from a combination of Protestant and Catholic missions who would offer the 'strongest opposition' to such a policy.[7]

Taking advantage of the government's deliberations, the CMS entered the debate in 1912 with a proposal to create officially recognized Christian *kiamas* or councils of elders to administer 'tribal law' to mission adherents. Before the First World War, CMS missionaries still saw the major obstacle to their efforts in the paganism of African society rather than in the materialism of European civilization, and saw in the idea of Christian *kiamas* an opportunity to remove their converts from the judicial control and the cultural influence of their pagan neighbours. Such action would also provide the mission with a more effective means of regulating its internal affairs as church discipline was applicable only to those who had been confirmed, a group which in 1913 accounted for only about one-third of the total number of mission adherents. But the government's view of missions as a threat to the control mechanism of colonial society spelled the end of the CMS scheme, for at the end of 1912, Governor H. C. Belfield decisively rejected any policy that would be destructive of 'tribal cohesion' or that might undermine the authority of chiefs.[8] No clearly defined policy emerged, however, and the matter was left largely in the hands of local administrators.

Missionaries resented colonial authorities not only for constraining their opera-tions but also for refusing to legislate on Christian morality. Kenya missionaries attempted to appropriate the power of the state on such issues as restricting the sale of beer, exempting Christians from swearing 'native oaths', and excusing people from performing public work on Sundays. Success was mixed. For example, on the question of the 'inheritance' of Christian widows, it required a decade's agitation on the part of various mission bodies to produce the Native Christian Marriage Ordinance in 1931.[9] But where action on such cultural issues was likely to provoke African sensibilities and generate political unrest, the government moved very cautiously. In spite of much mission urging to take a stand against female circumcision, the administration contented itself with general admonitions against the practice, unsupported by any legislation on the grounds of its political inexpediency. That the government was unable to persuade the missions to adopt a similarly moderate policy on the issue provoked a political and educational crisis of considerable proportions in Kikuyuland at the end of the 1920s.

All of these issues involved fairly standard missionary attempts to defend their own interests and those of the embryonic African church and as such represented normal conflicts in mission–state relations. What exacerbated and complicated CMS relations with the colonial establishment in Kenya was the presence of a sizeable and influential settler community numbering some 12,500 by 1925. Socially and economically, they were a diverse group – bored aristocrats like Lord Delamere whose social functions were being eroded by democracy at home, unemployed ex-soldiers who arrived after the First World War, Boers seeking a new beginning after their defeat by the English. What they had in common was a certain marginality to European life, a correspondingly intense attachment to their new homeland and a deeply felt belief in themselves as agents of civilization and progress. Their encounter with Anglican missionaries occurred in a variety of ways, each of which provided occasion for serious conflict as well as cooperation; socially, both settlers and missionaries were part of the white community of colonial Kenya; ecclesiastically, a segment of the settlers participated actively in Anglican church affairs; politically, missionaries and settlers were separate and frequently rival pressure groups seeking to influence government policy.

From the beginning of European settlement, the relationship between settlers and missionaries was one of distance, suspicion and frequently antipathy. At least in part this rift in the white community derived from the very different cultural traditions which each group represented. Norman Leys, a critical observer of Kenyan affairs, commented perceptively on the matter in the mid-1920s:

> It is important to realize that the Evangelical party, as the inheritors of the Puritan tradition are now called, have always been a minority party in the national life.... The Puritan tradition is, furthermore, notoriously unpopular among those classes of English people from which the Europeans in Kenya are chiefly drawn. It stigmatizes many of their pleasures, such as horse-racing and the use of alcohol. The emphasis it lays on private judgement is difficult to reconcile with authority and it is well known to be the parent of equalitarian and socialist ideas that are even more excessively disliked by Europeans abroad than by their friends in England. It may be added that most missionaries are adherents of the older theological ideas, now becoming less common in Europe.[10]

CMS missionaries, especially in the early days, had very little social contact with settlers at all. Bishop Peel complained vigorously about the 'aloofness' of missionaries towards the European community, and their reluctance even to conduct services for their settler countrymen. In thirty-two years at Mombasa, he noted, H. K. Binns had never entertained or been entertained by a non-missionary European. Peel feared that 'this unreal cleavage between CMS and properly conducted Europeans' would generate strong anti-CMS sentiment and adversely effect mission work.[11] For their part, settlers almost universally disliked and distrusted the 'mission boy', felt that missionaries tried to move Africans too quickly towards civilization and took insufficient account of their racial limitations. There was a debate of sorts among settlers as to whether Christianity should precede or follow civilization with an emphasis on the relationship between mission activity and the willingness of Africans to work for them. 'Civilize the native first by the Gospel of Work and the Gospel of Christ will follow' reflected one side of the argument, while more liberal elements felt that Christianity would encourage Africans to work without, however, removing the 'curse' of servanthood. Sensitive to these implied criticisms, missionaries responded both aggressively and defensively. Most settlers, charged one CMS missionary, have 'surrendered entirely any pretence at having a religion at all and a Christian servant of a quasi-heathen master of a race so far above his own is in a perilous position indeed.' Others were reduced to defending their enterprise on the ground that it induced a desire for a higher standard of living and was thus 'an increasingly important factor in the insurance of a steady labour supply'.[12] Such general antagonism made cooperation between the two groups difficult and tenuous. In 1926, for example, a joint settler–missionary appeal to the government for the suppression of 'indecent native customs' broke down when the Kenya Missionary Council refused to meet the settlers' condition for cooperation, namely that the missions use their contacts in the English parliament and press to defend the aims, character and actions of the European community in Kenya.[13]

Nor was cooperation within the church any easier than outside. In Nairobi Europeans resented Africans worshipping in the same building as themselves and insisted on holding their Sunday service at the unusual hour of 9.30 a.m. to avoid sitting on forms and chairs recently used by Africans. An active high church group in the Nairobi European congregation further alienated the evangelical CMS missionaries.[14] Likewise in Mombasa, CMS ownership of the Anglican cathedral gave rise to considerable anxiety on the part of the European congregation which insisted in 1918 on having their 'rights' in the cathedral officially recognized by the mission. In particular they wanted to appoint their own chaplain rather than accept the one the CMS gave them, to have sole control over the organ they purchased for the cathedral and to reserve certain church furniture for their exclusive use for reasons of 'cleanliness, wear and tear'. In the face of a virtual threat to secede and withold financial contributions to the cathedral, the CMS and Bishop Heywood capitulated to European demands on the organ and church furniture and took pains to appoint as chaplain a missionary acceptable to the European congregation.[15] Neither settler demands for separate recognition nor CMS willingness to compromise on the issue boded well for the development of a non-racial church.

It had taken the CMS from 1900 to 1921 to move from the formation of an embryonic African Church Council to the establishment of a synod which in Anglican practice was the next step towards the eventual creation of an ecclesiastical province, composed of several dioceses, which would be independent of Canterbury under its own archbishop. While the relatively slow growth of church membership in Kenya, compared with that in Uganda, was largely responsible for this interval, the presence of a sizeable European community, active in church affairs, considerably complicated the whole process of ecclesiastical evolution. When Bishop

Heywood began to push for a diocesan constitution and a synod, he set himself the unenviable task of accommodating the interests of the church's African and European elements. 'We don't want a racial church', he insisted shortly after his arrival in Kenya in 1918. 'Of course we realize that there must be separate congregations with language differences, etc., but evidently the ideal of a united church of both nationalities has caught on.'[16] The difficulties involved in articulating this ideal became apparent as the diocese of Mombasa moved towards the creation of a synodical structure. Some European church members expressed quite frankly their view that Africans must not 'swamp' the synod, a use of language that paralleled in the ecclesiastical arena the political and psychological concerns of the settler community deriving from their overwhelming numerical inferiority. So sensitive was Bishop Heywood to the 'danger of one race overbalancing the other' that in the eyes of some CMS missionaries he was 'more the Bishop of the European than of the African'. The outcome of these pressures was a decision that the number of African lay delegates to the synod should not exceed the number of European lay delegates. A diocesan conference in 1921 decisively rejected an African proposal for proportional representation based on one lay delegate for every one hundred communicant church members on the grounds that Africans were insufficiently educated.[17] This pattern of 'equal' representation of racial groups on the synod was, however, far in advance of anything that Africans were to achieve in the political sector for over thirty years, for not until 1944 was the first African admitted to the Legislative Council and not until the Lennox-Boyd constitution of 1958 did the number of African representatives equal that of communal European representatives. Nevertheless, settler pressure in the church had inscribed a pattern of racial corporatism in the structure of the synod, a development which helped to delay for decades the next step in the ecclesiastical evolution of the CMS communities in Kenya.

The creation of a diocesan synod, Bishop Heywood fervently hoped, would be but a step towards the development of an eastern African province stretching ideally from Northern Rhodesia and Nyasaland in the south to the Sudan in the north, and throughout his tenure as bishop he worked to this end. Within his own diocese of Mombasa, however, two factors combined to frustrate these plans and in fact no provincial structure was established until 1960. The first of these involved the old question of Anglican churchmanship, for the dioceses of Central Tanganyika, Mombasa, Uganda and the Upper Nile had received their missionary impulse from the evangelical CMS, while the southern dioceses of Zanzibar, Masasi, Northern Rhodesia and Nyasaland had been evangelized by the Universities Mission to Central Africa which represented the extreme Anglo-Catholic wing of the Church of England. In 1933 Heywood bowed to the strong evangelical missionary sentiment within his diocese and recommended now the formation of two provinces in eastern Africa – a northern one consisting of the evangelical dioceses and a southern one based on the high church tradition.[18]

If this move calmed missionary anxieties, it did nothing to allay the fears of African church members in Kenya whose concerns derived from a perception of the link between church affairs and matters of race and politics. Their reluctance to support the bishop's proposal was rooted in their fear that ecclesiastical self-government would cement white domination in the church, for as one group of church leaders from Murang'a confessed, 'we have no Bishops and Archdeacons of our own colour in East Africa.' Drawing a political analogy, this group of veteran CMS adherents elaborated their fears:

> In Kenya Legislative Council, we Africans are represented by Europeans, but, although they are very desirous to help, unfortunately they do not understand us well. It then becomes evident that if the Ecclesiastical Province takes place so early, we Africans will have to be represented in important meetings of the Church by Europeans who do not understand us.[19]

Those Europeans who represented Africans in the Legislative Council were in fact missionaries and often from the CMS. African rejection of the province thus expressed an indictment of the degree of ecclesiastical Africanization achieved by the mid-1930s.

But the provincial question went well beyond the internal mission–African conflicts and touched on sensitive political concerns in the larger colonial society, for many African churchmen feared that a wider church union under white control would encourage a similar move in the political arena. In particular they feared a revival of the 'closer union' scheme, a Colonial Office plan for the federation of Kenya, Uganda and Tanganyika which was seriously considered during the late 1920s and early 30s. Settler leadership had seen in this proposal a chance to solidify and extend white control in the creation of a Great White Dominion and had therefore endorsed the proposal on the condition that they be granted an unofficial elected majority on the Kenya Legislative Council, a position to which they had aspired for some time. African political groups strongly opposed closer union on precisely these grounds. 'It will conflict with our advancement by the establishment of the settlers' interests above our own,' declared the Kikuyu Association in 1928 and urged that they be left under the 'Home Government who will look after our interests'. Though closer union had largely collapsed in the enforced economies of the depression, the African Church Council of the CMS would agree to Heywood's modified 1933 proposal for an Anglican province only if 'self-government in the church will not lead to self-government in the state', an assurance that the bishop was in no position to give, and if the right of appeal to Canterbury were guaranteed, a condition which would have vitiated genuine provincial autonomy. When the matter was brought to a formal vote in the 1936 session of the Mombasa synod, it was defeated and Heywood resigned in great disappointment later in the year.[20] By shaping the structure of the synod and by conditioning the response of Africans to the idea of a province, the presence and political aspirations of the settlers had an important reflex impact on the development of the CMS communities.

While missionaries avoided the settlers socially and suffered their influence in church affairs more or less quietly, they were gravely disquieted by their pervasive impact on the government's African policy. While there was a range of opinion within the CMS, a substantial number had by the 1920s come to a position that Hooper referred to as a 'Christian imperialism that accepts the white man's burden as a genuine responsibility'. Missionaries who held such views perceived themselves as being in frequent and substantial opposition to the policies of a settler-oriented colonial government. While there was perhaps an element of sentimental regard for the passing of old Africa, their opposition was based much more on the economic and social distortions which the settler presence injected into what they regarded as the potentially liberating and uplifting impact of European civilization in Africa. That the old order was doomed was both inevitable and largely desirable.

The question was whether or not the colonial state would actively promote a just, progressive and viable alternative social order.

No missionary in Kenya articulated this sense of opposition so vigorously as Archdeacon W. E. Owen, whose missionary career in western Kenya was a frequent provocation to settlers and officials and a thorn in the flesh to his missionary colleagues. Believing that the only 'Christian justification for empire is service', Owen roundly condemned what he saw as the 'foreign exploitation of the soil' and outspokenly denounced government capitulations to settler pressure. From the early 1920s he favoured African representation in the Legislative Council and declared in a public sermon that church–state relations in Kenya would never be peaceful until this political change had occurred. All this was but a means to the larger end of an active government policy directed at African development or, as he put it, 'native states, running their own affairs under the guidance of an efficient Native Affairs Department'. Though Owen's active liberalism was laced with paternalism toward Africans, it was nonetheless upsetting in the extreme to those in authority. To settlers, he was 'Archdemon Owen', while to C. M. Dobbs, Provincial Commissioner of Nyanza during the 1920s, 'that awful Owen who is ruining the whole place' was nothing less than an 'out and out Bolshevist'.[21]

Owen's counterpart in central Kenya was Handley Hooper, stationed at Kahuhia from 1915 to 1926. Here, however, the direct influence of settlers and the threat of African political expression persuaded him to be more circumspect in articulating his views. Even so he admitted that government officials believed him to 'walk rather near the edge of the thin ice' in his advocacy of African interests. Working largely through local personal contacts rather than public declaration, Hooper was also the major CMS contact for J. H. Oldham, head of the International Missionary Council and leading spokesman for the missionary lobby in England. Like Owen, Hooper believed 'that the growing forces of industrial and commercial civilization will have to be combated by the strongest combination of forces possible, if a purely selfish and utilitarian policy is to be squashed'. In pursuit of this 'combination', Hooper attempted to weave a network of contacts in Kenya with sympathetic officials such as McGregor Ross and Norman Leys and helped his superiors at CMS headquarters to do likewise.[22]

Further south in Kiambu, Harry Leakey became an important CMS defender of African land rights. He opposed the soldier-settlement scheme as 'an act of treachery to the Kikuyu people' and consistently pressed for security of tenure on their remaining lands. Even a missionary of the older, more purely evangelical persuasion such as George Burns of Nairobi saw the missionary task as standing between those who wanted to push Africans too fast and those who regarded them only as 'agricultural implements'.[23]

Most of this sentiment was clearly a post-war phenomenon. Before the war there was very little missionary objection, particularly within the CMS, to the major land and labour policies of the colonial government. Leakey had in fact encouraged European settlement around Limuru in 1901, while Bishop Peel joined the settlers in opposing the Zionist scheme for large-scale Jewish settlement in Kenya. Citing their alleged lack of regard for Christ, morality and fair bargaining, Peel indicated a preference for Christian settlers who might act as 'living examples to the benighted Africans of the Christian life and Christian civilization which we are declaring to be God's message to man'.[24] Though much of this optimism had been eroded in the ensuing decades, no one regarded colonial rule as illegitimate and probably very few saw the settler presence as necessarily evil. Missionary recognition of the real political and economic power of the settlers made wholesale opposition impractical. It was better strategy, then, to counter the abuses of settler influence while not denying the white farmers a legitimate if more circumscribed place in the structure of the colony.

This was the stand that informed the Anglican position on the labour question, the first of those post-war issues that drew missionaries into the political arena. Settler pressure for increased supplies of labour had culminated in 1919 in Governor Northey's Labour Circular No. 1, which instructed administrative officers, chiefs and elders to 'exercise every possible lawful influence' to get men, women and children on to the labour market. The local missionary response to this initiative came in the Bishops' Memorandum signed by the Bishops of Uganda and Mombasa as well as by J. W. Arthur of the Church of Scotland Mission. On the one hand the document represented a sharp critique of government policy, especially in pointing to the widespread abuses likely to result from the involvement of chiefs in labour recruitment. The signatories were also appalled at the inclusion of women and children in what they recognized as a policy of disguised forced labour.

> The native has also his home, his crops, and his plans for development. The demands on his time may not be constant but they are insistent. To leave his own plantation, perhaps at a critical time, for the benefit of someone else's plantation; to leave his house unthatched, his crops unreaped, his wife unguarded perhaps for months at a time, in return for cash he does not want on the 'advice' of his chief – which he dare not disregard – is not a prospect calculated to inspire loyalty to the Government from which the advice emanates.

But on the other hand there was no fundamental questioning of the settler's position in Kenya nor of their right to African labour. Neither was compulsory male labour primarily for public purposes considered necessarily objectionable. In fact the thrust of the document was to urge the legalization and strict regulation of compulsory labour. The document did serve, however, to trigger off considerable on government policy. Settlers in fact were pleased at the mission's clear advocacy of compulsory labour. The document did serve however to trigger off considerable activity on the part of the missionary-humanitarian lobby headed by J. H. Oldham and thus initiated a train of events that ultimately resulted in the withdrawal of Northey's circular.[25]

The limits of CMS support for the settlers and the limits of their willingness to stand against settlers, both clearly revealed in the labour controversy, were likewise tested in the dispute over the role of Indians in Kenya's public life which came to a crisis in 1923. The issue was joined when local Indian demands for a greater equality of treatment in Kenya were given favourable consideration by the British government under pressure from the India Office, thus provoking a ferocious settler reaction which moved to the very edge of rebellion. As the crisis unfolded, missionaries picked their way cautiously through an issue of political and moral complexity. In a general sense most missionaries shared the settlers' unwillingness to allow further political or economic concessions to Indians, who outnumbered Europeans by three to one, for by the early 1920s a considerable body of anti-Indian sentiment had crystallized in the missionary community and was widely shared within the CMS. The Indian presence was regarded as detrimental to African development, in part because Indians occupied middle-level positions in the colonial economy to which Africans might aspire. Burns argued that granting the Indians' demands would 'retard the native for fifty years'. Nor were missionaries willing to share their trusteeship obligations for African interests with a racially and culturally alien population. Finally, missionaries as well as other Europeans had persuaded themselves that Indians were behind much of the African political movements, particularly the 'Thuku troubles', which had sprung seemingly out of nowhere in the early 1920s. Thus missions did not hesitate in aligning themselves with settlers in presenting a united European front on the issue. Local CMS missionaries sent an urgent telegram to their London headquarters urging immediate support for restrictions on Indian immigration 'for sake of native races', while the Presbyterian missionary J. W. Arthur joined the European delegation to London as a representative for African interests.[26]

Particularly within the CMS, however, the limits of support for the settler position soon became apparent. CMS headquarters in London declined to stand with the settlers on the grounds that it was a political matter that affected their interests in India as well as in Africa. In Kenya itself, as settlers prepared for rebellion, missionaries warned them strongly against the use of force and were prepared to go to jail if an oath of allegiance to a settler regime were demanded. More generally, local CMS leadership feared a heavy settler influence on Kenya almost as much as they did that of the Indians. Several expressed the view that both European and Indian immigration should be restricted on the grounds of 'giving natives a chance', while Mrs Hooper wished 'they would disenfranchise the whole country and put it back on a protectorate status'. Through his contacts with Oldham in London, H. D. Hooper in fact attempted to defend the Indians against what he regarded as hypocritical European criticism. Bishop Heywood hoped to turn settler fear of Indian domination into a positive settler commitment to African development.[27] While the local expression of such sentiments had little impact on the resolution of the larger controversy, they do show that the CMS did not simply offer an unambiguous endorsement of the settler viewpoint. While they felt a certain racial and cultural kinship with the settlers and recognized their powerful position in the colony, they likewise saw the dangers which settler aspirations posed to African interests for which they presumed to speak. It represents no justification of mission attitudes and policy on the labour and Indian questions to recognize that they felt themselves to be on the horns of an acute and sometimes agonizing dilemma in their participation in the politics of colonial Kenya.

THE POLITICS OF EDUCATION

While missionaries were convinced imperialists, they defined themselves against their fellows in the colonial establishment in two important respects – by their resistance to a pervasive and, many believed, nefarious settler influence on the government's African policies and by their opposition to the potential secularism of that policy. Nowhere were these twin concerns more acutely felt than in mission inter-action with the colonial establishment on educational matters. It is not a little ironic that while education was the area in which mission and colonial structures were most closely integrated, it was also here that government policy made missionaries most anxious, defensive and even hostile, for it engaged both their religiously defined self-interest and the concerns of Africans for whom they presumed to speak.

It was not until after the First World War that the colonial government of Kenya demonstrated any sustained commitment to an overall African educational policy.[28] Before this time the pressure of other priorities, the exigencies of finance, settler opposition to African education before European educational needs had been met and the dislocations of war combined to impede a serious effort in this area despite a variety of investigations, reports and plans. During the 1920s, however, conditions more favourable to a modicum of African educational development prevailed. In the first place, a succession of able Directors of Education energetically advocated African education in Kenya. Furthermore, the settler community proved willing to sanction a degree of technical education for Africans primarily to displace Asians in the colonial economy and thus render them politically impotent, while the colonial administration itself required a limited number of trained Africans to function effectively. Both groups felt that education of the 'right sort' could act as a solvent of the political tensions born of social change but feared that uncontrolled and inappropriate instruction would dangerously exacerbate those tensions. Finally, widespread demands by Africans for more and better education was a pressure difficult to resist altogether. The outcome of these conditions was a steadily rising curve of expenditure on African education during the decade of the 1920s from under £5,000 per annum at the end of the war to almost £90,000 in 1930. For the most part these monies were expended through the missionary societies operating in Kenya which received a variety of grants in aid for staff, buildings and equipment, upkeep and other educational functions. This was the 'policy of cooperation' which represented simultaneously an opportunity of tremendous proportions to the missions and a serious threat to their autonomy, integrity and interests.

The CMS responded enthusiastically to the possibility of an educational partnership with the colonial government. 'If we act now', declared Bishop Heywood in 1919, 'we can have the full support of the government; if we fail them, they may take up the work themselves and we find ourselves missing a grand opportunity.' By 1926 the 'grand opportunity' amounted to annual grants of more than £11,000 for nine mission educational centres,[29] resources which many hoped could solve some of the missions' most pressing problems. Among these was the difficulty of retaining the most highly qualified African teachers in the mission's educational system. The far higher wages available in various government departments and commercial agencies resulted in a 'constant drain of the most intelligent and ambitious of our younger teachers'. The only solution, concluded the mission, lay in a 'large increase in the scale of salaries and this is quite impossible without the assistance of government'. Furthermore, those who did remain were frequently not very well qualified and Hooper admitted in 1922 that many of the older first-generation teachers could no longer command the respect of their younger and more ambitious and experienced pupils.[30] For these reasons the CMS was receptive to government plans for the upgrading of teacher training facilities in the colony, the first of its post-war educational initiatives, and within a few years the CMS was receiving grants for normal school development at its Mombasa, Kahuhia and Maseno centres.

Nor was the 'technical' slant of the government's educational initiatives in a general sense out of line with the mission's own educational priorities. The CMS had tried repeatedly to introduce a technical or vocational focus into its educational system only to find itself stymied by inadequate financial resources. Many missionaries regarded technical training as an antidote to the disruptive and 'detribalizing' consequences of culture contact and appropriate to the racial limitations and social conditions of Africans. It provided, moreover, a firmer economic foundation for the African church which, many believed, 'can never become strong and self-supporting until a much larger number of its members are skilled artisans able to command remunerative employment'. Thus when the government's Education Commission of 1919, on which the CMS was represented, concluded that 'technical education shall be the principal aim and object of native schools', the CMS offered no fundamental objection. By 1923, in fact, the CMS had considerably enhanced its technical programme in eight of its schools with annual grants totalling £5,540.[31]

A further positive consequence of the policy of cooperation lay in the necessity to recruit more highly educated missionaries in order to qualify for government grants. Almost half (eighteen) of the thirty-seven new male missionaries who arrived in Kenya between 1919 and 1933 were men with university degrees. This was no doubt a source of gratification to Bishop Heywood who remarked in 1918 that 'this mission does need a larger proportion of men who are of a rather higher social standing than the majority here, . . . people who can meet with Europeans and make their influence felt.'[32] As the mission entered into a new and closer relationship with the state and the settler leadership, a greater degree of social and educational conformity with these elements of the colonial establishment was clearly desirable, while educational partnership with the government made it necessary. The new relationship with the state also served to introduce a number of trained technical people – joiners, builders, carpenters, farmers – into the mission community. The policy of educational cooperation, in short, marked the end of the age of the untrained general missionary of the pioneer era – that person who could preach, teach, build and practise medicine with equal facility – for as the entire enterprise became functionally differentiated, in part under government pressure, the missionary had to become a specialist.

Basically, of course, missions entered into a policy of cooperation in order to continue their monopoly on the provision of modern education, an increasingly popular commodity in post-war Kenya, for more than ever, they thought, the school was the major recruitment agency for the church. For many of the newer missionaries whose theology emphasized 'wholeness in this world' rather than the adventist hope, mission education was also a means of stamping a Christian imprint on African culture generally and more particularly on that rising group of educated Africans on whose side, they dimly perceived, the future lay. 'It is hardly necessary to say', wrote Hooper in 1922, 'that our main purpose in accepting Government grants for educational work is to secure that as large a percentage as possible of the new generation of trained Africans shall receive instruction for life, definitely built up upon the teachings of Christ.'[33]

Whatever the opportunities of a policy of cooperation, it was a relationship suffused on the mission side with anxiety, a sense of threat and a need continually to defend essential interests. One threat lay in those elements of the settler community that resisted any education for Africans at all or sought to limit that education to technical training of the most immediate economic benefit to themselves. When J. R. Orr, Kenya's first Director of Education, began to elaborate his post-war plans for educational development, he encountered, as he had expected, 'the utmost opposition from the European population if I attempt to develop native education before European education is more fully provided'. In submitting the 1921 estimates for the Education Department to the Legislative Council, Orr found the non-official members solidly opposed to any financial assistance to missions on the grounds that 'they occupy large tracts of lands and show no results'. It was only with the aid of mission statistics on the results of their previous technical efforts and the inability of the settler representatives to find their papers at the appropriate time that Orr's policy of cooperation with the missions was salvaged. Faced with these difficulties, Orr had actively sought missionary assistance. On one occasion he called a conference of one Presbyterian and two CMS missionaries to 'lay the foundations of a definite policy'. And he encouraged the CMS to pour both men and money into the colony.[34]

A more important occasion for this sort of alliance occurred during 1923–4 when settler pressure resulted in the funding of a very narrowly defined technical education programme in the estimates for the fiscal year 1924.[35] Out of the £13,000 budgeted to mission grants, £12,000 was earmarked specifically for technical education and the other £1,000 for literary training of pupils in a technical programme, while missions were allowed to receive government funds only for the training of indentured apprentices. Although most Europeans in Kenya favoured a technical emphasis for African education, this verbal consensus concealed widely different conceptions of an appropriate educational experience for Africans. Settlers were concerned to produce semi-skilled artisans for work outside the reserves with little concern for their general education. Illiterate masons, they had observed, could build excellent houses. For the Director of Education J. R. Orr, technical education served an entirely different function. With his educational philosophy for Africans rooted in the American Tuskeegee model, for the education of blacks, Orr was much more interested in the development of self-sufficient village communities, believed that technical training had to be built on a firm foundation of general literary education, and strenuously protested against a policy that 'shall provide education only for those African males who are willing to serve the European community as Artisans'. On this issue the missions were in full agreement with Orr, for they looked to technical education as a character-building device and as a means of improving the economic and social life of the reserves. Thus they acted vigorously to counteract a settler policy which Hooper sharply criticized as one in which 'the immediate interests of the European community must be the controlling factor in the determination of our native policy'. Locally, the Alliance of Missionary Societies, an agency of intra-mission cooperation, took up the issue. Citing a 'conflict between the ideals of the Missionary Societies and those of the Legislative Council', the Alliance flatly declared that missions were unwilling to spend their resources on expensive and highly specialized technical training and insisted that government funds be available on a much broader basis to include general elementary education, teacher training and schools for women. Here was an implicit mission threat to withdraw from the policy of cooperation unless some satisfaction were given to their points of view. In England, J. H. Oldham had been alerted to the situation by Hooper and stood ready to intervene with the Colonial Office on the grounds that the Kenya government had violated the 'native paramountcy' policy of 1923.[36] Mission action, then, had helped to turn a disagreement over the direction of technical education in Kenya into a crisis and a stalemate. It was only the coincidental arrival in Kenya of the Phelps-Stokes Commission, whose philosophy of adapted education for Africans appealed for various reasons to all of the contending parties, that temporarily resolved this political and educational crisis. It revealed, however, that when the vagaries of Kenya's educational politics focused on settler efforts to force African education into very narrow and self-interested channels, missions and certain elements of the administration, particularly in the Education Department, found themselves natural allies.

On other occasions, however, the threat to mission education derived more directly from the colonial government itself in the form of efforts to create government secular schools entirely outside the missionary framework. While many settlers favoured this policy, it was also advocated strongly by some of the administration's district officers, people who came most directly into contact with mission schools. Many of them simply felt that education ought to be a government function, perhaps because, owing to their management of local schools, missionaries represented a rival source of white influence. Furthermore, the inability of various denominational missions to work effectively together immensely complicated the jobs of the district commissioner. Most importantly, however, local officials had severe reservations about the social consequences of uncontrolled mission education. 'There is being created', warned a 1926 meeting of district commissioners, 'a detribalized, discontented and for the most part unemployable section whose education and training has neither been directed towards their own welfare nor to the social and economic needs of the country.'[37] Even in the Education Department, where cooperation with missions was a central feature of established policy, successive Directors of Education always left open the door to government schools where the missionary presence was ineffective or absent altogether.

A further pressure in the direction of non-mission educational alternatives emanated from the Local Native Councils, district-level advisory bodies of elected and nominated Africans, established in 1925 largely to channel political expression into acceptable directions. The creation of these institutions provided an important forum for the articulation of African dissatisfaction with mission education. By 1929 these bodies had taxed themselves almost £50,000 for educational purposes, but many of the LNCs refused to spend these funds on grants to missions, insisting rather on government or locally controlled schools. This development put the administration in a difficult position, for it was unwilling to jettison the policy of cooperation with missions but was equally reluctant to frustrate this important source of revenue and local initiative. In fact the coincidence of LNC opposition to mission education and the anti-mission sentiments of many district commissioners led missionaries to suspect an unholy collusion between the two groups.[38]

In their efforts to counteract these pressures for alternative educational opportunities, mission societies used a variety of arguments and resources. In the first place there was the argument of precedent. Ever since the Education Commission had recommended the policy of cooperation in 1919, missions had attacked any deviation from it as a breach of promise. Furthermore, missionaries repeatedly stressed the social dangers inherent in a policy of secular education. The Kenya Missionary Council warned in 1925 that 'no education can be safely given to animistic Africans which does not rest upon a definitely religious basis and is not permeated by Christian ideals.'[39] A more telling line of reasoning emphasized the cost involved in the creation of an alternative educational system. Even the Director of Education recognized that 'for a public authority to undertake the same work would be a far more expensive way of securing the same service.'[40] This was the mission's trump card and the major reason for the willingness of the colonial government to endure the vexations of dealing with a variety of competing mission groups in educational matters. Finally, mission societies had an array of contacts in England both through their denominational headquarters and through J. H. Oldham's International Missionary Council which had access to and some leverage in the Colonial Office.

While possible deviations from the policy of cooperation entailed obvious threats to mission interests, the policy itself contained more subtle but no less worrisome implications, for the CMS found itself increasingly enmeshed in a pervasive web of regulations and restrictions that substantially undermined mission control of their educational system. Subjected to periodic inspection, CMS schools were perpetually being threatened with the removal of grants owing to their 'inefficiency', lack of qualified staff, unavailability of funds, and so forth. From the government's viewpoint, the locus of educational responsibility in the colony had changed dramatically. 'Government should no longer be regarded as assisting the Missions. The Missions should be regarded as lightening the task of Government in the work of education ... It means that the voluntary agencies, under an efficient system of inspection, virtually become Government institutions....'[41] It was this process of incorporation that missions attempted with varying degrees of success to resist, for they often found themselves confronted with educational policies neither of their making nor to their own liking.

A case in point – and one that held considerable symbolic significance for the CMS – involved the conscience clause exempting unwilling students from compulsory participation in religious instruction. The refusal of missions to countenance such a provision had been in large part responsible for the collapse by 1912 of an early effort in mission–government cooperation designed to provide schools for the sons of African chiefs.[42] By the 1920s, however, the very real threat of government schools had persuaded the mission to accept the conscience clause as a means of forestalling the far worse possibility of public secular education. Nevertheless, when the Director of Education in 1924 required all village schools to post and periodically read a notice in the vernacular and English stating that students were 'encouraged but not compelled' to attend religious classes, CMS and other missions perceived a grave threat to their educational enterprise.[43] While they accepted the conscience clause policy, two aspects of the situation represented a sharp provocation to the missions. One was the necessity to read and post the notice publicly, an action, they argued, that would undermine school discipline. The other was the 'right of entry' implication in the policy, for they feared that representatives of Islam might ask for access to mission schools. Not a single student, vowed the CMS African Secretary Manley, would hear the teaching of Islam in an Anglican school. The missions counter-attacked these threats vigorously in a variety of arenas. Bishop Heywood personally discussed the issue with high officials in Kenya and was assured that right of entry did not apply to mission schools. Mission representatives on the Governor's Central Advisory Committee on Native Education used the issue to hammer through a resolution to the effect that where mission schools accepted the conscience clause and could meet the educational needs of a particular district, they should be supported by the government. It is effective testimony to missionary anxiety that they continually sought this type of formal reassurance. Back in England, Oldham interceded at the Colonial Office, while Anglican and Presbyterian missionary officials drafted a strongly worded protest to the Kenya government including the threat that missions might close schools in which large numbers of pupils took advantage of the conscience clause. The result of these various pressures was a series of concessions to the mission view: right of entry by other religions would not apply to mission schools; the notice had to be posted but not read; and the words 'but not compelled' would be omitted from the statement encouraging students to attend religious instruction. In fact the existence of the conscience clause had little effect on the operation of CMS schools, for the alternative to religious instruction frequently involved working in the school garden, an activity even less attractive to most students than Scripture classes.[44] Nonetheless the issue disclosed the intensity of mission anxiety regarding their incorporation into a state educational system and the limits of their ability to manoeuvre effectively within it.

While mission efforts could on occasion modify the implementation of educational policy, they had increasingly little power to affect the major lines of its formation. When a new Director of Education, H. S. Scott, was formulating an overall educational policy for the colony in 1929 and 1930, he informed the missions that while they might be consulted on matters of implementation, 'it is clearly impossible to ask Missionaries to consider the policy'.[45] Vigorous missionary objections to major features of Scott's proposals, such as the provision for teacher training in non-denominational schools with mission hostels attached and the incorporation of Local Native Council funding for, and thus influence on, African education at the highest levels of the system, were unable to prevent their acceptance as policy by the Kenya government and the Colonial Office. Even the active intervention of Oldham proved ineffective. The major reason for this state of affairs lay in the growing strength of African initiatives in educational matters largely growing out of the female circumcision controversy. African demands, wrote Scott, are becoming the 'dominating factor in the situation', for the government was more concerned to blunt African political assertiveness through judicious educational concessions than to forestall a serious cleavage with the missions.[46]

Inter-action with the state on educational matters during the 1920s had substantially reduced missionary control over their educational systems. On such a variety of issues as language of instruction, curriculum, placement of staff, frequency of outschool inspection and many others, missions were subject to government regulation or review. Frequent uncertainty and mountains of correspondence were for many the depressing outcome of their partial absorption into the state's educational system. 'It is no longer a matter of cooperation,' complained CMS missionary Pitt-Pitts in 1931, 'but they [the government] dictate terms all the time and terms which we unfortunately, through our lack of staff, have to agree to.'[47] Such sentiments provided the occasion for considerable individual soul-searching as to the wisdom of extensive mission involvement in the educational enterprise, even among some of the new and more socially concerned missionaries of the post-war era. Owen insisted in 1934 that he would do no more inspection work than he could accommodate with his more important pastoral duties. It became a common observation among CMS missionaries that 'the African has begun to lose his trustful spirit because we are very rarely in his villages'.[48] While the withdrawal of missionaries into their institutional responsibilities and their transformation into educational civil servants remained a matter of deep concern, the CMS never really undertook a fundamental reconsideration of its commitment to education or to the policy of cooperation. 'The marriage was stormy,' writes Professor Schilling, 'but it never led to divorce.'[49] The willingness of missions to continue the relationship, even under what they regarded as trying conditions, was in large measure responsible for the absence of any very extensive system of government schools in Kenya. Mission schools, in short, were encapsulated rather than supplanted.

The colonial setting of mission communities had a variety of impacts on their development. It had been the imposition of alien rule and the associated processes of economic and social change that had facilitated the flourishing of these communities. And as networks of inter-action between white rulers and black subjects, they functioned in many ways as mechanisms of cohesion in colonial society. But this reciprocity was not without its strains, for the colonial situation in Kenya frequently drew missionaries into the arena of white politics in opposition to aspects of established policy and practice, delayed and distorted the ecclesiastical evolution of mission churches, and deprived mission education of much of its previous autonomy. But none of these conditions posed questions so fundamental to the cohesion of mission communities as those associated with movements of African political assertion.

FOOTNOTES

1. G. Balandier, 'The Colonial Situation: A Theoretical Approach', *Social Change: The Colonial Situation*, ed. I. Wallerstein (New York, 1966), pp. 34–61.
2. A. J. Temu, *British Protestant Missions* (London, 1972), p. 132.
3. CMS/1901/199, Minutes of Executive Committee, 26 November 1901; 1911/110, Leakey to Baylis, 6 October 1911; CMS, 'Historical Records', 1927–8, p. 49.
4. CMS/1915/60, Rogers to Manley, 20 August 1915.
5. CMS/1910/70, Procedure with Regard to the Establishment of Native Catechists Among Native Tribes; 1910/88, Peel to Baylis, 4 July 1910; 1915/66, Rogers to Manley, 8 September 1915; KNA: Coast Province 9/272, 40/715.
6. KNA: Coast Province 64/252A, Memorandum by John Ainsworth, 22 April 1912; KBU/11, Dagoretti Sub-District Annual Report, 1917–18; PCEA: Education 1912–19, Orr to Bishops, 25 March 1912.
7. See correspondence in KNA: Coast Province 64/252A.
8. KNA: Coast Province 64/252, Binns to P.C., 31 July 1912; Minute by H. C. Belfield, 31 December 1912.
9. CMS/1913/52, UMC Resolution, 18–21 July 1913; 1909/87, Minutes of Mission Conference, 14–20 May 1909; Embu LNC Minutes, 29 May 1930; Leon Spencer, 'Defense and Protection of Converts', *Journal of Religion in Africa*, V:2 (1973), pp. 107–26.
10. Norman Leys, *Kenya* (London, 1973), pp. 226–7.
11. CMS/1907/52, Peel to Baylis, 21 March 1907.
12. *Advertiser of East Africa*, 21, 28 May, 11 June 1909; CMS/1898/176, *Taveta Chronicle*, September 1898; 1919/61, Hooper to Manley, 20 July 1919.
13. KNA: CMS/1/33, Gaitskell to Secretary, KMC, 18 June 1926; ENA: Box 235, Barlow to Oldham, 30 August 1926.
14. CMS/1916/109, Rogers to Manley, 14 November 1916; Hooper Papers, MCH to Mother, 5–11 August 1918.
15. CMS/1919/48, Sanderson to Manley, 12 May 1919; 1920/33, Interview: Manley and Pickering, 5 July 1920; KNA: DC/MBA 8/5.

16. CMS/1918/54, Heywood to Manley, 7 August 1918.
17. CMS, Annual Letters, Bishop R. Heywood, 14 December 1923; CMS/1921/76, Hamshere to Manley, 5 September 1921; 1921/21, Binns to Manley, 29 January 1921; KNA: CMS/1/124, Constitution, 1924.
18. CMS/1921/54, Heywood to Manley, 1 May 1921; 1921/21, Binns to Manley, 29 January 1921; KNA: CMS/1/124, Mombasa Synod Standing Committee, 28 November 1933; M. G. Capon, *Towards Unity in Kenya* (Nairobi, 1962), pp. 55–8.
19. Mbatea to Cash and Hooper, September 1937, in CMS, Acc. 85, Hooper mss.
20. KNA: CMS/1/103, Minutes of Central Council ACC, 30 July–2 August 1934; CMS/1/123, Mombasa Diocesan Synod, 7–9 January 1936; Hooper Papers, 'Church Affairs in East Africa'; RH: Coryndon 17/2, Memorandum of Kikuyu Association to Hilton Young Commission, 1928; Keith Cole, *The Cross over Mount Kenya* (Nairobi, 1970), p. 12.
21. W. E. Owen, 'Empire and the Church in Uganda and Kenya', *Edinburgh Review*, CCXLV (January 1927), pp. 43–57; CMS/1923/4, Owen to Manley, 30 November 1922; EHA, Box 241, Owen to Oldham, 7 September 1921; RH: C. M. Dobbs Collection, Memoranda, S.655, 16–17 June, 23 July, 7 October 1927. E. S. Atieno-Odhiambo, 'A Portrait of the Missionaries in Kenya Before 1939', *Kenya Historical Review* I:1 (1973), pp. 1–14.
22. EHA: Box 247, Hooper to Oldham, 27 January 1925, 19 January 1925; CMS, Annual Letters, Rev. George Burns, October 1923; CMS/1919/89, Hooper to Manley, 20 October 1919.
23. RH: Coryndon 17/2, Leakey to Secretary of State for the Colonies, 12 February 1919; Memorandum from Canon Leakey; CMS, Annual Letters, George Burns, October 1923.
24. CMS/1903/145, Peel to Eliot, 7 September 1903; M. P. K. Sorrenson, *Origins of European Settlement in Kenya* (London, 1968), pp. 263–70.
25. See Roland Oliver, *The Missionary Factor in East Africa* (London, 1952), pp. 246–57 and Norman Leys, *Kenya* (London, 1973), appendix. Also EHA: Box 247: Hooper letter, 22 June 1920.
26. B. K. McIntosh, 'Kenya, 1923: The Political Crisis and the Missionary Dilemma', *Transafrican Journal of History*, I:1 (January 1971), pp. 103–29; CMS/1923/30, Rogers to Manley, 8 March 1923; 1923/14, Telegram, 4 February 1923.
27. Hooper Papers, MCH to Mother, 17 February 1923; CMS/1923/17, Britton to Manley, 13 February 1923; CMS, Annual Letters, Bishop Heywood, 14 December 1923; EHA: Box 241, Hooper memo, n.d.; Box 247, Hooper to Oldham, 22 September 1923.
28. Three recent studies have examined the educational history of colonial Kenya: John E. Anderson, *The Struggle for the School* (Nairobi, 1970); K. J. King, *Pan Africanism and Education* (Oxford, 1971); Donald Schilling, 'British Policy for African Education in Kenya, 1895–1939', Ph.D. Dissertation, University of Wisconsin, 1972. For background information on government educational policy, I have relied mainly on Schilling's comprehensive study.
29. CMS/1919/70, Heywood to Manley, 2 September 1919; KNA: Education 1/575, Director of Education to Chief Native Commissioner, 2 June 1927.
30. CMS/1919/87, Rogers to Manley, 16 October 1919; Hooper Papers, HDH to friends, 20 August 1922.
31. KNA: CMS 1/628, Secretary to Lankester, 16 August 1923; British East Africa Protectorate, *Education Commission Report* (Nairobi, 1919); PCEA: Education Department 1923–4, Orr to Secretary of Protestant Alliance, 25 June 1923.
32. CMS/1919/13, Heywood to Manley, 30 December 1918; CMS, Register of Candidates, 1919–41.
33. Gordon Hewitt, *The Problems of Success* (London, 1971), p. xviii; EHA: Box 247, Hooper to Jones, 10 August 1922. For the clearest elaboration of the newer missionary theology of education, see James Dougall, *Missionary Education in Kenya and Uganda* (London, 1936), esp. pp. 33–4.

34. PCEA: Education 1912–19, Orr to Arthur, 7 June 1919; EHA: Box 247, Orr to Hooper, 17 August 1920.
35. For details of this crisis, see Schilling, 'British Policy', op. cit., pp. 206–69 and King, *Pan Africanism and Education*, op. cit., pp. 95–127.
36. EHA: Box 243, Hooper to Orr, 23 November 1923; Oldham to Hooper, 2 January 1924; CCK: Minutes of Representative Council of AMS, 19–22 November 1923.
37. KNA: PC/CP.8/4B/1, District Commissioner's Meeting, 3–4 August 1923, 8–9 March 1926; UCN:RPA, C/3/3(1), History of Grants in Aid Committee.
38. This paragraph is largely based on Donald Schilling's 'Local Native Councils and the Politics of African Education in Kenya, 1925–39', an unpublished paper.
39. KNA: CMS 1/33, Minutes of KMC, 20 February 1925.
40. KNA: Education 1/2143, Humphries to Chief Native Commissioner, 8 January 1927; Education Department, Annual Report 1922.
41. Education Department, Annual Report 1925, pp. 3, 17.
42. KNA: Education 1/587, Annual Report 1911–12; CMS/1913/30, Peel to Manley, 20 March 1913.
43. EHA: Box 243, Arthur to Oldham, 24 January 1925.
44. See correspondence in EHA: Box 243; PCEA: Advisory Education Committee, Minutes, 10 March 1925; Interview 4.
45. KNA: CMS 1/33, KMC Executive Committee, 5 December 1929; KNA: PC/NZA.3/10/1/4, H. S. Scott, 'Memorandum in Regard to African Education'. For details on the fate of Scott's plans, see Schilling, 'British Policy', op. cit., pp. 395–474.
46. PCEA: Loose Papers, Educational Policy in Kenya; Education Department, Annual Report 1929, pp. 8; EHA: Box 242.
47. EHA: Box 242, Pitt-Pitts to Oldham, 26 January 1931.
48. KNA: CMS 1/122, W. E. Owen, 'Notes on the Cost of Sector School Inspection'; CMS 1/378, Secretary to Beecher, 24 December 1937.
49. Schilling, 'British Policy', op. cit., p. 494.

CHAPTER VII

꙳꙳꙳꙳꙳꙳꙳꙳꙳꙳꙳꙳꙳꙳꙳꙳꙳꙳꙳꙳꙳꙳꙳꙳꙳꙳꙳꙳꙳꙳꙳꙳꙳꙳

The Challenge of African Politics

REBELS AND CHIEFS

From its inception the missionary enterprise in Kenya had inter-acted politically with African societies. Before the imposition of colonial control, of course, mission groups were almost wholly at the mercy of African political leadership, for they had no independent power base whatever, a condition that many accommodated only with great difficulty. But the advent of colonial rule completely transformed this situation as missions moved from a position of weakness to one of association with a far wider and more potent political structure than East African societies had ever before encountered. This change in status had a double impact on mission activity. While it provided powerful incentives for collaboration, it also ensured that movements of anti-colonial resistance or opposition might very well be directed against the missions as well as against the colonial state. A case in point was the Mazrui rebellion of 1895–6, in which elements of coastal Arab society reacted violently to the establishment of the East Africa Protectorate which they saw in part as another form of a hated Zanzibari domination. It is not surprising that the rebellion included attacks on CMS stations at Freretown, Rabai and Shimba,[1] for mission–Arab relations had hovered on the brink of violence for the better part of two decades owing to the mission's willingness to accept the runaway slaves of their Arab masters.

Likewise during the Giriama rebellion of 1914, the CMS as the major mission agency in the area felt the force of this widespread and bitter rising. Rebels burned the Anglican outpost at Jilore, raided the station at Vitengeni and forced the CMS evacuation of Kaloleni. Their anger, however, was directed not only at the European intruders but also at those Giriama who were most obviously associated with them, for at least in part the rebellion represented an attempt to regenerate Giriama society and to cleanse it from alien influences. 'Clearly', writes Cynthia Brantley whose history of the Giriama is the most comprehensive to date, 'much of this was aimed at Giriama who had gone to the missions and were wearing shirts and trousers and working to assist British administration.' The course and aftermath of the rebellion further revealed the mission–state link which had so provoked the Giriama. Government scouts were recruited from the mission; Jilore was used as a base for the King's African Rifles and proposed as a settlement for 'friendlies'; and the CMS shared in compensation for damages raised from forced levies on the Giriama.[2] The colonial situation rendered missions vulnerable as well as valuable.

When the CMS encountered African politics in the shape of major rebellions, their reaction to it was not very complex. Rather more ambivalent were their dealings with another group of African political actors – the chiefs. While many chiefs had facilitated the establishment of mission stations in the period of political adjustments immediately following the establishment of colonial rule in their respective areas, serious antagonism soon developed in a number of places as chiefs attempted to limit if not stop the flow of their people to the mission. In Murang'a, Karuri went so far as to pull down one of the CMS outschools in 1906; in Embu Chief Gutu tried to levy fines on those reading at the mission; while missionaries everywhere perpetually petitioned government officials about the 'secret opposition' of their local chiefs. This tension was also reflected in frequent complaints about the injustices which mission adherents experienced at the hands of chiefs and 'native tribunals'.[3] Here was a pattern of conflict rooted in the obstacles which the presence of mission communities presented to the exercise of the chiefs' authority. European leadership of such communities meant that their members had an alternative means of contact with the colonial establishment. Local people were well aware of this possibility and often used missionaries' contacts with district officers to avoid the labour obligations imposed by chiefs. H. D. Hooper, veteran of ten years' experience at Kahuhia, commented on the problem:

> To the mission adherents ... the missionary presence presented a heaven sent opportunity of taking his case over the heads of chiefs and elders since it was logical in his eyes to assume that being of the same race, the missionary's advocacy would weigh more heavily with the District Officer than would the Chief's allegations ... The chiefs, however came to recognize the insidious threat to their authority from such means of bypassing their local jurisdiction.[4]

Nor were missionaries simply passive channels of communication but rather they injected themselves actively, directly and deeply into local political affairs. The log books of CMS stations in the highlands are filled with cases of missionaries reporting the misdeeds of chiefs to local administrators. And in the early days when ill-conceived attempts to apply indirect rule went unchecked by officially recognized councils of elders or by frequent touring of European officials, abuses were common indeed, and missionary representations were in some cases responsible for the making and deposition of chiefs. Finally, the products of mission schools were increasingly being employed by the government as hut and poll counters, clerks, interpreters and medical agents. These were people much less under the influence of chiefs than their *njama* or retainers who had previously performed such lower-level administrative functions. McGregor reported in 1912 that his pupils had filled many of these positions in Fort Hall district and noted happily Karuri's displeasure at the sight of these young men running all over his district with orders from the government.[5]

The relations of chiefs and mission communities thus represents an early pattern of competitive collaboration with the colonial state. But by the 1920s the interests of these rivals had begun in some areas to converge. In the first place, mission Christians began to be recruited in greater numbers into positions as chiefs and headmen. The four major chiefships in Kiambu district of Kikuyuland were in the hands of staunch mission adherents by the early 1920s, and in the next decade four out of eight Taita headmen were Christians. Especially in the aftermath of Thuku's movement, the government made extra efforts to appoint Christians to official positions in order to co-opt mission adherents of the more militant political organizations. While the CMS certainly favoured and encouraged this development, it did present the mission with certain difficulties, for the temptations and demands of office frequently resulted in Christian chiefs falling away from active church participation. It was to avoid this possibility that the CMS at Kahuhia required Christian office holders to appear monthly before the assembled members of the Christian community to account for their actions.[6] While Christian and chief were no longer mutually exclusive categories, it was the rise to assertiveness of a new group of political 'communicators' that led chiefs and missions to re-evaluate their relationship. These were the politically conscious, impatient, mission-trained 'elite' who began in the 1920s to press their claims to speak for African interests. A CMS missionary who lived through the process observed that the growth of Christian communities

> went a long way to obviate the antagonism of chiefs who came to recognize such Christian organisms as useful allies in combating a breakdown in their own authority . . . [F]orces of disintegration were seen to be disastrous to chiefs as well as to Christian Missions.[7]

On a number of issues, including a general concern for order and discipline, opposition to secret meetings, the singing of the subversive dance-song *muthirigu*, and a preference for the politics of accommodation and petition, missions and chiefs found themselves in substantial agreement. But if social change and the growth of a new politics promoted a reconciliation between these erstwhile rivals, their impact on mission communities themselves was quite the opposite, since now for the first time the major thrust of African criticism and protest was coming from within those communities.

MISSIONS AND THUKU

The First World War marked in many respects a watershed in the history of Kenya, and mission communities, no less than other groups, were affected by the changes of the post-war era. Among these none was more significant than the growth of African political consciousness, a development which posed a major challenge to the CMS as well as to other mission communities. If the pre-war conflicts within the CMS were focused largely among the more established stations along the coast, the tensions of the 1920s found expression primarily among the mission communities of the Kikuyu highlands, for it was there that the new political awareness was most acutely experienced. Always uneven in its impact, colonial rule had been felt far more heavily in central Kenya than elsewhere, particularly in terms of land alienation and demands for labour on settler farms. The opportunities of Nairobi were nearby, while the fact that Kikuyuland had been a major target area for a variety of mission groups facilitated the emergence of an articulate leadership for the new political movements and made the missionary enterprise itself an important political issue.

At the heart of this process of politicization lay a change in the internal relationships of the mission communities, a growing divergence between European missionaries on the one hand and at least a section of their adherents on the other. This emerging split was occasioned by a twofold African challenge to the assumptions and practices of their European mentors. First the very participation of African Christians in movements of political protest created serious tensions, for missionaries saw in the new politics an effort that was misguided, presumptuous and dangerous alike to church and state. Moreover, the movement itself developed perspectives, ideas and aspirations which were either implicitly or directly critical of mission activity. The combined effect of these developments was to fracture the relative community of interests which had previously characterized the relationship of missionaries and their adherents in Kikuyuland. Missionaries found themselves unable to speak with confidence for their own followers, let alone for African interests generally. Their role as brokers between the African masses and the colonial state was being challenged by a new group of intermediaries who were themselves almost entirely mission products. Yet the extent of conflict within the various affected CMS communities was highly uneven, for neither the political challenge nor the missionary response was everywhere the same.

The post-war conditions under which these developments occurred are well known. The effects of the war on African expectations, the change of Kenya's status from a Protectorate to a Colony, higher taxes, lower wages, the introduction of the *kipande* (registration certificate), an increased demand for labour associated with the soldier-settlement scheme – all of these elements and more contributed to the heightening of social tensions and the consequent growth of a larger political consciousness which was articulated in a variety of explicitly political associations during the 1920s. Europeans found themselves startled at the apparent suddenness of this political explosion. To J. W. Arthur, head of the Presbyterian mission in 1922, 'the development of the native peoples in Kenya in one short year and a half is simply past thinking.' The district commissioner in Fort Hall likewise testified to the intensity of the new consciousness: 'the whole body of the male population is watching intently what is going on around them ... Political progression ... has come to stay for good or evil.'[8] It is at least arguable that a 'traditional' as well as a modern dynamism informed the political events of the decade, for the new politics, which involved a sharp challenge to the older leadership of chiefs and elders, coincided with the change of ruling generation sets among the Kikuyu. Preparation for the transfer of power had begun by 1919 and the process was still under way in 1927.[9] The politics of protest in the 1920s, then, may represent one of those crucial points of conjuncture between African and colonial history.

While social and political tensions were rising, the old hostility to missions was in certain respects declining as the economic value of education became apparent and aspirations for improvement more widespread. Elderly Christians in the early 1970s remembered how previously hostile attitudes towards them improved as the relationship between their education on the one hand and their enhanced social prestige and economic potential on the other was perceived. Furthermore, the proliferation of outschools substantially decentralized the mission community and allowed these new institutions to be assimilated into patterns of local life. With the erosion of the pioneer atmosphere of beleaguered persecution, African adherents no longer needed to depend so completely on mission communities for social and psychological support. They now had the credentials and increasingly the aspiration to become people of standing and leadership in the larger community.

It was in this context that the political associations of the 1920s arose. From the very beginning CMS adherents were among the most active members of these organizations. In fact, the CMS was instrumental in the establishment of what was probably the earliest of these bodies, the Kikuyu Association. It seems to have originated in late 1919 when the headmen in the vicinity of the CMS station at Kabete gathered under the guidance of the Rev. Harry Leakey to protest at the government's alienation of land in the area.[10] Koinange Mbiu and Josiah Njonjo, both of whom were CMS adherents and important chiefs in Kiambu, were among the association's early members. Here was the kind of African political activity of which missionaries could heartily approve. Rural in its social composition, oriented towards the issue of land, dominated by chiefs and headmen, the Kikuyu Association adopted a moderate, loyalist stance towards the colonial government which it approached through approved channels by means of polite petitions. The government reciprocated and encouraged the KA, noting that its meetings were normally attended by missionaries, whose presence, it was felt, helped to keep the organization on the 'right lines'. The KA, in fact, was eager for continued mission support. At a meeting of 27 July 1922 the Association resolved to invite missionaries to its meetings because 'they know our language and ways and they also understand the ways of the European'.[11] Such sentiments merely confirmed missionary views of themselves as the most appropriate 'communicators' of African needs to the colonial state and represented the clearest example of the missionary–chief alliance. Despite its conservative reputation, the Kikuyu Association's position on missionary representation did evolve during the decade in the direction of greater independence from mission paternalism. In 1924, the year in which a missionary was officially appointed as representative of 'native interests' on the Legislative Council, the Kikuyu Association looked forward to eventually representing themselves on that body. By 1928 the KA was insisting on twelve representatives of African interests on the Legislative Council – four missionaries, four Africans and four officials – all of whom were to be elected by Africans.[12] Nonetheless, given a base of support limited to southern Kiambu, its moderate political style and openness to missionary guidance, the KA posed no serious difficulty for the CMS community at Kabete.

Rather different was the East African Association.[13] Founded in mid-1921, it was active for less than a year and yet established the tradition of militant politics which dominated central Kenya for decades. In contrast to the rural Kikuyu Association, the EAA was urban in its origins. It grew out of discussions among African activists in Pangani, one of Nairobi's African quarters, and was stimulated in particular by European efforts to cut African wages by a third during the post-war depression in 1921, an issue of special concern to urban wage earners. Harry Thuku, a product of the Gospel Missionary Society and then a telephone operator at the government Treasury, emerged as the dominant figure in the association owing to his education, forceful personality and range of contacts in the city. Another mark of its urban origins lay in its multi-ethnic character, reflected even in the name of the organization. Though it was dominantly Kikuyu, it had been stimulated by contacts with Ganda elements of Nairobi, had an active connexion with the leadership of Kenya's Indian community and attempted to reach out to the Kamba and to the emergent political groups of western Kenya. Thuku's correspondence with Tuskeegee Institute imparted a certain pan-African dimension to the EAA as well. While the urban milieu of Nairobi was certainly responsible for this impulse to transcend ethnic and religious barriers, it is arguable that the effort was facilitated at least in Thuku's thinking by his mission background. 'I saw no difference', he wrote in 1922 only a month before his arrest, 'between the Kavirondo and the Kikuyu or between the Christian believer and the believer in Islam; and I was very pleased too that we fulfilled the command of the Lord God, that you should love your neighbour as yourself.'[14]

What distinguished the EAA so sharply from the Kikuyu Association was not so much the issues it articulated as the style and tactics it adopted. Land, forced labour, settler power, taxation, *kipande*, wages – these were common themes in the politics of the day, though Thuku's emphasis on the abuses perpetrated by government chiefs and his criticism of missions were grievances which were for obvious reasons not emphasized by the Kikuyu Association. But it was the practice of denunciation, the tone of demand and the implicit threat of civil disobedience which permeated EAA pronouncements and actions that so exasperated government officials and missionaries alike. Furthermore, Thuku's reluctance to go through appropriate channels in presenting EAA grievances further antagonized the authorities. It also resulted in an early and bitter break between the EAA and the Kikuyu Association.

The EAA's membership was primarily one of young mission adherents. In Nairobi these were African civil servants and houseboys, most of them the products of CMS schools or current students from Burns' schools. In Kiambu just north and west of Nairobi, the EAA had much less success due to the strength of the Kikuyu Association which had in effect inoculated the area against Thuku's overtures. Thus the CMS community at Kabete and the Presbyterian station at Kikuyu were little affected by the new movement.[15] But when towards the end of 1921 Thuku turned his attention further north to Murang'a, he found in the CMS communities of Kahuhia and Weithaga his most fervent reception. Unofficial branches of the EAA were organized to which delegates were sent from various mission centres and villages. Meeting in secret sessions, these 'cells' neither informed the government of their meetings nor invited chiefs to attend. They had come to the end of their tether, they informed Hooper, and felt it imperative to do something to make their grievances known to the world. Particularly incensed by the need to perform unpaid road work, they had resolved to refuse the next time it was demanded, though they made the decision over civil disobedience with great reluctance.[16] Here in the physical and spiritual heartland of Kikuyu country and among people who had been immersed in the Bible for years, there was a distinctly religious dimension to the way they regarded and received Harry Thuku. Gideon Mugo and other Christians at Kahuhia composed a prayer for 'our leader Harry Thuku and his associates' which drew an implied analogy between the experience of the Kikuyu and the liberation of the children of Israel from Egypt, as well as David's deliverance from Goliath and Saul. Harry Thuku was chosen for them, they claimed, 'because it is now that we are feeling the slavery which we did not have before the coming of the Europeans to East Africa'. The prayer concluded: 'and we also believe that before God there is no difference between whites and blacks; we are all human beings – equal in the sight of God.' Handley Hooper at Kahuhia pointed to the Old Testament context in which many people interpreted Thuku's movement: 'a big element of the Christian community, the mystical sector, are seeing in him a deliverer of the prophetic type and religious fervour is contributing to his popularity.' From Weithaga as well, McGregor reported unhappily that Thuku was seen as 'also their spiritual saviour'.[17] While there is little hard evidence on the point, it would seem likely that popular perception of Thuku drew on the prophetic tradition within Kikuyu culture as well as that in biblical literature. Heroic prophet figures such as Mugo Kiburu or Waiyaki have been assimilated into nationalist mythology and it seems at least possible that Thuku was seen in the same tradition. Certainly his supporters in Murang'a were not limited to mission adherents, for the invitation for him to appear at a mass meeting at Weithaga was issued distinctly by 'both Christians and non-Christians' and was attended by a broad spectrum of people.[18]

The solidity of support for Thuku within the CMS communities of Murang'a was demonstrated by their reaction to the visit of five Kikuyu Association delegates, at least four of whom were chiefs, on a tour which had been prompted by government and mission authorities to counteract Thuku's propaganda in the area. While the chiefs of Fort Hall district welcomed their counterparts from Kiambu, the latter were thoroughly rebuffed by mission adherents at a meeting in Weithaga. Pointing to such evidence of missionary and government benevolence as schools, the KA representatives claimed they had not come to ask for a repudiation of Thuku but rather to show that there were 'two ways' of expressing grievances. But after the reading of correspondence from Thuku critical of chiefs, district commissioners and missionaries alike, 'the meeting separated unagreed ... Their decision was Harry Thuku to be their leader'.[19] Here was a direct encounter between the Kiambu politics of moderation and the much more aggressive style of African assertion in Murang'a. Could the new politics be accommodated within the confines of mission communities? This was the question that confronted the CMS throughout the 1920s.

While the entire CMS staff in central Kenya had to respond to the Thuku movement in one way or another, the major burden fell to H. D. Hooper at Kahuhia and A. W. McGregor at Weithaga. The two men could hardly have been more different. McGregor, then fifty-seven, had been a grocer before his appointment to mission work in 1892. A staunchly evangelical pioneer of the old school, he was from an altogether different missionary mould than the thirty-one-year-old Cambridge-educated, socially concerned and well connected Handley Hooper. Yet their analyses of the Thuku affair were similar in most respects, even if their means of coping with it were not. Like all other CMS missionaries, they accepted as a starting point that the Kikuyu had 'real grievances', though they would have denied that these were inherent in a colonial society. What had started them on the wrong road of unconstitutional action, Hooper and McGregor agreed, was their own absence on furlough during much of 1921. This was a typical over-estimation of the degree to which African political movements were susceptible to missionary or other manipulation. In the same vein, missionary opinion was unanimous that the EAA was substantially controlled by Indians whose presence in Kenya was widely regarded as regrettable. Thuku's alliance with the Indians and his assertion that 'next to missionaries, Indians are their [the Africans'] best friends' had contradicted the missionary position that the Indian presence was harmful to African interests.[20] That Thuku made the assertion in a telegram to the Prime Minister over the heads of all local authorities only exacerbated missionary resentment and fear of Indian political activity.

If the origins of the Thuku movement provided occasion for mission regret, its potential consequences filled them with the most profound foreboding. We are at the crossroads, warned Hooper, between 'rebellion and the destruction of all that has gone before ... or on the other hand' 'a new shouldering of responsibility'. Likewise McGregor feared an 'insurrection against the government with possibly an enormous loss of life'. Talk of 'another India' or Ireland or a 'second Amritsar' was common in mission circles. What magnified these fears immensely were assumptions of a certain African racial immaturity, deeply rooted in even the most liberal missionary thinking. George Burns expressed the prevailing attitude:

The African native has reached a stage in his development when it is most difficult to know how to help him. He must be advanced, but it should be slowly and cautiously, for he is far from the point where he can control himself, much less his country ... To lead [them] to realize their own limitations and to help them to rectify such is the difficult but necessary task with which the missionary is at present faced.

Even Hooper, one of the missionaries most sympathetic to African concerns, expressed fear of an 'agitation, dangerous for an ordered people, but poisonous for a primitive folk like our own'.[21] In this analysis of the likely consequences of Thuku's movement, there was thus fused a conservative respect for the fragility of the social order with elements of missionary racism expressed in terms of the parent-child analogy.

The Thuku affair represented a political crisis of the first magnitude. But it also meant for the CMS a crisis in their own work. McGregor perceived in the movement a sort of spiritual competition, for allegiance to Thuku, 'their so-called saviour', seemed to correlate with a decline in 'love for spiritual things' among African Christians. More generally, however, the concern was for Thuku's 'definitely anti-missionary' stand and the impact this might have on his numerous mission-trained followers. 'In this district', warned Hooper, 'the future of mission work is trembling in the balance.'[22] While it is hard to distinguish Thuku's own attitudes towards missions from the ideas uncritically attributed to him, it seems clear that he hoped to wean his followers away from dependence on missionaries.[23] Thus he lashed out vigorously at those missionaries or African agents of missions who openly opposed his movement. In a scarcely veiled reference to McGregor, he labelled as a 'false prophet' a certain missionary who prayed that the country would remain in darkness and ignorance. Since McGregor was at that time busily collecting affidavits to justify Thuku's arrest, his antagonism was understandable. Simeon Kalume, CMS pastor in Nairobi, and a certain Joshua from Weithaga were likewise bitterly condemned in a series of pamphlets called *Tangazo* for mixing anti-Thuku politics with their religious teaching. Beyond a vigorous defence of himself against mission attacks, Thuku was implicitly critical of mission education, for in a letter to Tuskeegee Institute he asked for 'our own man, a skinsman brother ... for founding a Tuskeegee in the African wilds'. He was apparently reluctant to trust even the best-intentioned whites with the education of his people. Thuku further antagonized missionaries by taking credit for reforms, such as the withdrawal of the government's 'forced labour' policy which missionaries felt rightly belonged to themselves. And in his most bitter moments, he allegedly accused missionaries of being in the pay of settlers. Yet Thuku did make distinctions. He was particularly impressed with Hooper, who 'did not speak humbug' like the others. In fact he sent Hooper copies of his correspondence with the government 'so that you will see that I am doing everything in light, but not in darkness or secret', though he realized that even Hooper wanted to advise him. In fact a substantial part of missionary allegations that Thuku was anti-missionary probably derived from their offence at his lack of interest in their counsel and his refusal to accept the role implicit in missionary definitions of Africans as racial children.

If their analysis of Thuku's movement was similar, McGregor and Hooper responded to it in very different ways, a divergence which had important consequences for their respective communities. With a minimum of sympathy for the movement and little apparent respect for Thuku, McGregor sought to excise what he regarded as a 'cancer in the body'. He undertook an 'educational campaign' to persuade Weithaga Christians that missionaries rather than Thuku were responsible for securing Colonial Office intervention in the forced labour controversy. Most significantly, he worked closely with the government in gathering evidence and affidavits to justify Thuku's arrest. It was perhaps no wonder that he indicated to the District Commissioner that he might need protection for the station. Since the African leadership at Weithaga broke with Thuku's movement, the CMS there apparently lost close contact with the political elements of its constituency.[24]

At Kahuhia, on the other hand, Hooper's response to the Thuku movement solidified CMS relations with the most militant Christian politicians of the day even though it represented a paternalistic effort to guide the movement into a 'right channel'. Like some of his predecessors at Freetown and unlike McGregor, he practised a paternalism of conciliation rather than one of suppression. Hooper was genuinely sympathetic to African grievances, respected Thuku's sincerity of motive if not his tactics, and was shrewdly concerned that he should not become a nationalist martyr. His rapport with the political elements at Kahuhia was evident shortly after his return from furlough in December 1921, when he was invited to a secret meeting with the African Christians in the area. They indicated a desire not to hide anything from him and told him that they had been meeting regularly under the inspiration of Thuku. They had come to the point of feeling the need for a public and defiant gesture to express their deep sense of grievance. Hooper's initial impulse was to form a local political association patterned after the Kikuyu Association, which would operate with the knowledge and consent of the government and act as a safety valve in a very tense situation. Particularly anxious to establish the representative principle of political organization, Hooper feared that the 'instinctive' African method of free and open discussion for all was not sufficiently amenable to control. 'Any young ass', he predicted, 'may jump up and fire out a pot of heady nonsense which will defeat the ends in view.' Yet he recognized that such a course was impossible at the time. Not only would Africans be unlikely to accept it, but the government was discouraging any African political associations whatever. Under these conditions, Hooper was left with little more than a policy of personal persuasion, an effort 'to sway the fellows round to a more sensible method of tackling [their grievances]'.[25]

Apart from such therapeutic exercises as having his older students write essays on their grievances and possible solutions, Hooper's most interesting effort at persuasion lay in a series of interviews with Thuku himself in early 1922.[26] On the first such occasion, Hooper recorded that Thuku was evidently touched that a missionary should be willing to receive him. He questioned Thuku about his holding of secret meetings, association with Indians and lack of a constructive programme. 'I told him that he was trying to make men of children in twenty-four hours and that the rapidity of the method would be disastrous.' At their second interview, following Thuku's triumphant mass rally at Weithaga, Hooper took up the matter of Thuku's criticism of missionaries and tried to persuade him of the harm such a course was doing to his cause. Thuku's own account of this meeting is perhaps more revealing of his intentions. He recalled that the missionary referred to a crack in the wall and stated that if he wanted it repaired, he would call a skilled workman rather than someone who knew nothing about such matters. Though Hooper did not explain the parable, Thuku took it as a criticism of his political association with Indians and as an indication that Hooper wanted to become his adviser. These persuasive efforts were cut short by Thuku's arrest on 14 March 1922, an event that provoked a major and bloody demonstration in Nairobi and ended in his deportation to the coast. Yet Hooper's personal contacts with the political elements at Kahuhia had accomplished something very significant, for he created an atmosphere in which they could remain in the church without seriously compromising their political commitments and aspirations. It was one thing for missionaries to cooperate with 'establishment' associations such as the KA. It was quite another for them to maintain active links with the most 'advanced' expression of African political opinion during the 1920s, and in all of central Kenya this occurred only at Kahuhia. By cementing this connexion during the crisis of 1922, Hooper helped to ensure that the CMS station at Kahuhia would be on centre stage during the next phase of Kikuyu political protest.

THE CMS AND THE KCA

With Thuku's arrest and deportation, the EAA did not vanish but went partially underground. Rural branches in Murang'a continued to send delegates to Nairobi headquarters, funds were raised to pay for Thuku's lawyers, thus diminishing church contributions, and 'travelling propagandists' toured the countryside.[27] The transformation of the EAA into the Kikuyu Central Association, which emerged in 1925, was closely associated with the mission community at Kahuhia, whose politically active elements constituted a major 'cell' of post-Thuku activity. Oral tradition remembers Hooper urging these EAA people to alter the focus of their organization to one more strictly Kikuyu. And he lent them his typewriter, and doubtless his advice, when they wanted to prepare in 1924 a memorandum to the Ormsby-Gore commission, the first openly political act of the new organization. The leadership of the KCA apparently made contact with Hooper again after an official at the Native Affairs Department urged them to 'get some European to act as their President and adviser' as a condition of government support and recognition.[28] But in 1926 Hooper left for England where he had been appointed Africa Secretary of the CMS, though he kept in close touch with events in Kenya through numerous correspondents at Kahuhia. Thus the establishment of the KCA, the dominant expression of 'modern' Kikuyu politics throughout the inter-war era, had been facilitated by its mission contacts at Kahuhia.

It was not long, however, before the KCA was reaching out to re-establish old contacts and create new ones well beyond Murang'a. Thuku's pan-African emphasis was continued through correspondence with the West African Student Union in London, and in Kenya the link with Kiambu and Nairobi was re-opened by the establishment of an office in the capital city and by engaging Johnstone Kenyatta, then a reasonably paid employee of the municipal water works and a flashy man-about-town, as general secretary of the KCA and editor of its publication *Muigwithania*. As part of their pan-Kikuyu programme, the KCA also attempted to enlist support among mission circles in Embu and Gicugu and so confronted the CMS communities at Kigari and Kabare with their first taste of the new politics.

In August or September of 1928 a deputation of the KCA approached John Comely, missionary in charge of Kigari, asking that he identify himself with the Association in expressing opposition to forced labour and certain other local grievances. An ex-dairy farmer and a Cambridge graduate, Comely was among the most conservative of CMS missionaries in almost every respect and proved himself a bitter opponent of the KCA. Comely flatly refused to join the KCA in protest and justified his action to church elders on the grounds that the KCA was composed of non-Christians, that it was out to gain control of the church and that support for the KCA risked offending others and causing them to lose their faith. If he had any doubts about the KCA, they were erased the following year when people in his area began refusing to do government work, apparently under KCA leadership. At that point he found himself 'led by prayer' to rule that no KCA member could serve as a church elder in Kigari. About the same time, KCA representatives also approached W. J. Rampley, CMS missionary at Kabare, with a letter of introduction from Gideon Mugo, a staunch mission adherent and active KCA member from Kahuhia. A meeting was arranged where the KCA envoy presented his case to the Kabare and Mutira Christians, hoping to organize them into a branch association. It soon became clear that a working arrangement with the KCA was impossible, for Ramley's offence at their secrecy, exclusion of chiefs and 'lack of cohesion' coincided with a certain local antagonism of the Gicugu towards the 'Kikuyu proper'. With Rampley's support, plans were made to create a local and rival association which, they hoped, would prevent the establishment of a KCA branch in the area. At least one meeting was held, attended by four chiefs, a number of mission adherents and Rampley, where they decided unanimously to have nothing whatever to do with the KCA.[29] Thus at Kigari and Kabare, as at Weithaga, mission communities proved reluctant or unable effectively to assimilate the new politics.

Much the same was true at the Scottish mission station at Tumutumu, where even before the circumcision controversy broke out in 1929, the mission had for three years been fighting the KCA 'tooth and nail'. Here the initial issue was the mission's aggressive policy of agricultural education. Regarding their request for school garden plots as a step towards further land alienation, the KCA supported and may have organized the destruction of a large number of school gardens between 1924 and 1928. The issues soon became very basic. 'The vital point to me is not so much the gardens', wrote Presbyterian missionary Philp, 'but the fact that we are being bossed by these people. They are becoming the real governors of the country.' By 1927, twenty-three of Tumutumu's fifty-five outschools had been closed and the following year the mission suspended from church membership anyone who attended KCA meetings. By this time the KCA had taken up the circumcision issue and in fact contested Local Native Council elections on the platform of preserving tribal customs. In response, the Scottish mission sponsored the Progressive Kikuyu Association, a moderate pro-government group along the lines of the Kikuyu Association in Kiambu.[30]

Given this history of KCA–mission antagonism, the situation at Kahuhia was all the more remarkable, for there the mission community effectively assimilated the KCA with little indication of political tension. Evidence for this synthesis comes from the correspondence of Hooper and Gideon Mugo, a CMS adherent since 1911, an active Thuku supporter and leader of the KCA contingent at Kahuhia.[31] To Gideon Mugo, the KCA and the mission were twin agencies of Kikuyu improvement – 'so that our country may come out of darkness'. He spoke of the 'work which I am doing here at Kahuhia mission and in our country in the Association' with no sense of contradiction, for the KCA and the CMS were to him not only parallel means of progress but related ones. Thus to Mugo, 'the church is the father of the KCA without quarrelling because it is the KCA who are the children of the church.' He was particularly proud that people from CMS Kahuhia were known as 'leaders in speaking for the Kikuyu people' and that 'Kahuhia has unity between the church and the KCA', unlike any other mission centre in Kikuyuland. While 'loyal' church members in the Presbyterian mission had nothing to do with the KCA, at Kahuhia and nearby Kathukeini the majority of church council positions were filled by KCA activists. In fact, Mugo attempted to promote this sort of unity outside Kahuhia in several ways. Presbyterian missionaries at Tumutumu asked him to help reconcile opposing factions there. And in *Muigwithania* he insisted that the 'KCA is not the enemy of the church' and urged that both organizations be fully supported for 'each of these duties is ours'.

Yet the Kahuhia group was not reluctant to dispute the advice of their missionary associates when the situation demanded it. Such an occasion occurred in the course of Handley Hooper's relationship with Kenyatta who had been sent as a KCA representative to the imperial capital in 1929. It was not long before Hooper became disillusioned with Kenyatta's handling of money, his 'doubtful' morals and his trip to Russia. Therefore he advised Gideon Mugo and other KCA people at Kahuhia to recall or drop Kenyatta as their representative. To a missionary friend he explained his reasoning:

> Many of us who realize better than the Association what an infinitesimal unit in the empire their numbers are would do our best to secure that any reasonable statement should at least receive a hearing but to send a boy like Kenyatta is worse than not sending anyone and just makes the friends of Africa in this country sad ... I just don't want to drive the members of the Association any further into futile obstructionism. I wish that they would be content for the next five years to build a solid core to their movement by lending their help to any agencies busy with social development in their own country.[32]

Hooper's paternalism was clear and was resented back in Kenya. Gideon Mugo indicated that the Kahuhia people were 'uneasy' with this advice, rebuked Hooper for failing to talk to Kenyatta before writing to them, and urged him not to defame the KCA on account of its representative. No permanent breach of confidence grew out of the incident, however, and the KCA group at Kahuhia continued to regard Hooper, together with the Labour Party, as among 'those Europeans who are on our side'.[33]

How then can the uneven pattern of mission–KCA conflict be explained? Despite its reputation for radicalism among missionaries in Kenya, the KCA generally operated well within the colonial framework. Self-help was far more characteristic of its platform than self-government. Nor was its position essentially anti-mission. *Muigwithania* did give voice to an incipient cultural nationalism at least implicitly critical of missions. 'Unless you hold on to the Kikuyu characteristics at this time', wrote the editor Kenyatta, 'you will become like a little appendage on a goat, which is neither part of the meat nor of the skin.'[34] But unless confronted by a provocative mission policy on such critical issues as land or circumcision, the more significant thrust of the KCA position towards missions lay in an attempt to overcome the many rifts which a heavily denominational missionary presence had introduced into Kikuyu society. The strong pan-Kikuyu dimension of KCA concern thus set limits on the expression of anti-mission sentiment, for the organization was not so large that it could afford to antagonize a substantial segment of its potential Christian membership by general attacks on missionaries. Rather, mission adherents were urged over and again to associate themselves with the Kikuyu nation. Kenyatta summed it up succinctly:

> The KCA seeks night and day for that which will cause all Kikuyu to be of one mind, educated and uneducated, ceasing to ask each other what school or mission do you belong to or saying to each other, 'you are not a reader'. For if there could be an end of things like these, the country of the Kikuyu could go ahead in peace.[35]

And the support, if not the leadership and advice, of individual missionaries was still valued, as demonstrated by the abortive KCA approaches to Comely and Rampley. The Association was also concerned about the breach between itself and its mission critics, and so in early 1930, while the wounds of the circumcision crisis were still raw, the KCA made a gesture to the missions. In a firm but conciliatory letter to the heads of all churches and missions in Kikuyuland, acting president Jesse Kariuki observed that the KCA was being libelled by people who claimed that it 'spoiled the church'. Declaring that his goal was the 'unity of the KCA and the church', Kariuki requested mission leaders to provide him with specific evidence of KCA misdeeds so that he might deal with them. No one on the side of the Association, he warned, should 'spread bad reports or spoil the church'.[36] Thus it would be a mistake to interpret KCA–CMS conflict as a function of an implacable or general KCA hostility to missions, for the emerging politicians seemed open to a working arrangement with the missions.

The variable in the conflict appears to have been missionary attitudes and policies which were sometimes of a very individual and personal nature. In Kiambu, of course, the problem did not arise to the same extent as the Kikuyu Association largely insulated the area from the more assertive politics further north. But in the CMS communities at Weithaga, Kigari, Kabare and on the Scottish station at Tumutumu, it was the intransigent and hostile stand of resident missionaries, in allegiance with an important segment of local African leadership, that made the integration of the new politics and mission communities impossible.

The experience of Kahuhia showed that such integration was not out of the question. Hooper's successor at Kahuhia, Francis Green, continued the tradition of an active involvement with the political element there. Gideon Mugo praised him highly to Hooper, for 'he helps us in the work of the church and the association ... as you helped us when you were here at Kahuhia'. For example, Green allowed Parmenas Githendu, a CMS teacher at Kahuhia, to represent the Association before the Hilton Young Commission,[37] a use of mission employees that would elsewhere have been out of the question.

The absorption of the politics of assertion into the mission community at Kahuhia was clearly facilitated by the reputation of its resident missionaries for a willingness actively to advocate African points of view even at the risk of open disagreement with the colonial government. Hooper had earned his credentials by an energetic interest in African economic and social improvement and by his sympathetic intervention in colonial politics on their behalf. Gideon Mugo testified to his reputation for getting things from the colonial government and to his interest 'in taking black people ahead'.[38] Hooper, however, felt himself very much on a political tightrope and feared, for example, that his association with Thuku would erode his influence with government officials though he recognized that it was this connexion that gave him credibility at Kahuhia. Green was apparently in much the same mould as several other missionaries appointed in the 1930s. Some of these seriously antagonized the administration by cooperating with the KCA in bringing complaints about tax abuses before a commission investigating the issue.[39] In western Kenya, it was Archdeacon W. E. Owen's frequent and outspoken opposition to many aspects of colonial policy that gave him the necessary standing to convert the politically active Young Kavirondo Association into the moderate and welfare-oriented Kavirondo Taxpayers Welfare Association. W. J. Rampley at Kabare made the connexion explicit when he observed that the necessity for him to contend for 'native rights' and to prevent injustices being imposed on a backward people 'had the effect of checking native political activity unconstitutionally'.[40] A measure of conflict between missionaries and the colonial establishment – enough to be credible but not so much as to be ineffective – appears to have been a condition for the effective assimilation of the new politics into mission communities. If these communities were to function as mechanisms of cohesion in the larger colonial society, this divergence was, ironically enough, an integrative one. In the long run, missionaries perhaps did more for the stability of the colonial regime by selectively opposing its policies than by according it their unambiguous support.

The failure of the Kahuhia model to gain widespread acceptance within the CMS was responsible for the development of serious strains between missionaries and a substantial section of African Christians within the mission communities of Kikuyuland. 'The trust and confidence of the native Christians in the missionaries is not what it was,' reported the mission in the aftermath of the Thuku troubles. And at the end of the decade, Hooper confessed himself both perplexed and humiliated at the degree to which Africans had lost faith in missionaries. Younger and newly appointed missionaries in particular felt the decline of that deferential treatment which had been the unquestioned right of their predecessors.[41] Nor were the changes in attitude wholly one-sided, for as McGregor Ross perceptively noted, missionaries frequently viewed their politically active followers as objects of suspicion tinged with resentment'. Harvey Cantrell, who arrived in Kenya in 1931, came to regard as a menace and a contamination the 'strong political undercurrent' that he found in the mission during the 1930s. To the veteran missionary Crawford, many African church leaders seemed

> to stress the idea that it is quite as important to contend for tribal rights as it is to support the Church in its conflict against the powers of sin and darkness; in fact they practically declare that there is no difference between the world and the church.[42]

Herein perhaps lay the ultimate offence of the new politics, particularly for older missionaries, for to blur the distinction between the world and church, to deny the importance of separation from the world, was to erode the very conceptual foundation of mission as it was understood by conservative evangelicals.

The paternalistic assumptions on which mission–African relations had been predicated for several decades were no longer acceptable to many African Christians. Nowhere was this more evident than in the growing rejection of missionaries as legitimate spokesmen for African needs and aspirations. Thuku had implicitly embraced this position when he appealed directly to London, bypassing all local channels. Only two years after the appointment of a single missionary to represent

African interests on the Legislative Council, the KCA expressed what was becoming a more prevalent attitude:

> Now it is known to us that if we won't speak for ourselves, our country will be finished by encroachment. There is not any one can represent our grievances, there is no faithful person who can speak on our behalf. So if we keep quiet the Government will think we are satisfied.

By 1929, the KCA was openly expressing the racial dimensions of this position: 'No European can really and truly represent us. The only person capable of representing us really well is a man with a black skin.'[43]

What is even more significant is the extent to which this distrust of missionary spokesmen had gained ground among the staunch mission adherents in moderate organizations such as the Kikuyu Association, renamed the Kikuyu Loyal Patriots around 1932, and the Progressive Kikuyu Party in Nyeri. In 1931 Leakey, as the representative for African interests, was reported in the local press as having told the Parliamentary Committee on Closer Union that Kenya was 'entirely suitable as a white man's country'. This disclosure touched deep fears of further land alienation in Kiambu and provoked the two loyalist associations to protest strongly at Leakey's statement and to ask permission to send 'witnesses chosen by the community' to give evidence to the Commission. The head of the Presbyterian mission, J. W. Arthur, argued strenuously that they should not bypass their missionary intermediaries. They were making their association as bad as the KCA, he told them, and warned that they 'could no longer be trusted to keep a level head, especially when they refused to consult the Europeans who had stood by them all these years, and did things all on their own'. By this time Arthur, described by Hooper as an 'old Tory of the ruling caste', had lost almost all support among African Christians in Kiambu and was unable to prevent the Loyal Patriots, led by CMS adherents from Kabete, from telegraphing their repudiation of Leakey to Parliament, the Anti-Slavery Society, the *Guardian* and the *Times*.[44] Three years later, these 'moderate' political associations took another step away from dependence on missionary 'communicators'. In the process of rejecting the controversial report of the Kenya Land Commission, they actually joined the KCA in a further protest to the Colonial Secretary against missionary representation:

> [W]e do not want a self-Government to be born in Kenya, because we have no representatives to speak for us in the Legislative Council (in) whom we can fully confide. Those who are considered as our pleaders do not help us or speak for us as they ought.[45]

In such ways had the encounter with African politics altered the internal relationships of the CMS and other mission communities of central Kenya. It was, however, but the prelude to a more sharply focused and explosive crisis associated with the female circumcision controversy.

FOOTNOTES

1. CMS/1895/237, Jones to Baylis, 15 November 1895; 1896/44, Binns to Baylis, 21 January 1896; Binns Journals, 29 June 1896.
2. KNA: Coast Province 20/136, Handing Over Report, Nyika District, 13 November 1915; 5/336, DC to PC, 18, 20 September 1914; 20/101, DC to PC, 8 June 1915; Cynthia Brantley Smith, 'The Giriama Rising, 1914', Ph.D. Dissertation, UCLA, 1973.
3. KNA: CMS 1/639, Kabare Log Book, 12 July 1915; PC/CP.1/5/1, Embu District Record Book, 31 March 1914, October 1917; CMS/1907/44, Conference Review of 1906.
4. CMS, Acc. 85, Hooper typescript.
5. CMS/1913/16, Annual Letter, A. W. McGregor, 12 December 1912.
6. EHA: Box 236, Hooper letter, 5 January 1922.
7. CMS, Acc. 85, Hooper typescript. For a discussion of the concept of alternative communicators, see J. M. Lonsdale, 'Some Origins of Nationalism in East Africa', *Journal of African History*, IX:1 (1968), pp. 119–46.
8. EHA: Box 236, Arthur to Oldham, 4 March 1922; KNA: FH/4, Fort Hall District Annual Report, 1924. For a comprehensive discussion of the origins of the new politics, see Carl Rosberg and John Nottingham, *The Myth of Mau Mau* (New York, 1966), chs 1, 2.
9. KNA: PC/CP.1/7/1, Fort Hall District Record Book; FH/7, Fort Hall District Annual Report; John Middleton, 'Kenya', *History of East Africa*, eds Vincent Harlow *et al.* (Oxford, 1965), II, 359.
10. Rosberg and Nottingham, *The Myth of Mau Mau*, op. cit., pp. 41–2.
11. KNA: PC/CP.1/1/1, Central Province Political Record Book; RH: Coryndon 17/2, Kikuyu Association.
12. RH: Coryndon 17/2, Report of Meeting of KA, 11 October 1924; Memorandum of KA to Hilton Young Commission, 1928.
13. On the origins and development of the EAA, see Harry Thuku, *An Autobiography* (Nairobi, 1970), pp. 11–34; Rosberg and Nottingham, op. cit., pp. 36–55; K. J. King, 'The Nationalism of Harry Thuku', *TransAfrica* I:1 (1970).
14. Harry Thuku, *Tangazo*, 17 February 1922 in K. J. King, 'The American Background of the Phelps-Stokes Commission', Ph.D. Dissertation, Edinburgh University, 1968, appendix III.
15. EHA: Box 236, Arthur to Oldham, 19 March 1922; KNA: KBU/15, Kiambu District Annual Report, 1922.
16. EHA: Box 236, H. D. Hooper, 'Development of Political Self-Consciousness in the Kikuyu Native'.
17. RH: Coryndon Papers, 17/2/21, A Prayer for Mr Harry Thuku; EHA: Box 236, Hooper to Oldham, 4 March 1922; CMS, Annual Letters, A. W. McGregor, 1 October 1922.
18. Harry Thuku, *Tangazo*, 8 March 1922.
19. RH: Coryndon Papers, 17/2, The Five Delegates of the Kikuyu Association to Nyeri.
20. CMS/1922/19, Heywood to Manley, 20 February 1922; EHA: Box 236, Hooper to friends, 24 January 1922. Thuku, *Autobiography*, op. cit., pp. 23, 83.
21. EHA: Box 236, Hooper to friends, 24 January 1922; Hooper to Oldham, 4 March 1922; CMS, 'Historical Records', 1923–4, p. 38.
22. CMS, Annual Letters, A. W. McGregor, 1 October 1922; EHA: Box 236, Hooper to Oldham, 4 March 1922.
23. For Thuku's attitude towards missions, see Harry Thuku, *Tangazo*, 17 February 1922, 8 March 1922; Thuku, *Autobiography*, op. cit., pp. 1–34; EHA: Box 236, Hooper to Oldham, 4 March 1922; Thuku to Hooper, 2 March 1922; Thuku to Secretary, Tuskeegee Institute, 8 September 1921 in Appendix V of K. J. King, 'The American Background', op. cit.

24. CMS/1922/39, McGregor to Manley, 12 April 1922; 1922/19, Heywood to Manley, 20 February 1922.
25. EHA: Box 236, Hooper to friends, 24 January 1922; Hooper, 'Development of Political Self-Consciousness', op. cit.
26. EHA: Box 236, Hooper, 'Development of Political Self-Consciousness', op. cit.; Thuku, *Autobiography*, op. cit., p. 31.
27. EHA: Box 247, Hooper to Oldham, 1 August 1923; CMS, Annual Letters, A. W. McGregor, 1 November 1923.
28. Interview 21; CMS, Acc. 85, Watkins to Hooper, 21 October 1925; Jeremy Murray-Brown, *Kenyatta* (London, 1972), pp. 100–3.
29. KNA: CMS 1/637, Embu Log Book, 1 September 1928; CMS 1/638, Mutira Log Book, 4, 9 April 1929; CMS 1/639, Kabare Log Book, 4, 9 April 1929.
30. EHA: Box 236, Arthur to McLachlan, 15 February 1929; PCEA: Letters to DC, Nyeri, Philp to DC, 9 June 1928; Brian G. McIntosh, 'The Scottish Mission in Kenya, 1891–1923', Ph.D. Dissertation, University of Edinburgh, 1969, pp. 408–10.
31. See CMS, Acc. 85, Mugo to Hooper, 18 February 1928; 19 February 1930; 30 March 1930; n.d. I was kindly supplied with translations of these letters by Dr Jocelyn Murray. Also CMS, 'Historical Records', 1930–1, p. 88, and *Muigwithania*, June 1929.
32. CMS, Acc. 85, Hooper to Soles, 26 September 1929; Hooper to Gideon Mugo, 1929.
33. CMS, Acc. 85, Mugo to Hooper, 30 December 1929; 30 March 1930; 26 April 1931.
34. *Muigwithania*, May 1929.
35. *Miugwithania*, August 1928.
36. CMS, Acc. 85, Kariuki to the respected elder, 23 February 1930.
37. CMS, Acc. 85, G. H. M. Kagika to Hooper, 18 February 1928.
38. CMS, Acc. 85, Mugo to Hooper, 7 August 1926, 30 March 1930.
39. Hooper Papers, MCH to Mother, 11 March 1922; KNA: DC/FH.6/1, History of Fort Hall.
40. John M. Lonsdale, 'Political Associations in Western Kenya', *Protest and Power in Black Africa*, eds Robert Rotberg and Ali Mazrui (New York, 1970); KNA: CMS 1/639, Kabare Log Book, 10 June 1932.
41. CMS, Annual Letters, Highlands District Mission Annual Report, 1922; Interview 3; EHA: Box 242, Hooper to Oldham, 11 April 1929.
42. McGregor Ross, *Kenya From Within* (London, 1927), p. 225; CMS, 'Historical Records', 1933–4, p. 48; 1937–8, p. 48.
43. KNA: PC/CP.8/5/2, KCA to Sr. Commissioner, 10 July 1926; *Muigwithania*, February–March 1929.
44. PCEA: Legislative Council I, Arthur to Leakey, 17 April 1931; Progressive Kikuyu Party to Leakey, 6 May 1931; EHA: Box 242, Hooper to Oldham, 11 April 1929.
45. PCEA: Secretary to Council, Arthur to Barlow, 19 March 1934; 'Political, 1933', Koinange Mbiu and J. Kamau to Cunliffe-Lister, 13 October 1934.

CHAPTER VIII

written in conjunction with Dr Jocelyn Murray

The CMS and Female Circumcision

Before the outbreak of the Mau Mau revolt, few issues had engaged the passionate attention of so many people in colonial Kenya as the controversy over female circumcision. Involving a sharp missionary challenge to a central feature of Kikuyu identity, the circumcision crisis drove not a few African Christians to the point of rupture with their churches. But in a colonial setting such cultural issues readily take on the function of expressing resistance to the foreign order and so for a time the circumcision matter became in the hands of the Kikuyu Central Association an important means of political mobilization. It touched too on the immensely sensitive problem of land, for popular belief had it that Europeans would marry uncircumcised Kikuyu girls and through them gain access to still more Kikuyu land. The control of outschools, those local symbols of modernity and mobility, likewise became a point of contention in a crisis which decisively broke the missionary monopoly on education in central Kenya. Thus the circumcision crisis, potent enough in its own right, was linked with many of the other tensions of colonial Kenya both within mission communities and in the larger society.

Yet this is not to imply, as some have done, that female circumcision was merely the occasion for an inevitable political and educational crisis which would have found some other *casus belli*,[1] for the specific handling of the issue at various mission centres largely determined the intensity of the crisis in particular locations. Nor is it very useful to discuss the controversy simply in terms of 'the missions and the Kikuyu',[2] for the missions were by no means agreed on the matter, the CMS being the major dissident element, while without a measure of real anti-circumcision sentiment among the Kikuyu there would have been no crisis at all. Even those studies that have recognized the relatively more flexible CMS position on the issue have failed to perceive the great variety of policy, practice and impact within CMS communities and the tortuous process by which these various positions were reached.[3]

THE DEVELOPMENT OF A CULTURAL CRISIS

At the heart of Kikuyu rites of passage marking the entrance for both men and women to adult status was the physical operation of circumcision. Performed at puberty, the operation for girls is more correctly termed clitoridectomy. Local variations in the extent of cutting had persuaded government officials and some missionaries that there were two forms of the operation, a minor one limited to the excision of the clitoris and a major or 'brutal' form involving cutting of the *labia minora* and *majora* as well. This belief played an important role in shaping European strategies for dealing with the custom. However it was performed, the operation itself was embedded in a richly symbolic set of rituals, was associated with much singing and dancing, and held a profound significance for the initiates and their families. It marked the coming of mature status, the passing from an asexual to a sexual world and as such was a prerequisite for marriage as well as for membership in 'age sets', one of the major integrative institutions of Kikuyu society.[4] If Kikuyu women in the 1970s still regard an uncircumcised woman as less than mature, a social anomaly and unable to participate fully in adult relationships,[5] the immensity of what missionaries were asking them to abandon a half-century earlier can be imagined. Uncircumcised girls are so scorned by their neighbours, wrote Tabitha Wangui in *Muigwithania*, that they seek to escape this reproach in Nairobi where they become prostitutes. 'In what way are they women?' she asked, 'If you want prostitutes to increase largely, you should say that circumcision is to be abandoned.' The depth of feeling occasioned by threats to the practice is reflected in the reply of one Wambugu, a member of the Nyeri Native District Council, to a suggestion by the District Commissioner that it be abandoned:

> You white men came among us and we seeing that you were good men welcomed you with both hands; we readily do all that you wish us to do: ... you impose taxes upon us and we pay without a murmur; when your taxes become more than we can pay, we will come as suppliants and tell you so. But in this matter of our girls, we cannot see eye to eye to you and we cannot agree to obey you even if you attempt to coerce us.[6]

To most missionaries in Kikuyuland, female circumcision was simply abhorrent. From a medical viewpoint they regarded it as nothing less than mutilation which often had, they felt, terrible consequences during childbirth. But even where no physical harm occurred, the associated rituals and festivities represented to the missionaries an occasion for unsurpassed spiritual degradation. To Cicely Hooper, it was 'a disgusting ceremony', while Leonard Beecher objected to the 'unnecessary attention which any puberty rite calls to the non-spiritual aspects of sex'.[7] But in all this there was never any discussion whatever of the effect of clitoridectomy on women's participation in sexual relations, though whether this silence derived from a residual Victorian reluctance to discuss issues of such delicacy or from ignorance of the physiology of sexual response is unclear. Almost everywhere, then, there had been teaching against the practice and efforts to strengthen the resolve of girls and their families against it. From the first, the Church of Scotland Mission had led the attack on female circumcision and by the early 1920s it was a rule that baptized church members undergoing the operation or allowing their daughters to do so would be disciplined by suspension from church membership.[8] The African Inland Mission soon followed suit. While the CMS fully shared in resolutions condemning the custom and periodically raised the question for discussion within the mission, no station had imposed such a law on its adherents.

These efforts had not been without some success and by the end of the 1920s there were groups of mission adherents in Kikuyuland who had come to oppose the practice of female circumcision. 'We find it our duty,' declared a group of African Christians from Kiambu just as the crisis was breaking, 'to take up our stand on the matter and show that it is not the Europeans that make the law against circumcision of women but we Kikuyu ourselves.'[9] But personal opposition to female circumcision, usually among the earliest converts, did not always imply a willingness to press the pace of cultural change by legislating against the practice. Nor did it mean that church elders were necessarily able to persuade their wives and daughters to abandon the custom. Yet without this support, clearly even the most determined of Scottish missionary crusaders would not have been able to carry the campaign through.

If core groups of African Christians represented one ally for the missionaries in their anti-circumcision struggle, they hoped to find another in the colonial government. From the government they expected at least protection and support for Christian girls who refused to undergo circumcision, but some hoped for much more. As early as 1918 the Alliance of Mission Societies resolved that the government 'should be approached to legislate for its abolition among the heathen'.[10] In 1925 the government went on record strongly condemning the practice of female circumcision and offered legal support for individuals who chose to refuse the operation. 'Native law and custom' was not to over-ride the individual decisions taken by African Christians and the right to bring legal action in cases of enforced circumcision was ensured, though all this proved much more contentious in practice than the authorities had envisaged. But fearing that 'premature action might have the effect of uniting native authorities against the Government in defence of old customs', the authorities would move no further towards actually abolishing the custom than attempting to secure the opposition of Local Native Councils. This latter effort had some impact, for by 1928 the Kiambu, Fort Hall and Embu LNCs had passed resolutions limiting the operation to excision of the clitoris,[11] though these were observed more on paper than in practice. The noticeable reluctance of the government fully to support mission efforts for wholesale suppression of female circumcision was in large measure responsible for limiting the political impact of the crisis, though it opened up a considerable breach between the more conservative missions and colonial authorities.

By the mid-1920s all the elements for a potential clash were in place. But exactly what precipitated the crisis is extremely difficult to disentangle. The Scottish position held that the KCA launched a deliberate anti-mission campaign with circumcision as its rallying cry, while the nationalist point of view saw intemperate mission action as responsible for the crisis.[12] While we may never know precisely who fired the first shot, clearly it was in Nyeri at the CSM station of Tumutumu that the issue first became political and led African Christians to an open, if reluctant, break with their church. The issue of school gardens had for several years provoked hostility between the KCA and the CSM. Furthermore Tumutumu was the station of Dr H. R. A. Philp, a strongminded missionary who was uncompromisingly hostile to both female circumcision and the KCA. Thus in March of 1928 the KCA announced that it would contest the forthcoming elections to the Local Native Council by defending traditional Kikuyu culture including female circumcision. And in April the Tumutumu Kirk Session demanded a declaration of loyalty on circumcision from all baptized church members on pain of suspension. No compromise was possible and about two hundred people, seven per cent of the Tumutumu congregations, were put under church disipline.[13] Thus the issue had been joined. No doubt the Scottish missionaries felt justified and emboldened by the results of a 'United Native Conference' of African representatives from all the Protestant missions in Kikuyuland held at Tumutumu in March of 1929. There the African delegates – the missions' own people – voted unanimously that female circumcision was 'evil and should be abandoned by all Christians', and thirty to nine in favour of enforcing church discipline on those who submitted to it.[14] Significantly all nine dissenting votes were cast by CMS delegates from Kigari, Kabare and Kahuhia stations. Nonetheless, African church leaders had seemed to put their stamp of approval on the CSM actions.

Events of the rest of the year escalated on both sides as a kind of chain reaction effect set in. The precipitating event was a court case regarding a Kiambu girl circumcised, allegedly, against her will. This was the sort of affair that the Kiambu missionaries had been using to pressurize the government into a stronger stand on behalf of those who refused the operation. In this case, however, the verdict of the magistrate, upheld on appeal to the High Court, resulted in only a very minor fine for the offenders, a decision which so infuriated J. W. Arthur, head of the Presbyterian mission at Kikuyu, that he took his case to the press. Arthur's determined and uncompromising stand on the issue at this time was a major factor in the crisis and may have been related to his awareness of an impending change in the colony's criminal law from one based on the Indian penal code to new codes based on English law. A solid show of support for the anti-circumcision viewpoint might mean the introduction of measures in the new penal code favourable to the mission position, perhaps even outlawing the practice for all Kenyans. But if this was Arthur's intention, it backfired. Within a week of his letter to the press, the KCA took up the challenge and in a letter addressed to 'all the chiefs of Kikuyu country' accused him of issuing a law against circumcision and warned that 'if we are compelled to comply with it, it will cause us much trouble'.[15] Thus by September of 1929, female circumcision was being discussed in many forums – the Governor's Executive Council, the councils of the KCA, in church services and at elders' meetings. Emotions were raw and while Arthur retained the staunch backing of the four Christian chiefs of Kiambu district, he was rapidly losing whatever support he might have had among the people in his area. 'You did not come forth to the Kikuyu for the sake of God's word', went a virulent anonymous letter to Arthur,

> but for the sake of trade and lies and you have added to the commandments of God a commandment of circumcision ... Has God spoken to you this time and informed you that those who circumcise will not enter into God's place? It is better for a European like you to leave speaking about things like this because you can make the Gospel to be evil spoken of.[16]

At the same time the dance-song called *muthirigu*, abusing missionaries, administrators, loyal church elders and Kiambu chiefs alike, spread like wildfire through Kikuyu country. And in January of 1930 the murder of an elderly AIM missionary, Hulda Stumpf, injected a note of violence into the unfolding crisis.

Under these conditions, the CSM decision to force the issue among its own adherents could only result in disaster. In early October, 1929, the paid agents of the mission at its Kikuyu station in Kiambu district were required to declare their loyalty to the Presbyterian position on circumcision and to forswear membership of the KCA. Twelve out of fifty-three refused to do so and left the mission. Several weeks later church elders were asked to make a similar declaration, though the question of KCA membership was left open. Again, eighteen of fifty elders refused to so commit themselves. Finally the CSM insisted that church members affirm their opposition to female circumcision, at which fully ninety per cent of the mission's communicants balked, surely an indication of a substantial gap between the church's leadership and its members. The educational side of the mission's work was equally affected as total CSM outschool attendance dropped from an average of 728 in December 1928 to only eighty-seven a year later, and as parents refused to accept as teachers those who had declared their loyalty to the CSM on circumcision. 'It is well that you send us the teachers we want,' wrote the elders of Riruta outschool to Arthur, 'for in our school it is our children who read and pay fees. ...' The mission's right to occupy the land on which outschools were located was being questioned and an increasing demand for government or independent schools punctuated the debate. The AIM followed similar policies and experienced similar consequences. By the end of 1930 twenty AIM outschools had been closed in the Fort Hall area alone and the people there declared that no power on earth could persuade them to return to the mission.[17]

Around the events of 1929 there hovered a certain air of inevitability. Given an issue so central to Kikuyu identity, an aggressive political organization in need of issues to mobilize and unite its members and missionaries such as Arthur for whom 'the cause is a righteous one' and the issue worthy of a 'fight to the death', it is difficult to see what other outcome was possible. Neither side sought a moratorium on the subject and the colonial referee pursued a policy of masterly inactivity except when law and order were threatened. Events rather than actors seemed in charge. For the Church of Scotland Mission and the Africa Inland Mission, the climax of the crisis had passed by early 1930 and it remained to begin rebuilding their churches and schools on a new foundation. But for the CMS the whole question of how to deal with female circumcision had only begun.

THE MAKING OF A CULTURAL POLICY

The impact of the female circumcision crisis within the CMS communities in Kikuyuland was considerably less intense than it had been among the other major Protestant missions. With the important exception of the region around Kigari in Embu, very few independent schools or churches were established in CMS areas and relatively fewer CMS adherents felt pushed to an open break with their mission. This situation was due almost wholly to the refusal of the CMS to take so inflexible a position on the issue as had the other mission societies. Nor was this an entirely new divergence among the competing mission groups in Kenya, for the CMS had earlier proved reluctant to legislate decisively on such matters as smoking and drinking, a policy which had already strained the bonds of mission comity. This greater tolerance was basically a product of the more comprehensive and inclusive character of the Church of England as a whole rather than a uniquely local phenomenon. Such attitudes enabled the leadership of CMS communities, both African and European, to keep in touch with their members, rendered them more willing to be guided by popular opinion on crucial matters, and made it possible for CMS missionaries to view the crisis more in political than ideological terms. Yet the CMS was by no means united on the matter and in fact the initial impact of the crisis was to provoke a major internal debate from which emerged a series of increasingly lenient compromises.

Most deeply involved in the crisis during its early stages was the CMS community at Kabete, where the Rev. Harry Leakey had been in charge since 1902. Located on the southern frontier of Kikuyu settlement, many of Leakey's early students were among the first generation to be born in the area – people of pioneering stock, enterprising, hard-working and open to change. Kabete's location only eight miles from Nairobi gave a peculiar advantage to the literate young Kikuyu who emerged from the school there. Thus the Leakeys gained the support of an able and progressive group of Kikuyu men and women such as Stefano Kinuthia, chief interpreter to the Supreme Court, his brother Matthew Njoroge, Josiah Njonjo who became a chief and Koinange Mbiu, later a senior chief. Finally Kabete's proximity to the CSM station at Kikuyu meant frequent contact with the Presbyterians, an involvement in the circumcision matter earlier than any other CMS station, and intense pressure to fall into line with the strict stand of the other Kiambu missions.

Kabete's policy on female circumcision had been one of reluctant accommodation. Leakey had permitted it so long as it was not accompanied by 'heathen customs'. But by 1929 there had developed at Kabete a group of men led by Yusufe Magu, the first ordained African there, and by Stefano Kinuthia, who were not only personally opposed to the practice but wanted to make it a penal offence in the church. Leakey was inclined to back them and seems to have denied baptism to some who actively supported circumcision for girls. These were not positions widely supported at Kabete. Most of the women, wrote a missionary who was there at the time, still favoured the practice 'as they do not wish their girls to remain children forever in the eyes of the tribe'. And the people most directly affected by the whole affair, the uncircumcised boarders in the Kabete girls' dormitory, were feeling the strain of the situation. The propaganda of the *muthirigu* songs, the abuse of outsiders and the taunts of their own relatives made it impossible for them to go on any longer rejecting the ceremony which they believed would make them fully adult women. So what the missionaries so feared happened on 29 December 1929:

> Our hopes were dashed to the ground today ... when twelve girls from the compound returned their school clothes, donned their blankets, and went off to be circumcised. Six more are on the verge of going and they may take the rest of the uncircumcised girls with them.

This was the situation at Kabete on the eve of a major CMS decision on the issue. Despite these expressions of opposition to a firm policy on circumcision, at a meeting in early December of all Kikuyu clergy – both European and African – to advise the bishop on the question, Kabete's delegates urged a strong stand against the practice with church discipline for offenders.[18]

Kigari in Embu was represented at the meeting by John Comely, missionary in charge there since 1915. Comely had hoped to institute at Kigari a service of renunciation at which parents of maturing girls together with their daughters would publicly repudiate the practice of circumcision. But at the all-clergy meeting he admitted that the majority of his elders and congregation were still very much in favour of the operation. W. J. Rampley from Kabare reported that his Pastorate Committee had gone even further and actually passed a resolution favouring the retention of female circumcision.[19] An unrepresented but very real force at this crucial gathering was the opinion of the already committed missions who were increasingly concerned at the apparent hesitancy of the CMS to align itself fully with them. The missionary arm of the established church, after all, still had some prestige and CMS hesitancy was preventing the formation of a united missionary front just when it was needed most.[20]

All of this was hammered out at the December meeting. The policy which emerged from these deliberations was a carefully worded compromise issued by Bishop Heywood as a pastoral letter on 1 January 1930.[21] It strongly condemned female circumcision but stopped just short of absolutely forbidding the practice on pain of church discipline. It declared that 'those who have children, both fathers or mothers, if they consent to their girls being circumcised deliberately expose themselves to being disciplined by the Church'. The nature of the discipline, however, was not specified nor did it appear to be mandatory. Rather, each case was to be considered by the relevant Pastorate Committee 'so that they may find out how far the people are to blame'. A later paragraph was a little stronger. 'Those who persist with this thing, knowing full well what they do, must be brought under discipline.' But there was still an escape clause – did they really know full well what they were doing? – and the letter expressed an attitude far removed from the simple and definitive prohibition of the Church of Scotland. By not enforcing a declaration of loyalty on those already baptized, thus purging the mission of pro-circumcision sentiment, church councils might still contain a majority of men favouring the practice and so make any kind of discipline impossible to enforce. Nonetheless, the CMS had decided something and it remained to see if it would be acceptable to the rank and file of mission adherents.

It was at Kabete, where the CMS stand contrasted sharply with that of neighbouring missions and where a substantial group of African elders wanted a strong stand on the issue, that the policy worked best. In 1930 Leakey had required all new candidates for baptism to take a vow against female circumcision, but by refusing so to test the loyalty of those already baptized, he avoided a major confrontation with his congregation and a major exodus from his churches and schools such as had decimated the CSM and AIM missions.[22] Yet this was not immediately apparent and in late 1929 it looked to one missionary at Kabete as if 'we may practically have to begin a new work here'. Indeed most of the eleven outschools around Kabete experienced a certain loss of students at least temporarily, though some actually gained pupils, defectors from the CSM. At several outschools there were more serious incidents. At one called Gacharage, Joshua Macheru, who had given the land on which the school stood and who was an ardent supporter of circumcision, wanted the school to become *karinga*, independent from the mission. When he violently disrupted a church service and attacked the teacher there he was arrested, but a group of his followers armed with sticks arrived shortly and began to tear the school down. Only the timely arrival of the missionary, Cecil Bewes, prevented its destruction. At Kirangari outschool another dispute over the ownership of the school plot led to the formation at Mukoi of the only independent school in the CMS sphere of influence. Defections from the girls' dormitory also continued as parents came to reclaim their daughters.[23] Yet in the end the crisis petered out at Kabete. Disaffected individuals left, but no wholesale defections occurred. That the mission policy of refusing to impose retrospective vows could have such an impact points to the fundamentally cultural rather than political nature of the crisis and to the powerful attractions of the mission community.

The response at Kahuhia to the bishop's letter was rather different. Here in the heartland of Kikuyu country there was a greater tendency towards cultural conservatism. And as the only mission station in Kikuyuland effectively to assimilate the new politics, any attempt by missionaries to push the issue would have had disastrous consequences. So there was little inclination among prominent church elders to move forcefully on the question of female circumcision. In 1926 in fact, the daughters of several leading men including the Rev. Levi Gacanja, Kahuhia's first African clergyman, had been circumcised without any great show of disapproval

from their fathers. Frequent discussions of female circumcision and other traditional customs took place in Pastorate Committee meetings and while there was
some inclination to take individual action against Christians who participated, there
was strong aversion to any general 'law'.[24]

Thus the initial reaction to the bishop's letter was confusion. 'Elders asked many
questions,' reported Ethel Soles when the letter was first read out to the congregation.[25] Nor could the subject be dropped in Pastorate Committee meetings.
In March of 1930, three months after the letter had been issued,

> Johana Mbira asked to be told clearly what had been decided. Bwana Green
> replied that Bwana Bishop and his clergy had seen that female circumcision was a
> sin, therefore the Bishop and his clergy met together, discussed and decided that
> any uncircumcised girl who got circumcised should be suspended from church
> privileges, together with her mother and father.

The elders immediately expressed grave doubts as to whether these aims could be
achieved by force. Green could scarcely argue with them since he had admitted to
the meeting that the CSM and AIM were experiencing great difficulties. Someone
then asked the deliberately embarrassing question – whether if circumcision of
black people stopped, blacks and whites would now inter-marry. Green replied
rather lamely that it would be better for them to remain separate. It was a difficult
meeting for the missionary. Again in May one of the elders, John Gicaga, raised the
question by asking why the bishop had made a law concerning female circumcision
when the Christian religion was based not on law but on love. Leonard Beecher,
who had by then replaced Frank Green at Kahuhia, answered that it was not
a law; the bishop had simply entreated the clergy and lay leaders to get rid of
this evil custom.[26] Green said it was a law; Beecher said not. Was it or was it
not a law?

Uncertainty in this case served the CMS well, for the fact of the matter was
that the elders at Kahuhia had no real intention of taking any decisive action on
the circumcision question. There was a number of younger men who had, it seems,
made some personal commitment to have nothing to do with the custom, but their
own daughters were still too young for them to have the matter brought to the test.
The teaching of the New Testament, as they understood it, certainly prescribed no
prohibition on the practice, and Galatians 5:6 was a favourite text: 'neither circumcision nor uncircumcision is of any avail'.[27] Given the prevailing climate of opinion
in Murang'a, these elders knew that to have taken any other stand would have
split their church completely. This they were not willing to do. Their missionary
mentors were new and younger men (Beecher was only twenty-four in 1930) of
broader views, who lacked in any case sufficient stature to force the issue even had
they been inclined to do so.

Thus in the CMS outschools in Fort Hall, reported the district commissioner,
the situation was 'normal' and attendance good. So attractive did CMS schools
appear to nearby adherents of the AIM that a number of them transferred their
allegiance to the Anglicans, thus provoking considerable tension between the two
missions. While there were scattered CMS defections, only one independent
school, Githithi, was established in the area served by Kahuhia and Weithaga, and
this may have had more to do with internal factional disputes than with the
circumcision issue.[28] The ambiguity of CMS pronouncements had thus prevented
the necessity of choosing between obedience and schism, between being a Christian
and being a Kikuyu.

Uncertainty was not the problem at CMS Kabare across the Tana River in Gicugu country. Occupied initially in 1910, it was not until 1921 that Kabare received a permanent resident missionary in the person of W. J. Rampley. He had come to Kenya in 1913 as an AIM missionary but joined the CMS four years later. The son of a farmer, Rampley had worked as a coachman on an estate in Sussex and perhaps this rural background facilitated his adjustment to life in Kenya. He became known in the mission for his efforts, in the best Venn tradition, to hand over responsibility to the local church. In cultural matters, he adopted a generally liberal and tolerant attitude. As the leading figure in the controversy over the *itwika* ceremony marking the change of generation sets, Rampley felt it should be possible for Christians to partake fully in Kikuyu handing-over rituals but strongly opposed their participation in the 'heathen sacrifices' normally associated with the process. In the circumcision controversy as well Rampley would try to satisfy the traditionalists without sacrificing what he regarded as Christian principle.

The reaction to the bishop's letter at Kabare was clear – they simply could not accept it. Members of the Pastorate Committee had watched the crisis decimate the Presbyterian station of Chogoria and felt that acceptance of the bishop's ruling would have a similar impact at Kabare. They would go no further than recommending the minor operation as a step towards eventual abolition. This decision was taken over the strong objection of John Comely, who in the absence of Rampley on leave had temporary oversight at Kabare.[29] Upon his return in early 1931, Rampley began to search for a compromise solution that would satisfy a Christian conscience without alienating the Christians from their families, clans and communities. In this pursuit he was influenced by the efforts of H. E. Lambert, the unusually sensitive Embu District Commissioner, to make a reality of the minor or modified operation in his district. Rampley also knew of the experiments of Bishop Lucas in Tanganyika with the Christianization of male initiation rites including circumcision. Bishop Heywood himself, aware that his earlier position was probably unworkable, had begun to think along these lines as well. There was much to be said, he wrote, in June 1931, for 'an endeavour to Christianize the African idea of three weeks' or so initiatory training, even with a purely superficial operation in private'.[30]

Thus in July 1931 the Kabare Pastorate Committee, with Rampley's support, came to a significant decision: not only would they permit the minor operation at puberty but they would conduct it under the auspices of the church. Four Christians, two men and two women, were chosen as operators for boys and girls respectively. All 'repugnant customs' traditionally associated with the rite were forbidden except the payment of certain goats due to the uncle of the initiate. No publicity was permitted and only those directly involved were allowed to be present.[31] This policy admitted what so many missionaries had never recognized, that the male and female operations were in Kikuyu eyes functionally equivalent. But there was no suggestion of an initiation school where Christian teaching regarding sexuality, marriage, family life or anything else would be given. And perhaps here Rampley was being led by, rather than leading, the Kabare elders. For the fact of the matter seems to be that, to the Kikuyu, the basic and essential part of the initiation ceremony, the *sine qua non* of adult status, was the actual physical operation itself, rather than the rituals surrounding it. Thus there seems to have been relatively little resistance to young men being circumcised at mission hospitals. Among other peoples – the Tiriki of western Kenya for example – the performance of the mere physical operation has not proved an acceptable substitute for the traditional initiation. To Tiriki elders even Christian circumcision rites incorporating as much as possible of the traditional ceremonies and teaching, and with the initiates sworn to secrecy in the customary way, have been highly suspect and men circumcised in hospitals have been generally despised.[32] Kikuyu initiates were traditionally secluded only for the length of time it took their wounds to heal. There was much colourful ceremony and dancing in the course of the rites and incidental teaching about adult life and sexual behaviour in the words of the songs, but the Kikuyu did not incorporate a formal period of systematic teaching as is customary in many other puberty rituals. The education and training of young Kikuyu men and women culminated in, but was not so dependent upon, the actual period surrounding the operation as seems to have been the case in many societies. This may be important in explaining the readiness of the Kikuyu to accept a truncated ceremony – in fact a non-ceremony – so long as the physical operation took place.

The Kabare experiment at any rate was widely accepted in the mission community there and was continued for about twenty years. When one of Rampley's successors raised the question of abolishing female circumcision altogether in 1937, he found the elders 'solidly opposed to any change in the present system'.[33] The ceremonies were held at homesteads with only the girls and Christian women present. No hymns were sung; there were prayers, but little ceremony. One or two women gave instruction to the girls in the style of exhortation. Such ceremonies must have been rather bleak proceedings and very much more painful to the girls than an operation performed during the course of an emotionally charged ritual.[34]

The Kabare compromise served its purpose well, for no outschools left the CMS to link themselves with an independent church/school organization. But its consequences were felt well beyond Kabare. What happened there, coupled with Kahuhia's refusal to cooperate, in effect meant that the bishop's policy on the circumcision question was a dead letter. Heywood himself admitted that only a 'distinct minority' of the clergy and laity were willing to carry out his proposals and complained that many church elders shielded offenders, making the policy extremely difficult to enforce.[35]

But the Kabare experiment and the weakening resolve of the bishop to maintain a firm policy on circumcision also provoked an extremely strong reaction from the other major Protestant missions in Kikuyuland. What made these reactions so important to the CMS was that they threatened the foundations of Protestant unity in Kenya as expressed in the Alliance of Missionary Societies. Created in 1918 after considerable controversy, the Alliance was composed of the CMS, CSM, AIM and the Methodist mission and had as its aim the overcoming of denominational differences and ultimately the creation of a united African church.[36] But the Bishop's need to accommodate the widespread opposition to his policy within the CMS threatened the very existence of the Alliance. When Heywood informed Arthur that the CMS was considering meeting with its African clergy and elders to discuss the possibility of a private or even Christianized circumcision ceremony, Arthur bluntly replied that a decision along these lines 'would probably burst the Alliance'. Moreover, in an appeal to the racial feelings of his fellow missionary, he deplored Heywood's intention to 'approach Africans with your suggestion before meeting with your fellow *European* and *American* Christian brethren of the Alliance'.[37] At a special and acrimonious meeting of the Alliance in September

1931, Arthur sharply attacked the CMS for breaking the unity of the missions on the circumcision question and declared that a United African Church 'may be out of the question'. Had the CMS 'come into line', Arthur claimed, the government would have been faced with a solid bloc of mission opinion and thus given firmer support to the mission cause. Furthermore, Arthur was incensed at the participation of CMS adherents in the KCA, infected as it was by the 'spirit of bolshevism', and decried the unwillingness of Anglican missionaries to prevent their people from criticizing other missions. Finally, and perhaps behind much of his outrage, Arthur was concerned that the CMS might accept disaffected Presbyterian Christians into their own schools and churches, thus undermining further the authority and discipline of the CSM.[38]

And so the bishop was caught between the pressures of his own missionaries and African church leaders to change his policy and those of the other missions to hold firm. He promised Arthur not to suggest any Lucas-type plan for a Christianized circumcision ceremony to his African clergy, but further than that he could not go. Avoiding a major split in Anglican church was a far more pressing matter than preserving perhaps distant hopes for a united African church. In any event, he rationalized, differences over some questions of discipline should not prejudice unity. Thus in a second pastoral letter, issued on 12 October 1931, Heywood bowed to the dominant body of opinion in the CMS community. Female circumcision would no longer be forbidden if it was conducted privately, caused no physical injury and if all associated 'heathen practices' were abandoned. Thus the question raised so often at Kahuhia was answered – there was no CMS 'law' forbidding female circumcision. But, always the conciliator, Heywood issued a supplementary letter to those Pastorate Committees prepared to abolish female circumcision immediately. While he could not sanction excommunication of those who adhered to the mission's minimal standards, he did rule that where a Pastorate Committee decided to condemn female circumcision entirely, only persons of such persuasion could become members of that committee. He further agreed to support clergymen from such places who declined to baptize children whose parents supported circumcision.[39] In this action the CMS nodded to the hardliners but essentially reaffirmed a policy of moderation and, albeit with some reluctance, distinguished in this case between culture and Christianity. By doing so, they had quite simply preserved the integrity of their communities. Indeed to this day independent churches have little strength in those districts served by CMS stations of Kabete, Kahuhia, Weithaga and Kabare. To all of this, however, there was one major and dramatic exception, for at Kigari in Embu district the CMS experienced the head-on clash which Anglicans had elsewhere avoided. That the mission community at Kigari adopted the most rigid opposition to female circumcision provides a fascinating study in contrasts.

Established in 1910, the CMS station at Kigari remained under the supervision of John Comely from 1915 to 1938, and during these years the history of Kigari was decisively shaped by the attitudes and personality of this determined missionary. Born in rural Shropshire, Comely had worked as a young man in his family's milk business in London. After a brief and abortive term as a missionary among the Dinka of southern Sudan, he read for a degree at Cambridge and was appointed to Kigari as a CMS missionary in 1915. There he and his wife lived a life of Spartan and self-sacrificing simplicity. He shot game for local people during the famine of 1918, loaned them money for taxes, and pioneered in coffee growing when it was still illegal in other parts of Kikuyu Province. In these and other ways he won a good deal of affection and gratitude from the people of the area.[40] Yet he was a person of great strictness and unyielding determination once he had made up his mind on an issue. Thus he had been 'led by prayer' in 1929 to exclude KCA members from the Pastorate Committee in Kigari. But he was not altogether insensitive to African opinion and on occasion delayed taking a stand until he was sure he had the support of leading Christians.

This was the case in the female circumcision issue. Despite his own strong objections to the practice, when the promulgation of the bishop's first letter produced a strong negative reaction, especially in Kigari's outschools, Comely had copies of the letter withdrawn and by March of 1930 had decided that its instructions could not be applied. Thereafter tension over the issue subsided.[41] By the end of the year, however, Comely found his own objections to 'the unclean thing' matched by the growing doubts of a group of his leading elders. With the support of men such as Petero Gacewa, the medical assistant, Johana Muturi, recently ordained deacon and outschool teachers Musa Njiru and Paul Gatema, he felt able to press the matter. By January 1931 he felt 'led by prayer to see that either circumcision must go in its present form or the church will lose its power and disappear. It is a sign of a covenant and the conditions are of darkness.' Thus on 23 January, Comely and his church elders unanimously ruled that any communicant allowing female circumcision in his or her family would be stricken from the church roll and that all candidates for baptism or confirmation had to repudiate the custom.[42]

The response to these decisions was immediate and represented in Comely's words 'nothing less than a crash'. Within a month thirteen out of thirty-eight outschools were closed and eighteen out of sixty teachers had left the mission. Particularly significant was the reaction at the larger centres. At one outschool where a congregation of five hundred usually worshipped, only twenty remained. At Kagaari, one of the largest outschools, all of the teachers and evangelists joined the opposition, while at Ena only two teachers and three or four students remained by the end of February. In both of these places and others, demands were made that the mission leave and turn over the school and equipment to local people. When these demands were refused, church services were disrupted and school furniture removed by force. Those who remained loyal to the mission were subjected to intense pressure and abuse. Comely reported that they were regarded as outlaws, frequently removed from their land, beaten and threatened with losing their wives. Week after week, Comely dutifully recorded in the Kigari Log Book the decimation of fifteen years' work.[43] Given the absence of other political issues such as the loss of land and the lack of much political activity before 1929, the reaction at Kigari indicates just how potent the circumcision issue itself really was.

Steadfastly Comely resisted all efforts at compromise. He regarded as 'a great blow' a suggestion from the bishop that he consider allowing the minor operation. A local African proposal to have Christian girls circumcised at a different time than the usual ceremony was likewise ignored. And when Chief Arthur Mairani, himself a firm Christian and an opponent of female circumcision, agreed to the compromise suggestion of Lambert, the District Commissioner, that he supervise the circumcision of *infant* girls of Christian parents, Comely promptly put him under church discipline.[44] Thus there was no way out and the situation continued to deteriorate. In 1932 Lambert reported an 'extreme distrust of the mission by the people and an almost universal antagonism to the Pastorate Committee'. School attendance fell from 1,734 in 1930 to 346 in 1931. Adult baptisms dropped from 107 in 1930 to fifty-four a year later and only fourteen in 1932.[45] Thus Comely's adamant refusal to compromise − despite numerous opportunities − resulted in an estrangement at Kigari far more profound than at any other CMS station.

But in addition to the circumcision issue, there were at Kigari a series of 'amplifiers', issues not in themselves fundamental but capable of aggravating the crisis. One of these was Comely's almost total political isolation in Embu. The anti-circumcision efforts of the Presbyterians and the AIM in Kiambu had received the strong support of the most important chiefs in the district, all of whom were associated with the moderate and pro-government Kikuyu Association. But in Embu the chiefs, with the exception of Arthur Mairani, vigorously opposed Comely's position on female circumcision in alliance with an increasingly militant branch of the Kikuyu Central Association. When the KCA in Embu split in 1932 into moderate and radical factions, it was primarily young ex-CMS adherents who constituted the more militant wing, described by Lambert as having a 'pan-African anti-European bias'. Under the leadership of Kanini wa Ireri, they found a potent issue in the circumcision question and at one point demanded that the mission positively require the rite of its members. But the moderates were little comfort to the CMS either. Their leader, Kamwochere wa Ndhiga, had been sent to prison on evidence supplied by Chief Arthur for holding unauthorized meetings to collect money with which to buy back mission property including Kigari. Nor could Lambert, who was trying hard to establish the modified form of circumcision as standard practice in the district, support Comely whose efforts meant nothing but trouble for himself.[46]

Comely's only ally in the struggle was a narrow circle of elders, most of whom served on the Kigari Pastorate Committee. This body had remained substantially unchanged since 1924 and ninety per cent of its members were men from Kigari itself. Thus when CMS adherents at Kigari's many outstations received the abrupt order to give up female circumcision, they experienced it as a directive from outsiders, for it had been issued by a body on which they were not represented. Most of the teacher-catechists who served these outlying centres were likewise men from Kigari. Thus, the *aregi*, those who refused, were rejecting not only the rule about circumcision but outside control over the schools and churches which their initiative and energy had created. The dissidents attempted to regain their autonomy by expelling those who had avowed female circumcision, many of whom were resident on the land they cultivated only by permission of its owner, and by claiming ownership of the school and churches to which they frequently had legal title. With Comely on furlough during much of 1932, Kigari was under the missionary supervision of Rampley, who enlarged the Pastorate Committee from seventeen to thirty members to ensure a broader representation, a move which did encourage some return to the mission.[47] Thus the perception of outside interference amplified the impact of Comely's adamant position on circumcision.

So too did Kigari's educational backwardness. Comely's intense fear of an overemphasis on education and his persistent refusal to accept government or Local Native Council grants for his schools, 'on the grounds that the schools are in a special sense God's', meant that the standard of education remained very low. Of seventy-nine students on the roll of the central school at Kigari in 1933–4, twelve were in Standard III, thirteen in Standard II, twelve in Standard I, and forty-two in sub-standard classes. Only three teachers in the entire Kigari system had any formal teacher training. So poor was the education offered there that the District Commissioner had difficulty finding sufficient qualified students to fill Embu's quota in the government primary school at Kagumo. Even his most loyal supporters allowed that in this matter Comely had done harm to people of Embu.[48] The continued growth of independent schools in Embu district, Education Department and administrative officials agreed, was directly traceable to Comely's refusal to cooperate with the government in educational matters.[49] It was also becoming an embarrassing political question. The policy in Embu – to withhold financial assistance from the independents in the hope that they would collapse – was based on the existence of a reasonably efficient mission educational system and one that was receptive to government direction and assistance. Comely's continued intransigence clearly endangered this policy as the demands of the independent schools for government assistance could hardly be denied if the mission was unwilling to utilize available funds. Only a virtual ultimatum from the CMS Secretary and bishop – accept government aid or be removed from Kigari – persuaded Comely to capitulate, though even then he fought a rearguard action to maintain strict control over the use of those funds.[50] By the time he died in 1938, a teacher training centre had been established and a start made towards improving the standard of education in Embu, an ironic spin-off of the circumcision crisis that Comely's actions had done so much to precipitate.

It was too late, however, to prevent the permanent rupture of the CMS community at Kigari. Although Comely and his elders were ultimately required to conform to the bishop's second letter, their actions had by 1935 fostered at least six independent schools in the vicinity of Kigari, while the number of mission outschools dropped from thirty-eight in 1930 to twenty-two in 1934. Former CMS adherents also swelled the ranks of the Salvation Army which had been introduced into Embu in 1928 by migrant labourers returning from Nairobi and other towns.[51] It was an ideal protest vehicle for the dissidents as it combined the prestige of a European-sponsored mission without interfering white supervision. The Salvation Army sent no European-sponsored missionaries to Embu, and polygamists and those who had left the CMS over female circumcision easily became members.

The CMS experience thus casts some interesting light on the circumcision controversy. Though there were plenty of tensions within mission communities and in the larger colonial society, this particular clash was hardly inevitable. Through a policy of nuance, studied ambiguity and accommodation, the CMS had for the most part maintained in somewhat uneasy juxtaposition people with a wide range of responses to the process of cultural change. There were the mission stalwarts such as those at Kabete who had come to a firm rejection of circumcision, the educated dissidents at Kahuhia who saw no necessary incompatibility between circumcision and Christianity and the compromisers of Kabare who actively sought a measure of reconciliation between their traditional culture and their new faith. As to the crisis itself, culture not politics seems to have been its driving force and the circumcision issue a sufficient 'cause' for the emergence of independent schools and churches. The major real difference, after all, between the situation at CMS Kabete

149

and CSM Kikuyu or between the CMS at Kahuhia and the AIM at Githumu was mission policy on the circumcision question. There is little evidence to suggest that mission adherents saw the issue primarily as an occasion for more fundamental political or other protest, for where a break with the mission occurred, it was usually an action taken with reluctance and only as a last resort. The independents regarded themselves not so much as protesters but as Christians whose 'old European helpers had cast them off'.[52] Yet the very success of the CMS in retaining the loyalty of its own potential 'independents' meant that more than any other mission it was forced to confront the consequences of its rivals' failure.

THE CMS AND THE INDEPENDENTS

Although outside Kigari the CMS had spawned very few independent schools and churches, it soon became apparent that the mission would have to define its attitude towards these emergent groups. The attempt to do so represented a last chance for the Protestant missions as a whole to repair the damage to their communities which the circumcision controversy had occasioned. Several contradictory possibilities emerged in the course of CMS inter-action with the independents. On the one hand, friendly relations growing out of the CMS's more conciliatory stand on the circumcision issue were not out of the question. The CMS might have been able to woo a portion of the independents into its own community, or at least establish a degree of Anglican influence among them, thus mitigating what many Europeans regarded as both a religious and a political danger. Yet any serious CMS negotiations with the independents greatly intensified the already considerable antagonism between the Anglicans and the other major missions in Kikuyuland. Most of the independents, after all, had been members of non-Anglican churches which came to consider CMS overtures to the rebels as a stab in the back.

By early 1933 the various independent schools and churches had begun to organize themselves into loose regional groupings. Committees were formed in Kiambu, Fort Hall and South Nyeri Districts to coordinate the activities of the individual schools and churches in these areas.[53] During 1933 several of these groups approached one or another of the Protestant missions for certain specific and limited assistance, primarily training for their teachers and pastors. Their 'independent' status did not, apparently, lessen their felt need for a sense of religious legitimacy associated with a mission connexion. It was still a colonial world. Given recent events, it is not surprising that they chose to approach the Anglican mission. The most important of these requests came from the Independent Schools Committee of Fort Hall which asked that several of its members be admitted to the CMS Divinity School 'to be taught how to baptize in our schools'. While these men were being trained, the Committee further requested that 'a good black man be elected by you to come to baptize our people who are ready for Baptism'. They were careful to make clear that after training and ordination, their men 'would not in any way be subject to the jurisdiction of the CMS'.[54] Thus with recent history very much in mind, they sought a friendly relationship with the CMS but one based on full equality. One of the rules of the association, in fact, was to be that no one could speak against the Europeans or refuse their advice 'unless the Europeans refuse to be friendly or try to force ... any course of action'. Other such requests for assistance came from a South Nyeri committee and a number of individual independent schools.[55]

The general attitude within the CMS to these overtures was favourable. Missionaries saw it as an opportunity to prevent the development of an independent church with 'heretical tendencies'. Or, as one of them put it: 'If we do not do something for them, they will go to Rome or form a schismatic church of their own.' Leading African churchmen as well urged the bishop to respond sympathetically to these requests.[56] The other Protestant missions were equally concerned about the development of an 'Ethiopian church' outside the orbit of European control. As a result, they agreed that the CMS could render assistance in the form of theological training and ordination to the Fort Hall Independent Schools Committee but insisted that the independents be fully incorporated into the Church of England.[57] In other words, they demanded that the independents completely disband as a condition of CMS assistance.

The non-Anglican missions had agreed to CMS negotiations with the independents with some reluctance, for, if successful, it would have given the CMS a foothold in what had been formerly CSM or AIM areas, thus representing a breakdown of the old 'spheres of influence' system, whereby a mission exercised a religious and educational monopoly in its own area. This policy had recently come under attack by the government and by African Christians who argued for its abolition on the eminently reasonable grounds that they had not been consulted when spheres were defined. Moreover, the circumcision crisis had itself weakened the sphere system by provoking a considerable movement of mission adherents from the stricter CSM or AIM to the more lenient CMS. In order to preserve what was left of the spheres policy, the non-Anglican missions insisted that this arrangement with the independents be limited to the Fort Hall area,[58] apparently hoping that the other independent groups would drift back to the missions with which they had broken.

Although the Fort Hall Independent Schools Committee publicly reaffirmed its earlier decision not to compromise its independent status, its leadership did agree to enter into negotiations with the CMS. In the discussions that followed, however, the issue of ultimate authority in the independent schools and churches seems to have been blurred. The bishop assured them for example that 'a school can be carried on by a Committee of Independent people who would have control over their own buildings, and choose their own teachers, and make their own rules for the children.'[59] This may have been a deliberate move on the part of the CMS to ensure successful negotiations or it may have represented a tactical compromise by the independents to gain the training which they seemed to want so badly. In any event, it was announced in February 1934 that the Independent Schools Committee had given satisfactory assurances regarding their loyalty to Anglican church discipline and episcopal authority.[60] It remained then only to choose those members of the independent churches who were to undergo theological training, leading to ordination.

Yet when the independents submitted the names of three men – David Maina of Fort Hall (ex-CMS), Elijah Kibaci of Kiambu (ex-CSM) and Stefano Wacira of Nyeri (ex-CSM) – in May of 1934, there was a major outcry by the non-Anglican missions. In the first place, they were offended that two of the proposed candidates were from outside Fort Hall district, a fact which they felt threatened the breakdown of the spheres policy throughout Kikuyuland and violated the agreement that only the Fort Hall area was being considered in these discussions. But they were even more outraged that the CMS would consider training two ex-CSM men, both of whom had been excommunicated for their political activities and bitter opposition to the church policy on circumcision, for they felt that such an action seriously undermined the authority of the CSM. Bluntly threatening the end of all hopes for a United African Church, by now a common tactic, the Presbyterian missionaries regarded the CMS actions as 'simply an insult' and observed that the Europeans feel it a 'real slap in the face'. Arguing that the independents 'simply want ordination to run an Ethiopian church', they considered it 'the maddest possible thing to do to give them standing'.[61] Here again was the conflict between a paternalism of suppression and one of conciliation. The ends were similar, but the divergence in means occasioned considerable bitterness and recrimination.

It is conceivable, though by no means certain, that the CMS would have been able to come to terms with the independents, had it not been for this extreme pressure from the other missions. After all, the Fort Hall Independent Schools Committee, which by late 1934 had become the more inclusive Kikuyu Independent Schools Association (KISA) was not a militant organization. Unlike certain other independent groups, it did not require female circumcision but left the matter up to individual choice and stressed religious and educational rather than political objectives. There are hints that the CMS was considering an arrangement with them short of their outright incorporation into the Church of England.[62] Such a policy would surely have been in the interests of the CMS as it would have tempered competition between the Anglicans and the independents and would have allowed for considerable CMS influence within the independent organization. In any event, this policy became untenable in light of the opposition of the CSM and other missions. Faced with a clear choice between loyalty to their fellow European missionaries and rendering assistance to the independents, the CMS chose the former by agreeing to insist that all independent candidates for ordination must become members of the Church of England before being ordained. By the end of 1934 this position had been made clear to the KISA with the result that they broke off negotiations with the CMS, for they refused to thus compromise the independence and autonomy of their organization.[63]

After 1934 the KISA turned to Daniel W. Alexander, Archbishop of the African Orthodox Church in South Africa, for the theological training and ecclesiastical legitimacy they could not obtain from the CMS, which soon found itself, therefore, in active competition with the KISA for students and adherents in Kikuyuland. By 1936, for example, KISA was responsible for a considerable drop in CMS school attendance in Fort Hall district, since one of the main attractions of the independent schools was their willingness to teach English even in the very lowest grades. At the same time the CMS was taking special measures to establish itself in the area south of the Maragua River where Archbishop Alexander had centred his activities. Two years later the Anglican African Church Council took a hard line towards the African Orthodox Church, refusing to recognize as valid the ordinations, baptisms, communion or instruction classes of the independent church.[64] Ironically enough, the CMS which had coped so successfully with internal dissident opinion could not escape association with other mission groups in Kenya and was driven ultimately into a hostile relationship with the independents outside their own communities.

FOOTNOTES

1. F. B. Welbourn, *East African Rebels* (London, 1961).
2. John Middleton, 'Kenya: Changes in African Life, 1912–1945', *History of East Africa*, eds Vincent Harlow *et al.*, (Oxford, 1965), II, pp. 362–6.
3. Carl Rosberg and John Nottingham, *The Myth of Mau Mau* (New York, 1966), pp. 120–1; A. J. Temu, *British Protestant Missions* (London, 1972), pp. 154–64.
4. For descriptions of the ceremonies and their significance see Jomo Kenyatta, *Facing Mount Kenya* (New York, 1970), pp. 125–48; John Middleton, *The Kikuyu and the Kamba of Kenya* (London, 1965), pp. 56–9; S. K. Gathiriga, *Miikarire ya Agikuyu* [The ways of life of the Kikuyu people] (London, 1959); Godfrey Muriuki, *A History of the Kikuyu 1500–1900* (Nairobi, 1974), pp. 118–22; L. S. B. Leakey, 'The Kikuyu Problem of the Initiation of Girls', *Journal of the Royal Anthropological Institute* (1931), pp. 277–85.
5. For this conclusion see a survey taken in 1973 and reported in Jocelyn Murray, 'The Kikuyu Female Circumcision Controversy', Ph.D. Dissertation, UCLA, 1974, pp. 334–59.
6. *Muigwithania*, June 1929; May 1929; PCEA: Minutes of Nyeri Native District Council, 4 June 1921. For a vivid account in fiction of one girl's struggle with the problem, see James Ngugi wa Thiong'o, *The River Between* (Nairobi, 1965).
7. Particularly active in detailing the medical effects of the operation was Dr H. R. A. Philp, a CSM doctor at Tumutumu. See his 'Native Gynaecology' *Journal of the Kenya Medical Service* 1:8 (1924). Also, KNA: EBU/32, Misc. Correspondence, Resolutions of United Conference of Missionary Societies, 1918; M. C. Hooper, *Property in the Highlands of East Africa*; Notes on Beecher's copy of Leakey, 'The Kikuyu Problem', op. cit.
8. PCEA: G/2, Kikuyu Native Church Laws, June 1922.
9. W. B. Anderson, 'The Development of Leadership in Protestant Churches in Central Kenya', an unpublished paper. See also CMS, Acc. 85, Karimu to 'all Kikuyu Christians', 1 August 1927; RH: Coryndon 17/3, Circumcision of Girls.
10. Hooper Papers, MCH to Mother, 18 September 1918.
11. KNA: DC/EBU/8/2, Watkins to All Sr. Commissioners, 24 September 1925; DC/KBU/7/3, DC Kiambu to DC Fort Hall, 1 April 1927; PC/CP.8/1/1, DC Fort Hall to PC, 4 January 1929; Embu LNC, 25 November 1925; South Nyeri LNC, 8–10 March 1927.
12. The Presbyterian apologia is found in Church of Scotland Mission, *Memorandum by the Kikuyu Mission Council on Female Circumcision*, mimeo, 1931, while the most recent nationalist view of the crisis is in Temu, *British Protestant Missions*, op. cit., pp. 154–64.
13. Rosberg and Nottingham, *The Myth of Mau Mau*, op. cit., pp. 116–17; CSM, *Memorandum*, pp. 32–3.
14. PCEA: D/2, Minutes of a Conference of Kikuyu Church Elders, 8–12 March 1929.
15. PCEA: G/2, Arthur to Barlow, 10 November 1929; KNA: PC/CP.8/7/1, Kangethe to 'all the chiefs of Kikuyu country', 19 August 1929.
16. PCEA: G/2, Anonymous letter to Arthur, 8 August 1929.
17. CSM, *Memorandum*, pp. 46–55; PCEA: G/2, Arthur to DC, Kiambu, 6 November 1929; KNA: PC/CP.8/1/1, Scott to Colonial Secretary, 10 January 1930; FH/10–11, Fort Hall District Annual Report, 1930, 1931.
18. This paragraph is based on the diary of the Rev. Cecil Bewes, then a young missionary at Kabete, who kindly allowed the authors access to this important source. Entries for 17 June, 23 June, 24 October, 3 December, and 29 December 1929.
19. Bewes diary, 3 December 1929; KNA: CMS 1/637, Embu Log Book, 4 October 1929.
20. PCEA G/2, Meeting of Representatives of Protestant Missions, 17 October 1929; Bowden diary, 30 January 1929.
21. Bishop's letter of 1 January 1930 in CSM, *Memorandum*.

22. PCEA: Native Church Matters, Kikuyu Church Annual Report, 1930.
23. Bewes diary, 29 December 1929, early 1930; Interviews 9, 11, 15, 17, 18; KNA: PC/CP.8/7/1, DC Kiamba to PC, 1 May 1931.
24. CMS/Acc.85, Gacanja to Hooper, 20 April 1926; Kahuhia Pastorate Elders' Meeting, Minutes of 30 November 1928; Murray interview with Mrs M. C. Hooper, 26 August 1971.
25. Hooper Papers, Soles to Hooper, 26 January 1930.
26. Kahuhia Pastorate Elders' Meeting, Minutes for 14 March 1930 and 26 May 1930.
27. T. F. C. Bewes, 'The Work of the Christian Church among the Kikuyu', *International Affairs*, XXIX (1953), pp. 319–30. Also Murray interviews with Kahuhia elders.
28. KNA:FH/9–11, Fort Hall District Annual Reports, 1929–31; AIM Archives, Davis to Campbell, 25 November 1931 (kindly supplied by David Sandgren); Interviews 3, 22, 23, 26, 28.
29. KNA: CMS 1/639, Kabare Log Book, 22–9 January 1930.
30. KNA: PC/CP.8/1/2, Lambert to LaFontaine, 15 July 1931; PCEA: Loose Papers, Heywood to Arthur, 6, 16 June 1931; T. O. Ranger, 'Missionary Adaptation of African Religious Institutions: The Masasi Case', *The Historical Study of African Religion*, eds T. O. Ranger and Isaria Kimambo (Berkeley, 1972), pp. 221–47.
31. Kabare Log Book, 21 July 1931.
32. Walter H. Sangree, *Age, Prayer and Politics in Tiriki, Kenya* (London, 1966), pp. 138–40, 150.
33. Kabare Log Book, February 1937.
34. Murray interviews with Jessie Samuel, 8 February 1971 and Sylvia Bewes.
35. CCK: Minutes of Representative Council, 3 September 1931; AIM: letter to Campbell, 4 September 1931.
36. See M. G. Capon, *Towards Unity in Kenya* (Nairobi, 1962). In 1924 a larger and more inclusive body, the Kenya Missionary Council, was formed to coordinate mission approaches to the government on educational and other matters, but it did not supersede the original Alliance.
37. PCEA: Loose Papers, Arthur to Bishop, 12 June 1931.
38. PCEA: D/3, J. W. Arthur, Address to the Representative Council, September 1931; AIM: letter to Campbell, 4 September 1931.
39. KNA: PC/CP.8/1/2, Bishop of Mombasa to Clergy and Pastorate Committees, 12 October 1931.
40. Murray interviews with Ruth Comely, Cicely Hooper, Canon Musa Njiru; Daudi N. Petero, *Jubilee A. C. Kigari and A. C. Kabare, 1910–1960* (1960); Amos Kiroro, 'Church Growth among the Embu of Mount Kenya', an unpublished paper, 1968.
41. KNA: DC/EBU/1/2, Embu District Annual Report 1930.
42. Embu Log Book, 7, 23 January 1931.
43. Embu Log Book; CMS, 'Historical Records', 1931–2, p. 37. KNA: DC/EBU/1/2, Embu District Annual Report 1931.
44. Embu Log Book, 18 May, 9 July, 16 July 1931; KNA: PC/CP.8/1/2, Lambert to Rampley, 9 July 1931.
45. KNA: DC/EBU/1/2, Embu District Annual Reports, 1930, 1931, 1932; Embu Log Book.
46. KNA: DC/EBU/1/2, Embu District Annual Reports, 1931–4; Embu Log Book, December 1931.
47. KNA: CMS 1/370, Rampley to Pitt-Pitts, 1932; Embu Log Book, 11 December 1932.
48. Donovan, 'Report of Kigari Schools' in Embu Log Book; KNA: DC/EBU/1/2, Embu District Annual Reports, 1933, 1934; Kiroro, 'Church Growth', op. cit.; Murray interview with Canon Musa Njiru; Embu Log Book, 25 July 1935.
49. KNA: DC/EBU/9/1, Donovan to Director of Education, 1 April 1935; Vidal to Director of Education, 12 March 1935.

50. See correspondence in KNA: CMS 1/378.
51. KNA: DC/EBU/9/1, Lindsay to PC Nyeri, 6, 24 March 1935; CMS, 'Historical Records', 1931–2, p. 37; Donovan, 'Report on Kigari Schools', op. cit.
52. PCEA: Council Memoranda Reports, Minutes of Kahuhia Conference, 13–16 October 1933.
53. PCEA: D/3, Barlow to Heywood, 8 November 1933. On the Kikuyu independent churches, see John Anderson, *The Struggle for the School* (London, 1970), pp. 112–31; F. B. Welbourn, *East African Rebels* op. cit.; Rosberg and Nottingham, *The Myth of Mau Mau*, op. cit., pp. 125–31; J. B. Ndingu, 'Gituamba and Kikuyu Independency in Church and School', *Ngano*, ed. B. G. McIntosh (Nairobi, 1969), pp. 131–52.
54. PCEA: D/3, David Maina and Justus Kangethe to Heywood, 5 July 1933; Minutes of a Meeting of Government Officers with Independent Schools Committee, 28 June 1933.
55. PCEA: D/3, Barlow to Heywood, 8 November 1933; Minutes of a Representative Council of the Alliance, 14–15 August 1933; CMS, 'Historical Records', 1933–4, p. 60; Council Memoranda Reports, Minutes of Kahuhia Conference, 13–16 October 1933.
56. CMS, 'Historical Records', 1933–4, p. 60; PCEA: D/3, Butcher to Irvine, 6 August 1934; KNA: CMS 1/360, Minutes of African Church Council, 18–19 August 1933.
57. PCEA: Council Memoranda Reports, Minutes of Kahuhia Conference, 13–16 October 1933.
58. PCEA: Representative Council of the Alliance, 1930–4, Scott to Heads of Missions, 19 August 1933; Council Memoranda Reports, Minutes of Kahuhia Conference, 13–16 October 1933; D/3, Ed. Cooperation in the Fort Hall Area, 11 September 1933; AIM: Davis to Campbell, 25 November 1931.
59. PCEA: D/3, Statement by KISA Delegate, 13–16 October 1933; Heywood to Kangethe, 27 December 1933.
60. PCEA: D/3, Representative Council of the Alliance, 23 August 1934.
61. Ibid.; KNA: CMS 1/114, Clive to Arthur, 8 July 1934.
62. PCEA: D/3, Heywood to Kangethe, 27 December 1933; Butcher to Irvine, 6 August 1934; KNA: CMS/1/103, Minutes of the Central Council of the ACC, 30 July 1934.
63. PCEA: D/3, Minutes of Conference of Alliance Missions, 21–22 September 1934; KNA: CMS/1/102, Minutes of Highlands District of ACC, 5 December 1934; DC/EBU/4/5, Report and Constitutions of KISA, 1938; UCN–RPA: C/1/1, African Independent Church and School at Gituamba, transcript of interview with Hezekiah Gichui.
64. KNA: CMS 1/288, Beecher to Smith, 4 August 1936; CMS 1/103, Beecher to Owen, 27 January 1936; CMS 1/105, Minutes of Coast District of the ACC, 23–4 August 1938.

CHAPTER IX

҉҉҉҉҉҉҉҉҉҉҉҉҉҉҉҉҉҉҉҉҉҉

Conclusion: Conflict and Cohesion in Mission Communities

Not unnaturally, the study of colonial societies and institutions has emphasized the elements of conflict and discontinuity. Thus the initial thrust of the new African historiography concerned itself with resistance, protest and nationalist movements of all kinds leading ultimately to the demise of colonial societies and the emergence of new independent states. Mission communities have mirrored the tensions of colonial society in many respects. In fact, part of what has given mission history its contemporary vitality has been the attempt to locate the roots of those many independent church movements which grew out of the strains within mission communities or the dissatisfactions with mission Christianity. Much of the voluminous literature on the subject has emphasized the element of political or social protest, and thus the search for origins has focused on missionary attitudes and policies on matters of race, education and Africanization of the church hierarchy. A few of the older studies as well as many of the more recent ones have shifted the emphasis to cultural conflict generally, and more particularly to the incompatibility of mission Christianity and traditional religious sensibilities. Horton's thesis on the inability of mission Christianity to meet the African needs for an instrumental religion of explanation, prediction and control has been the most general formulation of this approach. Robert Mitchell's examination of the origins of the Aladura movements of western Nigeria found the roots of schism in the inability of mission churches to provide an adequate religious response to the practical problems of life – healing, unemployment, sterility – and in the incompatibility between Christian notions of evil as the breach of an abstract moral principle and traditional views of evil as real and personal power. Central African studies in particular have stressed the inadequacy of mission response to the problems of witchcraft in explaining the popularity of Zionist independent churches.[1]

Yet these tensions by no means always broke through the surface in the form of independent churches, and to study them only at the point of rupture is to miss what David Barrett has called 'the rest of the iceberg' and to avoid examining the ways in which some conflicts could be resolved in colonial settings. Within the CMS communities of Kenya the question of authority, for example, continued to disturb the mission, from the protest of the Bombay Africans in the 1880s to the insistence of the African Church Council in the 1930s for greater power in the affairs of the church. And throughout this half-century, missionaries remained reluctant to devolve the building of an African church into African hands. Issues involving the pace, extent and direction of cultural change likewise generated an undercurrent of tension which occasionally erupted into crisis, most dramatically in the circumcision controversy. That affair illustrated clearly the dual sources of cultural conflict within the mission, for while it represented primarily a 'protest of conservation' aimed at defending a vital feature of traditional life, there were also elements of a 'protest of transformation' concerned to enhance Kikuyu ability to cope with the modern world through the provision of more and better education.[2] Such internal tensions were frequently amplified through inter-action with their larger colonial setting. It was in part the establishment of the Protectorate in 1895 that led to the undermining of William Jones' authority at Rabai and thus to a mass resignation of CMS employees. And African resistance to an Anglican ecclesiastical province drew much from their opposition to closer union, which they felt would consolidate white control over their lives. Yet all of this occurred without provoking separatism.

Thus there arises the problem of cohesion and continuity in mission communities and churches. So much scholarly attention has been paid to separatist movements that a major issue confronting mission history now involves explaining the continued attractiveness of main-line mission communities for many people despite their internal conflicts and the competition from independent movements. In Kenya, for example, while the independents have been active and numerous, they have hardly swept the field. By mid-1972 they represented about 14.6 per cent of Kenya's population and twenty-two per cent of those affirming some sort of Christian identity. The Western churches, according to the most recent survey, 'are still growing at a phenomenal rate of five per cent per year'.[3] While the question of the persistence of mission communities and churches involves issues of enormous complexity, it may not be out of place here to speculate briefly on some possible avenues of further research.

One obvious explanation for this element of institutional and cultural continuity in modern history lies in the view that mission communities represented a rational adaptation to a colonial situation and to the process of modernization. These communities, after all, were everywhere viewed as highly important mediators of modernity, a means to overcoming the power and status gap between Europeans and Africans. A recent study has suggested that many Igbo Christians of an orthodox persuasion still regard independent churches as backward-looking and full of 'ignorant dirty people', while mission Christianity is seen as both progressive and consonant with traditional values.[4] Even among the Scottish communities in Kenya most heavily affected by the circumcision crisis, church and school attendance regained previous levels within a few years and continued to increase steadily throughout the colonial period, while independent schools were never able to cater for more than a small percentage of school-age children in Kikuyuland. By the 1930s in Kenya, the status and material interests of not a few Africans were very closely linked to their respective mission communities which provided them with respectability, employment opportunities, the chance for appointment to chiefships, and generally the most advanced education available in the colony. Moreover, a mission connexion imparted a legitimacy that even the independents seemed reluctant to forego and represented an important source of external funding for their churches and teachers for their schools. It was also largely through missions that the government grants were distributed to village schools which were by then a source of much pride and hope for local communities. The missions also mediated religious values and concepts that operated on a scale commensurate with the enlarging world of political and economic intercourse to colonized people who did not necessarily know that the colonial world was coming to an end. In a variety of ways, then – both religious and secular, cultural and material – mission communities remained an important means by which subordinate peoples could tap the resources of their rulers.

This is a 'modernist' viewpoint which suggests that mission communities flourished during the colonial era and even after because they responded to and articulated with the new world of the twentieth century. But could these institutions really be viable unless they also established contact with the old world of African values, concepts, sensibilities and patterns of behaviour? There is, in fact, some evidence for the view that mission Christianity practised in mission churches could also be adapted to traditional ways of life and thought. It might even serve on occasion to support and enhance traditional identities and values by casting them in a modern and Christian framework. It has been argued, for example, that Christianity among the Igbo, particularly in its patriarchal Roman Catholic variant, served to reinforce the values of male dominance which new and independent economic opportunities for women tended to undermine.[5] Others have suggested that Christianity came to express the collective aspiration of certain peoples, at least as articulated by their elites. Margaret Read has remarked that a number of Christian Ngoni began to articulate the traditional concept of an Ngoni mission or task in terms of the Christian missionary purpose.[6] Or in Buganda Christianity as well as Islam symbolized for many that greater destiny towards which their country had been striving for centuries, while conversion to Catholicism among the Padhola served to distinguish their identity from that of their Baganda and largely Protestant conquerors.[7]

At a popular level, it seems clear that the Africanization of Christianity was not a process exclusive to the independent churches. African Christians frequently made unplanned and perhaps unconscious adjustments of concept and practice within the framework of mission communities and without the inspiration or approval of their European mentors. One such pattern of adjustment was simple eclecticism, a legacy perhaps from a traditional habit of religious pragmatism. African clergymen who wore protective charms and communicants who consulted customary religious specialists put this pragmatism into practice and frequently subjected themselves to severe church discipline for doing so. In the eyes of African Christians, however, it was missionary absolutism, not Christianity, that created the problem. And with the proliferation of mission outstations after the First World War and the withdrawal of many missionaries into the central institutions of the church, this pattern of adjustment doubtless became easier.

The reinterpretation of Christian rites and practices in terms of traditional belief represents another mode of adaptation that was altogether possible within mission churches. African Dominican sisters in Rhodesia, we are told, regard themselves as equivalent to the traditional *mbonga*, virgins who served at the shrine of Mwari, the Shona High God. Professor Ranger has shown how baptism could become a healing rite and St Andrew a rain-giver, and how African clergy might on occasion be assimilated into the role of customary religious practitioners.[8] Indeed there was much in mission teaching, and especially in the Old Testament, that met African needs for an instrumental religion related to real 'this-worldly' problems. It has in fact been argued that mission Christianity on occasion adapted itself all too successfully to traditional modes of religious thought. Philip Turner claims to have found in Uganda Protestantism 'a form of Christianity which fits easily with many aspects

of traditional culture' in that it is ecclesiastically conservative, legalistic or prover-
bial in its use of the Bible and pragmatic in the sense of being essentially unconcerned with theological issues.[9] There is some evidence that adaptation may also
take the form of outright incorporation of traditional practices into the life of the
church. The *Rukwadzano* and *Wabvuwi*, Rhodesian Methodist associations of
women and men respectively, regularly experience miraculous healings and practice
exorcism during their meetings. That such phenomena normally occur in the
absence of missionaries and African pastors suggests that this is a popular adaptation from below, and the fact that participants justify their behaviour by reference
to New Testament parallels indicates that they feel it is unnecessary to venture
beyond the framework of mission Christianity to meet these needs.[10] Clearly, then,
a considerable range of cultural and religious adaptation was possible within mission
churches without provoking schism. We have perhaps under-estimated the extent
to which some Africans in some mission churches could find a real measure of
religious fulfilment even if they had to create it themselves.

Nor were missionaries themselves always an active obstacle to this sort of adaptation. There seems, in fact, to be some correlation between the extent to which
missionaries allowed or encouraged such adjustments and resistance to the attractions of independent churches. The relative absence of independency in Tanzania
may owe something to the leadership of men like Bishop Lucas whose efforts to
Christianize the male initiation rites around Masasi met with considerable success.
In his study of south Shona independent churches in Rhodesia, M. L. Daneel has
carefully compared the attitudes and policies of the Roman Catholic missions and
the Dutch Reformed Church Mission in an effort to explain why the former lost
far fewer adherents to the independents than the latter. He concluded that the
willingness of the Catholics to Christianize elements of Shona ritual and to be flexible in practice on matters such as polygamy, bride-wealth and ancestor worship
was the most important reason.[11] Certainly CMS flexibility on the circumcision
issue and its unwillingness to impose rigid standards on smoking and drinking
distinguished it from those missions whose posture on such cultural issues was more
unbending.

More generally, the willingness of the CMS authorities to compromise with their
dissident adherents and the ability of men like Price, Peel and Hooper to blur the
issue of authority was instrumental in preserving the integrity of CMS communities. During the period under study here, the institutionalization of means of
African participation in mission affairs roughly kept pace with African demands
for participation. The African Workers Council at Freretown was not suppressed;
an African Church Council was established in the aftermath of the troubles around
the turn of the century; and in the inter-war era the quickening pace of ordinations,
the decentralization of the ACC and the growing authority of Africans in local
church councils all indicated a new degree of responsiveness on the part of mission
authorities and a revival of an active Venn tradition after the long night of its
neglect.

With a foot in both worlds, then, mission communities represented an important
arena for the making of a new African culture. Despite the many strains and tensions which accompanied the process, they remained in many cases and for many
people institutions of sufficient flexibility and responsiveness to ensure their continuity to the present day.

FOOTNOTES

1. Robin Horton, 'African Conversion', *Africa*, XLI:2 (April 1971), pp. 85–108; R. C. Mitchell, 'Religious Protest and Social Change', in *Protest and Power in Black Africa*, eds Robert Rotberg and Ali Mazrui (New York, 1970) pp. 458–96; Jocelyn Murray, 'Inter-relationships Between Witchcraft Eradication Movements and Christianity in Central Africa', an unpublished paper.
2. For these categories, see Robert Rotberg and Ali Mazrui, *Protest and Power in Black Africa*, op. cit., p. 1185.
3. David B. Barrett, 'The Expansion of Christianity in Kenya, AD 1900–2000', in *Kenya Churches Handbook* (Kisumu, Kenya, 1973), pp. 157–77.
4. Frank Salamone, 'Continuity of Igbo Values After Conversion', *Missiology*, III:1 (January 1975), pp. 33–44.
5. Ibid.
6. Margaret Read, 'The Ngoni and Western Education', in *Colonialism in Africa*, ed. Victor Turner (Cambridge, 1971), III, p. 353.
7. D. A. Low, 'Converts and Martyrs in Bugunda', in *Christianity in Tropical Africa*, ed. G. Bäeta (Oxford, 1968), pp. 150–63; B. A. Ogot, 'On the Making of a Sanctuary', in *The Historical Study of African Religion*, eds T. O. Ranger and Isaria Kimambo (Berkeley, 1972), pp. 122–36.
8. Sister Mary Aquina Weinrich, 'An Aspect of the Development of the Religious Life in Rhodesia', in *Themes in the Christian History of Central Africa*, eds T. O. Ranger and John Weller (Berkeley, 1975), p. 227; T. O. Ranger, 'Missionary Adaptation of African Religious Institutions: The Masasi Case', in *The Historical Study of African Religions*, op. cit., pp. 231–3.
9. Philip Turner, 'The Wisdom of the Fathers and the Gospel of Christ', *Journal of Religion in Africa*, IV (1971), pp. 45–68.
10. Marshall Murphree, *Christianity and the Shona* (New York, 1969), pp. 73–7; F. D. Muzorewa, 'Through Prayer to Action: The Rukwadzano Women of Rhodesia', in *Themes in the Christian History of Central Africa*, op. cit., p. 258.
11. Ranger, 'Missionary Adaptation', op. cit.; M. L. Daneel, *Old and New in Southern Shona Independent Churches* (The Hague, 1971), I, pp. 244–65.

Bibliography

PRIMARY MATERIALS

I. *Archival Sources*

A. African Inland Mission Archives (AIM), Brooklyn, New York
B. Christian Council of Kenya Archives (CCK), Nairobi
C. Church Missionary Society Archives (CMS), London
   1. Main Archival Series
      a. CA 5 (to 1881)
         Letter Books (L)
         Mission Books (M)
         Original Letters (O)
      b. G3 A5 (since 1881)
         Letter Books (L)
         Précis Books (P)
         Original Letters (O)
   2. Historical Records
   3. Candidates' Papers
   4. Register of Candidates
   5. Annual Letters
   6. Accession 85: H.D. Hooper Papers
D. Edinburgh House Archives (EHA), London
E. Kenya National Archives (KNA), Nairobi
   1. Provincial and District Records
   2. Church Missionary Society Deposit
   3. Ministry of Education Deposit
F. Presbyterian Church of East Africa Archives (PCEA), Nairobi
G. Rhodes House Archives (RH), Oxford
H. University of Nairobi: Research Project Archives (UN:RPA), Nairobi

II. *Private Papers*

A. Rev. T. F. C. Bewes, Diary
B. Rev. H. K. Binns, Journal (available through the Co-operative Africana Microfilm Project, Center for Research Libraries, Chicago)
C. Miss Lorna Bowden, Diary and Letters (now on deposit in CMS Archives)
D. Rev. and Mrs H. D. Hooper, Letters and Papers
E. Saint John's Church, Kahuhia, Minutes of Elders' Meetings
F. Rev. George Wright, Diary

III. *Interviews*

A. Interviews by Robert W. Strayer
  1. Mrs May Wright, 24 October 1969
  2. Mrs M. C. Hooper, 27–29 October 1969
  3. Mr Harvey Cantrell, 30 October 1969
  4. Canon T. F. C. Bewes, 7 November 1969
  5. Archbishop Leonard Beecher, 2 December 1969
  6. Miss E. M. Wiseman, 17 January 1970
  7. Miss Mary Rickman, 17 January 1970
  8. Mr Evanson Muriithi, 27 January 1970
  9. Chief Josiah Njonjo, 28 January 1970
  10. Rev. Mbongo, 29 January 1970
  11. Mr Zakayo Muigai, 29 January 1970
  12. Mr Moses Njoroge wa Ruringa Chege, 30 January 1970
  13. Mr Ishmael Ithongo, 30 January 1970
  14. Mr Paul Muite wa Kamami, 30 January 1970
  15. Mr Jeremiah Njuria, 3 February 1970
  16. Mr Onesmus Muiruri, 3 February 1970
  17. Mr Zephaniah Boro, 3 February 1970
  18. Rev. Andrew Macua, 3 February 1970
  19. Rev. Paulo Mbatia, 5 February 1970
  20. Rev. Levi Gacanga, 6, 11 February 1970
  21. Canon Nathanael Gacira, 6 February 1970
  22. Mr Stefano Gikuri, 7 February 1970
  23. Mr Lazerus Gaceru, 7 February 1970
  24. Mr Nathaneal Mwanyagi, 7 February 1970
  25. Mr Jockton Kamonjo, 9 February 1970
  26. Mr Jason Githumbi, 9 February 1970
  27. Mr Daniel Mugetha, 9 February 1970
  28. Kiruri elders, 9 February 1970
      Mr Cornelius Karinga
      Mr John Gakobo
      Mr Jonathan Kiiru
      Mr Sampson Ndugire
      Mr Esbon Mbatia
  29. Mr Ben Nyahu, 10 February 1970
  30. Mr Elijah Gacanja, 10 February 1970
  31. Mr Stefano Gicui, 11 February 1970
  32. Mr Paulo Gatema and Mr William Njuguna, 13 February 1970
  33. Mr Petero Gacewa, 13 February 1970
B. Interviews by Jocelyn Murray
C. Saint Paul's Divinity College (SPDC), Limuru: Transcripts of interviews

IV. *Published Primary Materials*

A. Official Documents
    Parliamentary Papers
    British East Africa Protectorate, Education Commission, *Report* and *Evidence*,
    Nairobi, 1919
    Kenya Colony, Education Department, *Annual Reports*

B. Journals, Periodicals and Newspapers
    The Advertiser of East Africa, Nairobi
    Church Missionary Intelligencer, London
    Church Missionary Review, London
    Church Missionary Society, *Extracts of Annual Letters*, London
    East African Standard, Nairobi
    International Review of Missions, London
    Mombasa Diocesan Magazine, Mombasa
    Muigwithania, Nairobi
    Proceedings of the Church Missionary Society, London
    Taveta Chronicle, Taveta, Kenya
    Tangazo, Nairobi

C. Books and Articles
    Bewes, T. F. C., *Kikuyu Conflict: Mau Mau and Christian Witness*, London, 1953.
    ——, 'The Work of the Christian Church Among the Kikuyu', *International Affairs*, XXIX, 1953.
    Boyes, J., *A White King in East Africa*, New York, 1912.
    Britton, J., 'Missionary Task in Kenya', *IRM*, 1923.
    Burton, R. F., *The Lake Regions of Central Africa*, London, 1860, 2 vols.
    ——, *Zanzibar: City, Island and Coast*, London, 1872, 2 vols.
    Buxton, T. F. V., 'Glimpses of Work in British East Africa', *CMI*, 1905.
    ——, 'Industrial Work in East Africa', *CMR*, 1909.
    Church of Scotland Mission, *Memorandum of Female Circumcision*, Nairobi, 1931.
    Cranworth, Lord, *Profit and Sport in East Africa*, London, 1919.
    Crawford, E. May, *By the Equator's Snowy Peaks: A Record of Medical Missionary Work and Travel in British East Africa*, London, 1913.
    Dawson, E. C., *James Hannington, First Bishop of Eastern Equatorial Africa: A History of His Life and Work*, London, 1887.
    ——, *The Last Journals of Bishop Hannington*, London, 1888.
    Dougall, J. W. C., 'The Case For and Against Mission Schools', *Journal of the African Society*, 1939.
    ——, *Missionary Education in Kenya and Uganda*, London, 1936.
    'The East Africa Mission', *CMI*, 1881.
    Eliot, Sir Charles, *The East Africa Protectorate*, London, 1905.
    Fitzgerald, W. W. A., *Travels in the Coastland of British East Africa and the Islands of Zanzibar and Pemba*, London, 1898.
    Frere, Sir Bartle, *East Africa as a Field for Missionary Labour*, London, 1874.
    Gregory, John Walter, *The Foundation of British East Africa*, London, 1901.
    Heywood, R. S., 'First Impressions of British East Africa', *CMR*, 1919.
    Hobley, Charles W., *Kenya from Chartered Company to Crown Colony: Thirty Years of Exploration and Administration in British East Africa*, London, 1929.
    Höhnel, Lt Ludwig von, *Discovery of Lakes Rudolf and Stefanie*, London, 1894, 2 vols.
    Hooper, H. D., *Africa in the Making*, London, 1922.
    ——, 'Carols', *CMR*, 1924.
    ——, 'The End and the Means in Missionary Enterprise', *IRM*, 1943.
    ——, 'The Expression of Christian Life in Primitive African Societies', *IRM*, 1924.
    ——, 'Kikuyu Churches in United Action', *CMR*, 1919.
    ——, *Leading Strings – Native Development and Mission Education in Kenya Colony*, London, 1921.
    ——, 'A Synthesis in Missionary Field Work', *CMR*, 1925.

Hooper, M. C., 'Beauty from Ashes', *CMR*, 1923.
——, *New Patches*, London, 1935.
——, *Property in The Highlands of East Africa*.
——*The Way of Partnership: With The CMS in East Africa*, London, 1939.
Hutchinson, Edward, *The Slave Trade of Africa*, London, 1874.
Huxley, Elspeth, *White Man's Country: Lord Delamere and the Making of Kenya*, London, 1953, 2 vols.
Huxley, Julian, *Africa View*, London, 1931.
'Industrial Training in Africa', *IRM*, 1914.
Johnston, H. H., *The Kilimanjaro Expedition*, London, 1886.
Jones, Thomas Jesse, *Education in East Africa*, London, 1925.
Kenyon, E. R., 'A Visit to British East Africa and Uganda', *CMR*, 1914.
Kikuyu Independent Schools Association, *Report and Constitution of the KISA*, 1938.
Kiragu, D. M., *Kiria Giatumire Independent Igie*, Nairobi.
Krapf, J. L., *Travels, Researches, and Missionary Labours*, London, 1968, 2nd edition.
Lenwood, F., 'Industrial Missions as a Policy', *CMR*, 1918.
Leys, Norman, *Kenya*, London, 1925.
Lugard, F. D., *The Rise of Our East African Empire*, London, 1893.
Manley, G. T., 'Industrial Education in Africa', *CMR*, 1920.
Mbotela, James Juma, *The Freeing of the Slaves in East Africa*, London, 1956.
McDermott, P. L., *Imperial British East Africa Company*, London, 1893.
McGregor, A. W., 'Kikuyu and its People', *CMR*, 1909.
Mockerie, P. G., *An African Speaks for His People*, London, 1934.
Oldham, J. H., 'Christian Civilization in Africa', *IRM*, 1927.
——, 'Christian Missions and African Labour', *IRM*, 1921.
——, 'The Educational Policy of the British Government in Africa', *IRM*, 1925.
Orr, J. R., 'Education in Kenya Colony', *CMR*, 1922.
Owen, W. E., 'Empire and Church in Uganda and Kenya', *Edinburgh Review*, 1927.
——, 'The Relationship of Missionary and African in East Africa,' *CMR*, 1927.
Peel, W., 'Among the Wadigo and Wagiriama of British East Africa', *CMR*, 1911.
Perham, Margery, ed., *The Diaries of Lord Lugard*, London, 1959.
Petero, Daudi N., *Jubilee A. C. Kigari and A. C. Kabare (1910–1960)*.
Price, W. S., *My Third Campaign in East Africa*, London, 1890.
Ross, W. McGregor, *Kenya From Within*, London, 1927.
Stock, Eugene, 'CMS Native Church Organization', *IRM*, 1914.
——, 'Future Independent Churches in the Mission Field', *CMI*, 1901.
Thomson, Joseph, *Through Masai Land*, London, 1963, 3rd edition.
Thuku, Harry, *An Autobiography*, Nairobi, 1970.
Tucker, Alfred R., *Eighteen Years in Uganda and East Africa*, London, 1908, 2 vols.
Willoughby, Captain Sir John C., *East Africa and Its Big Game*, London, 1889.
Wiseman, E. M., *Kenya: Then and Now*, London.
World Missionary Conference, *Reports of Commissions II and III*, 1910.
Wray, J. A., *Kenya, Our Newest Colony*, London.
Wright, George W., 'Mombasa: Its Position and Possibilities', *CMR*, 1911.

SECONDARY SOURCES

I. *Published works*

Ajayi, J. F. A., 'Henry Venn and the Policy of Development', *Journal of the Historical Society of Nigeria*, I, 4, 1959.
Ajayi, J. F. A. and E. A. Ayandele, 'Emerging Themes in Nigerian and West African Religious History', *Journal of African Studies*, I, 1, 1974.

Anderson, John E., *The Struggle for the School*, Nairobi, 1970.

Atieno-Odhiambo, E. S., 'A Portrait of the Missionaries in Kenya Before 1939', *Kenya Historical Review*, I, 1, 1973.

——, 'Some Reflections on African Initiative in Early Colonial Kenya', *East African Journal*, 1971.

Axelson, Sigbert, *Culture Confrontation in the Lower Congo*, Falkoping, 1970.

Bäeta, C. G., *Christianity in Tropical Africa*, London, 1968.

Balandier, Georges, 'The Colonial Situation: A Theoretical Approach', I. Wallerstein, ed., *Social Change: The Colonial Situation*, New York, 1966.

Barrett, David B., *African Initiatives in Religion*, Nairobi, 1971.

——, *Schism and Renewal in Africa*, Nairobi, 1967.

Beidelman, T. O., 'Social Theory and the Study of Christian Missions', *Africa*, XLIV, 3, 1974.

Bennett, George, 'Paramountcy to Partnership: J. H. Oldham and Africa', *Africa*, XXX, 4, 1960.

Bennett, Norman R., 'The British on Kilimanjaro, 1884–92', *Tanganyika Notes and Record*, LXIII, 1964.

——, 'The Church Missionary Society at Mombasa, 1874–1894', *Boston University Papers on African History*, Boston, 1964.

Brokensha, David, *Social Change in Larteh, Ghana*, Oxford, 1966.

Cagnolo, Fr. C., *The Akikuyu*, Nyeri, 1933.

Cairns, H. A. C., *Prelude to Imperialism: British Reactions to Central African Society 1840–1890*, London, 1965.

Capon, Martin G., *Towards Unity in Kenya*, Nairobi, 1962.

Cashmore, T. H. R., 'Sheikh Mbaruk bin Rashid bin Salim el Mazrui', Norman Bennett, ed., *Leadership in Eastern Africa*, Boston, 1968.

Chadwick, Owen, *The Victorian Church*, New York, 1966.

Champion, Arthur, *The Agiryama of Kenya*, London, 1967.

Channock, M. L., 'Development and Change in the History of Malawi', B. Pachai, ed., *The Early History of Malawi*, Evanston, 1972.

Cole, Keith, *The Cross over Mount Kenya: A Short History of the Anglican Church in the Diocese of Mount Kenya, 1900–1970*, Nairobi, 1970.

Colson, Elizabeth, 'Converts and Tradition', *Southwestern Journal of Anthropology*, XXVI, 2, 1970.

Coupland, Reginald, *The Exploitation of East Africa*, London, 1939.

Curtin, Philip, *The Image of Africa*, Madison, 1964.

Daneel, M. L., *Old and New in Southern Shona Independent Churches*, The Hague, 1971.

Ekechi, F. K., 'Colonialism and Christianity in West Africa: The Igbo Case, 1900–1915', *Journal of African History*, XII, 1, 1971.

——, *Missionary Enterprise and Rivalry in Igboland, 1857–1914*, London, 1972.

Fernandez, James, 'Fang Representations Under Acculturation', Philip Curtin, ed., *Africa and the West*, Madison, 1972.

Fisher, Humphrey, J., 'Conversion Reconsidered: Some Historical Aspects of Religious Conversion in Black Africa', *Africa*, XLIII, 1973.

Foster, Philip, *Education and Social Change in Ghana*, Chicago, 1965.

Gann, L. H. and Peter Duignan, *Burden of Empire*, New York, 1967.

Goody, Jack R., ed., *Literacy in Traditional Societies*, London, 1968.

Groves, C. P., *The Planting of Christianity in Africa*, London, 1948–58, 4 vols.

Hallden, Erik, *The Culture Policy of the Basel Mission in the Cameroons, 1886–1905*, Uppsala, 1968.

Heiss, David R., 'Prefatory Findings in the Sociology of Missions', *Journal for the Scientific Study of Religion*, VI, 1967.

Hewitt, Gordon, *The Problems of Success: A History of the Church Missionary Society, 1910–1942*, London, 1971.

Hodge, Alison, 'The Training of Missionaries For Africa: The Church Missionary Society's Training College at Islington, 1900–1915', *Journal of Religion in Africa*, IV, 1971.

Hollis, Claud, 'Notes on the History and Customs of the People of Taveta, East Africa', *Journal of the Royal African Society*, I, 1901–2.

Holway, James D., 'CMS Contact with Islam in East Africa Before 1914', *Journal of Religion in Africa*, IV, 1972.

Hopkins, Raymond F., 'Christianity and Sociopolitical Change in Sub-Saharan Africa, *Social Forces*, XLIV, 4, 1966.

Horton, Robin, 'A 100 Years of Change in Kalabari Religion', John Middleton, ed., *Black Africa*, London, 1970.

——, 'African Conversion', *Africa*, XLI, 2, 1971.

Illife, John, *Tanganyika Under German Rule*, London, 1969.

Inglis, K. S., *Churches and the Working Class in Victorian England*, London, 1963.

Isichei, Elizabeth 'Ibo and Christian Beliefs', *African Affairs*, LXVIII, 27, 1969.

——, 'Seven Varieties of Ambiguity: Some Patterns of Igbo Response to Christian Missions', *Journal of Religion in Africa*, III, 3, 1970.

Johnson, Hildegard Binder, 'The Location of Christian Missions in Africa', *The Geographic Review*, LVII, 2, 1957.

Kenya Churches Handbook, Kisumu, 1973.

Kieran, John, 'A Route to the Galla', *Hadith*, 3.

King, K. J., *Pan Africanism and Education*, Oxford, 1971.

——, 'The Politics of Agricultural Education for Africans in Kenya', *Hadith*, 3.

Lamphear, John, 'The Kamba and the Northern Mrima Coast', Richard Gray and David Birmingham, *Pre-Colonial African Trade*, London, 1970.

Langergnen, David, *Mission and State in the Congo*, Uppsala, 1970.

Leakey, L. S. B., 'The Kikuyu Problem of the Initiation of Girls', *Journal of the Royal Anthropological Institute*, LXI, 1931.

Linden, I., *Catholics, Peasant and Chewa Resistance in Nyasaland, 1889–1939*, Berkeley, 1974.

Lonsdale, J. M., 'European Attitudes and African Pressures: Missions and Government in Kenya Between the Wars', *Race*, X, 2, 1968.

——, 'Some Origins of Nationalism in East Africa', *Journal of African History*, IX, 1, 1968.

Mangat, J. S., *A History of the Asians in East Africa c. 1886 to 1945*, Oxford, 1969.

Markowitz, Marvin D., *Cross and Sword: The Political Role of Christians Missions in the Belgian Congo*, Stanford, 1973.

Mbiti, John S., *New Testament Eschatology in an African Background*, New York, 1971.

Middleton, John, *The Kikuyu and the Kamba*, London, 1953.

Mitchell, R. C., 'Toward the Sociology of Religious Independency', *Journal of Religion in Africa*, III, 1, 1970.

Mungeam, G. H., *British Rule in Kenya, 1895–1912*, Oxford, 1966.

——, 'Masai and Kikuyu Response to the Establishment of British Administration in the East Africa Protectorate', *Journal of African History*, XI, 1, 1970.

Munro, John Forbes Staples, *Colonial Rule and the Kamba*, Oxford, 1975.

Muriuki, Godfrey, *A History of the Kikuyu, 1500–1900*, Nairobi, 1974.

Murphee, Marshall, *Christianity and the Shona*, New York, 1969.

Murray-Brown, Jeremy, *Kenyatta*, London, 1972.

Ndungu, J. B. 'Gituamba and Kikuyu Independency in Church and School', *Ngano*, Nairobi, 1969.

Ngugi wa Thiong'o, James, *The River Between*, London, 1965.

Oliver, Roland, *The Missionary Factor in East Africa*, London, 1952.

Parkin, David, 'The Politics of Syncretism: Islam among the Non-Muslim Giriama of Kenya', *Africa*, XL, 1970.

Patterson, K. David, 'The Giriama Rising of 1913–14', *African Historical Studies*, III, 1, 1970.

Pauw, B. A., *Religion in a Tswana Chiefdom*, London, 1960.

Peel, J. D. Y., 'Religious Change in Yorubaland', *Africa*, XXXVII, 3, 1967.

Philp, H. R. A., *A New Day in Kenya*, London, 1936.

Pollock, J. C., *A Cambridge Movement*, London, 1953.

Ranger, T. O., 'African Attempts to Control Education in East and Central Africa, 1900–1939', *Past and Present*, XXXII, 1965.

——, *Dance and Society in Eastern Africa, 1890–1970*, Berkeley, 1975.

Ranger, T. O. and I. Kimambo, *The Historical Study of African Religion*, Berkeley, 1972.

Ranger, T. O. and John Weller, *Themes in the Christian History of Central Africa*, Berkeley, 1975.

Rosberg, Carl G., and John Nottingham, *The Myth of Mau Mau: Nationalism in Kenya*, New York, 1966.

Rotberg, Robert and Ali Mazrui, eds, *Protest and Power in Black Africa*, New York, 1970.

Routledge, W. S., *With a Prehistoric People: The Akikuyu of East Africa*, London, 1910.

Salamone, Frank A., 'Continuity of Igbo Values after Conversion', *Missiology*, III, 1, 1975.

Sangree, Walter H., *Age, Prayer, and Politics in Tiriki, Kenya*, London, 1966.

Spencer, Leon, 'Defense and Protection of Converts', *Journal of Religion in Africa*, V, 2, 1973.

Stock, Eugene, *The History of the Church Missionary Society*, London, 1889–1914, 4 vols.

Stovold, K. E., *The CMS in Kenya*, Nairobi, 1945.

Strayer, Robert W., 'Mission History in Africa: New Perspectives on an Encounter', *African Studies Review*, XIX, 1, 1976.

——, 'Missions and African Protest', *Protest Movements in Colonial East Africa*, Syracuse, 1973.

Sturt, Mary, *The Education of the People*, London, 1967.

Sundkler, B. G. M., *Bantu Prophets in South Africa*, London, 1948.

Tanner, Ralph, *Transition in African Belief*, Maryknoll, New York, 1967.

Taylor, John V., *The Growth of the Church in Buganda*, London, 1958.

Temu, Arnold J., *British Protestant Missions*, London, 1972.

——, 'The Role of the Bombay Africans on the Mombasa Coast, 1874–1904', *Hadith*, 3.

Turner, Philip, 'The Wisdom of the Fathers and the Gospel of Christ', *Journal of Religion in Africa*, IV, 1, 1971.

Urch, George E., 'Education and Colonialism in Kenya', *History of Education Quarterly*, XI, 3, 1971.

Warren, Max A. C., *The Missionary Movement from Britain in Modern History*, London, 1965.

——, *Social History and Christian Mission*, London, 1967.

Welbourn, F. B., *East African Rebels*, London, 1959.

Welbourn, F. B. and B. A. Ogot, *A Place to Feel at Home*, London, 1966.

Wright, Marcia, *German Missions in Tanganyika, 1891–1941*, Oxford, 1971.

II. *Unpublished Works*

Anderson, William B., 'Development of Leadership in Protestant Churches in Central Kenya'.

——, 'The Experience and Meaning of Conversion for Early Christian Converts in Kenya'.

Dena, Lawrence C. T., 'A Comparative Study of the Impact of the Differing Traditions of Christianity on Some of the Coastal Tribes of Kenya'.

Kibicho, Samuel G., 'The Interaction of the Traditional Kikuyu Concept of God with the Biblical Concept'.

Kiriro, Amos K., 'Church Growth Among the Embu of Mt. Kenya, 1900–66'.

Macharia, Ephantus G., 'The Establishment of the Anglican Church, Kahuhia'.

Mathu, George W., 'Gikuyu Marriage: Beliefs and Practices'.

McIntosh, Brian G., 'The Scottish Mission in Kenya, 1891–1923,' Ph.D. Dissertation, University of Edinburgh, 1969.

Muriuki, G., 'Background to Politics and Nationalism in Central Kenya'.

Murray, Jocelyn, 'Interrelationships Between Witchcraft Eradication Movements and Christianity in Central Africa'.

——, 'The Kikuyu Female Circumcision Controversy', Ph.D Dissertation, University of California at Los Angeles, 1974.

Mwangi, Matthew, 'History of Weithaga'.

Mwaniki, H. S. K., 'The Politics of Nationalism in Embu During the 1st Quarter of the 20th Century'.

Rennie, John K., 'Christianity, Colonialism and the Origins of Nationalism among the Ndau of Southern Rhodesia, 1890–1935', Ph.D. Dissertation, Northwestern University, 1973.

Richards, Charles G., 'History of the CMS in the Highlands of Kenya'.

Saint Stephen's Church, Njumbi, Jubilee, 1968.

Sandgren, David P., 'Kikuyu Society and the African Inland Mission'.

Schilling, Donald G., 'British Policy for African Education in Kenya, 1895–1939', Ph.D. Dissertation, University of Wisconsin, 1972.

'A Short History of Saint Stephen's Church, Thimbigua', 1965.

Smith, Cynthia, 'The Giriama in the 20th Century'.

——, 'The Giriama Rising, 1914: Focus for Political Development in the Kenya hinterland, 1850–1963', Ph.D. Dissertation, University of California at Los Angeles, 1973.

Spear, Thomas F., 'The Mijikenda ca. 1550–1900'.

Wambaa, Rebmann M., (with the assistance of Kenneth King), 'The Political Economy of the Rift Valley: A Squatter Perspective'.

White, Gavin, 'Kikuyu, 1913: An Ecumenical Controversy', Ph.D. Dissertation, University of London, 1970.

Index